Thomas Hardy on Screen

The novels of Thomas Hardy have often been regarded as cinematic in their scope and power, and they have inspired some of the most absorbing adaptations of fiction for the big screen. This collection of essays by prominent international Hardy scholars explores both successful and unsuccessful attempts to transfer Hardy's novels to the screen. It provides a fascinating illustrated history of the interpretation and recreation of Hardy's work, from the silent era to television. The essays highlight the challenging nature of Hardy's work, which finds its most powerful reflection in films by controversial directors such as Roman Polanski and Michael Winterbottom. Adaptations on screen have introduced Hardy's novels to new generations of readers, reinforcing the continuing relevance of his works. This collection offers a stimulating starting-point for the study both of Hardy's novels as films, and of the ways in which cinema and television adaptations illuminate aspects of the novels.

TERRY WRIGHT is Professor of English Literature at the University of Newcastle. He is the author of, among other books, *Hardy and the Erotic* (1989) and *Hardy and His Readers* (2003).

Thomas Hardy on Screen

Edited by

T. R. WRIGHT

CAMBRIDGE
UNIVERSITY PRESS

CAMBRIDGE UNIVERSITY PRESS
Cambridge, New York, Melbourne, Madrid, Cape Town, Singapore, São Paulo

Cambridge University Press
The Edinburgh Building, Cambridge CB2 2RU, UK

Published in the United States of America by Cambridge University Press, New York

www.cambridge.org
Information on this title: www.cambridge.org/9780521600521

First published 2005

Printed in the United Kingdom at the University Press, Cambridge

A catalogue record for this book is available from the British Library

ISBN-13 978-0-521-84081-1 hardback
ISBN-10 0-521-84081-3 hardback
ISBN-13 978-0-521-60052-1 paperback
ISBN-10 0-521-60052-9 paperback

Contents

Illustrations

Contributors

PHILIP ALLINGHAM is Acting Head of Undergraduate Studies in the Faculty of Education at Lakehead University (Thunder Bay, Ontario). Having gained his doctorate at the University of British Columbia, he has published on various aspects of nineteenth-century serialisation, in particular illustration in the novels of Dickens and Hardy, both in print and on the Victorian Web, for which he is currently Contributing Editor.

SIMON GATRELL is Professor of English at the University of Georgia. His work on Hardy includes critical editions of *Under the Greenwood Tree*, *The Return of the Native*, and *Tess of the D'Urbervilles*; editions of the manuscript materials relating to *The Return of the Native* and *Tess of the D'Urbervilles*; and three books: *Hardy the Creator: A Textual Biography*, *Thomas Hardy and the Proper Study of Mankind*, and *Thomas Hardy's Vision of Wessex* (with which is associated a Wessex website).

DALE KRAMER is Professor Emeritus of English at the University of Illinois at Urbana-Champaign and Courtesy Professor of English at the University of Oregon. He has written *Thomas Hardy: The Forms of Tragedy* and *Hardy: Tess of the D'Urbervilles* (Cambridge University Press). He has edited critical editions of *The Woodlanders* and *The Mayor of Casterbridge* and several collections of essays about Hardy, including *The Cambridge Companion to Thomas Hardy* (1999).

JUDITH MITCHELL is an Associate professor in the Department of English at the University of Victoria, British Columbia. She has published articles on gender issues in the work of George Moore, Thomas Hardy, and George Eliot, and is the author of *The Stone and the Scorpion: The Female Subject of Desire in the Novels of Charlotte Bronte, George Eliot and Thomas Hardy* (Greenwood Press, 1994).

ROSEMARIE MORGAN, editor and publisher of *The Hardy Review*, has taught at Yale University since 1984. She is President of the Thomas Hardy Association and a Vice President of the Thomas Hardy Society.

Her publications include *Women and Sexuality in the Novels of Thomas Hardy*, *Cancelled Words* (both Routledge), and an edition of *Far From the Madding Crowd* (Penguin Classics). She has contributed to *The Oxford Reader's Companion to Hardy* (2002) and *Thomas Hardy Studies* (Palgrave, 2004) and is currently producing a student guide to Hardy for Greenwood Press.

RICHARD NEMESVARI is Associate Professor of English and Chair at St Francis Xavier University. His edition of Hardy's *The Trumpet-Major* was published by Oxford University Press, and his article 'Hardy and His Readers' recently appeared in *Thomas Hardy Studies* (Palgrave, 2004). He has also published an edition of *Jane Eyre* with Broadview Press, and he is currently working on a book entitled *Disproportioning Realities: Thomas Hardy and Sensationalism*.

ROY PIERCE-JONES lectures in Drama and Performance Studies at University College Worcester. He has also lectured at several other universities in literature/film studies. He writes for the theatre and is currently completing a new play. He is also working on a study of British film-acting styles.

JOHN PAUL RIQUELME is Professor of English at Boston University. His publications focus on authors from Wilde to Beckett, literary theory, and Gothic modernism, including an edition of *Dracula*. He is editing *A Portrait of the Artist as a Young Man* and writing a book about Wilde. He has edited *Tess of the d'Urbervilles* and published essays on Hardy's fiction and poetry, including one on poetic modernity in *The Cambridge Companion to Thomas Hardy*.

ROBERT SCHWEIK is Distinguished Teaching Professor, Emeritus, of the State University of New York. He is editor of the Norton Critical Edition of *Far From the Madding Crowd* (1986), and author of *Hart Crane: A Descriptive Bibliography and Reference Sources in English and American Literature*. He has contributed to fourteen other books and written articles on Hardy, Tennyson, Browning, J. S. Mill, analytic bibliography, rhetoric, and cultural history in the nineteenth and early twentieth centuries. He is a Vice President of the Thomas Hardy Society and the Thomas Hardy Association.

ROGER WEBSTER is Professor of Literary Studies and Dean of the Faculty of Media, Arts, and Social Science at Liverpool John Moores University. He has published a number of essays on Thomas Hardy following his doctoral thesis on 'Hardy and the Visual Imagination'. Publications include a volume on suburbia, and essays on working-class literature and on literary theory. He is currently working on film depictions of Conrad's London.

PETER WIDDOWSON is Professor of Literature at the University of Gloucestershire. He has written extensively on Thomas Hardy and on Hardy on film (in *Hardy in History* and in *Thomas Hardy and Contemporary Literary Studies*, which he edited with Tim Dolin). He has also published *Literature* (Routledge, 1999), *The Palgrave Guide to English Literature and Its Contexts, 1500–2000* (2004), *Graham Swift* (Northcote House, 2005), and (with Peter Brooker and Raman Selden) *A Reader's Guide to Contemporary Literary Theory* (5th edition, Pearson Education, 2005).

KEITH WILSON is Professor and former Chair of English at the University of Otawa and President of the Association of Canadian College and University Teachers of English. He is the author of *Thomas Hardy on Stage* (Macmillan, 1995), editor of *The Mayor of Casterbridge* (Penguin, 1997), and co-editor (with the late Kristin Brady) of *The Fiddler of the Reels and Other Stories* (Penguin, 2003). He has published numerous articles on a range of nineteenth- and twentieth-century writers and is currently working on the representation of London in modern British literature.

TERRY WRIGHT is Professor of English Literature at the University of Newcastle upon Tyne. He has written two books on Hardy: *Hardy and the Erotic* (Macmillan, 1989) and *Hardy and His Readers* (Palgrave Macmillan, 2003). He has also written books on *The Religion of Humanity: The Impact of Comtean Positivism on Victorian Britain*, D. H. *Lawrence and the Bible* (both Cambridge University Press), *Literature and Theology* (Blackwell), and *George Eliot's 'Middlemarch'* (Harvester Wheatsheaf).

Acknowledgments

The most difficult part of this project was gathering the illustrations. I would like to thank all those film companies who responded promptly and positively to my requests for help, in particular Pathé Renn Production, their representatives Sylvie Coen, Claire Chevauchez and Tim Burrill for giving permission to reproduce the illustration on the front cover; Pathé Distribution Limited of Kent House and Simon Osborn their representative for permission to reproduce the theatrical poster and a still image from *The Woodlanders* (the poster courtesy of nostalgia.com); London Weekend Television and their picture publicist Sandra Powell for providing both the still from their production of *Tess of the D'Urbervilles* and permission to reproduce it. I have tried hard to contact all the other film companies whose work is still in copyright from whom I have taken stills. Since these stills are discussed in the relevant essays, however, and are not used for merely decorative purposes, I assume that the 'fair dealing' provision applies.

For the photograph of the painting by Edouard Manet and permission to reproduce it, I would like to thank Emma Hayes and the Samuel Courtauld Trust of the Courtauld Institute of Art Gallery. For the painting by J. M. Turner similarly and permission to reproduce that, I would like to thank Emma Hayes of the National Gallery Picture Library. The photograph of the illustration by Robert Barnes from *The Graphic* was supplied by the National Library of Scotland. I would like to thank them too for permission to reproduce it.

Many people have helped me in completing this project. I would like to thank Philip Powrie for helping me obtain stills from DVDs and video cassettes. These couldn't be used in the book itself but were helpful in identifying which stills I wanted. I would like to thank Rosemarie Morgan, Chair of the Symposium on 'Hardy on Film' at the Sixteenth International Thomas Hardy Conference held in August 2004 at which versions of three of the essays in this volume were delivered (those by Richard Nemesvari, Keith Wilson, and myself). This and the email Forum Discussion Group of the Thomas Hardy Association enabled much discussion of the issues in this volume to take place informally, helping to clarify and develop our ideas. I would also like to thank students of my module on 'Narrative Theory: Novel to Film' for their part in the development of my own ideas.

Additional thanks are owing to Peter Stebbing, who compiled the filmography, to the staff of the Robinson Library at the University of Newcastle upon Tyne for their unfailing help, and my editor at Cambridge University Press, Linda Bree, and her assistant Maartje Scheltens for responding quickly and positively to all my queries. My copy-editor Caroline Howlett also deserves credit for picking up and correcting a number of errors in the original typescript. Finally, as always, I want to express my indebtedness to my family, especially my son Andrew, who is much more technically adept than I am, and my wife Gabriele for helping me to complete the project.

Note on references and abbreviations

References to Hardy's novels are given in brackets in the text. Individual contributors have decided which edition is most appropriate for their own chapters, but for those with different editions they provide chapter numbers in lower-case roman numerals as well as page numbers in arabic numerals. Where the novel is also divided into books (as in *Jude the Obscure*) these are given in upper-case roman numerals (e.g. I, vii, 25). The titles of the novels are abbreviated as follows:

DR   *Desperate Remedies*
FMC   *Far From the Madding Crowd*
J   *Jude the Obscure*
MC   *The Mayor of Casterbridge*
RN   *The Return of the Native*
T   *Tess of the D'Urbervilles*
W   *The Woodlanders*

Introduction

Terry Wright

In the long-running 'war of independence' between film and literary studies,[1] in which film is often taught (with some resentment) as an extra dimension within English departments, it is common for film critics to deplore attempts to discuss adaptation of literary 'classics' as 'jejune' and 'moribund'.[2] Dudley Andrew calls it 'the most narrow and provincial area of film theory'[3] while Robert Ray complains of the 'same unproductive layman's question (How does the film compare with the book?), getting the same unproductive answer (The book is better)'.[4] Such studies, we are told, often lack 'diacritical specificity', failing to recognise the differences between the two media and their 'respective materials of expression'.[5] Attempts to discuss the 'fidelity' of films to their original novels can also degenerate into exercises in pedantry, expressions of critical disappointment that a director's interpretation of the novel fails to match their own.

All the contributors to this volume are aware of these problems surrounding the discussion of adaptation. Many of them may be better known for their work on Hardy than on film. But none of them underestimates the power of film and the difference of its conventions from those of literature. Occasionally, it is true, they do claim that the book is 'better', or at least more complex. But one of the arguments that emerges frequently in the essays that follow is that the most 'faithful' adaptations, the most literal attempts to transfer Hardy to screen, are often the least successful as films. While remaining true to the 'letter' of his novels they fail to capture the 'spirit' of his writing, that quality so difficult to define which satisfies an audience that a film is genuinely 'Hardyesque', achieving similar effects on its viewers as the novel on its readers. I place these terms under erasure, within scare quotes, to draw attention to their problematic status, since it is precisely the 'essence' of Hardy's work which is under discussion. It is this that makes the study of adaptation such a useful pedagogic tool within departments of literature (and therefore, perhaps, so suspect in the eyes of those film critics, who are, with perfect justification, interested in films for their own sake).

1

There is an additional irony in the field of Thomas Hardy studies at the moment, as Peter Widdowson, one of the contributors to this volume, has observed, in that

[w]here contemporary literary criticism is busy recasting Hardy's work as radically subversive in form and content — finding in a late nineteenth-century writer one whose texts simultaneously deconstruct issues of class and gender in particular . . . the most prevalent and popular late twentieth-century modes of reproducing his work, film and television, seem to return us to the older more conventional Hardy of Wessex, 'Character and Environment', and humanist tragedy.[6]

This is by no means universally the case; some of the film adaptations of Hardy's work, as we shall see, are as challenging in their own time and medium as the novels. But there is no doubt that some of the television adaptations to be discussed in this volume do appear to reproduce a somewhat outmoded version of Hardy: the 'good, little Thomas Hardy', producer of pastoral tragedies beloved and patronised by his contemporaries. What literary critics have come to regard as his strengths, his genuinely radical vision of the world, his experimentation with genre, his refusal to accept the moral and political conventions of his day, are not always reflected in those adaptations which are geared to filling the 'classic serial' slot for television, meeting the demands for entertaining, undemanding, acceptable family viewing.

Hardy himself, as I have argued elsewhere,[7] struggled to overcome similar expectations (the serial versions of his novels in family magazines such as *The Graphic* being the contemporary equivalent of television serials). Although at first he had to conform to some extent to the demands of his primary audience, and was only able to subvert them indirectly, he became increasingly open in his opposition to those demands. This may explain why similarly radical film-makers such as Roman Polanski and Michael Winterbottom, also prepared to shock audiences out of their complacencies, make the most powerful interpreters of his work.

This, however, is to prejudge the issue. The essays that follow will test these generalisations against the detailed evidence of a wide range of films, all of which are based more or less closely upon Hardy's work. In some cases, such as *Way Down East*, D. W. Griffith's silent movie of 1920, the reference to Hardy is not even acknowledged. In others, such as the series of BBC plays of the 1970s based upon his short stories, there is a deliberate attempt to reproduce on screen the authentic 'Wessex' of the tales. John Schlesinger goes out of his way to film some of the scenes of *Far From the Madding Crowd* in their 'actual' settings while Polanski and Winterbottom think nothing of transferring Stonehenge to France, Christminster to Scotland, or Casterbridge to California. What results, I hope, is a fascinating history of reception, interpretation, and recreation which follows our understanding of Hardy and his 'meaning' through nearly a century of screening from the silent movies of 1913 and 1915 to the present day.

The first three essays address general questions about screening Hardy, questions of narrative, of visual awareness, the 'painterly' qualities of his writing, and the difficulties of reproducing 'Wessex' on screen. My own contribution investigates earlier claims that Hardy was a 'cinematic' writer, deliberately renouncing some of the modes of representation characteristic of written narratives in order to reproduce modes of 'seeing' which anticipate cinema. I focus on three aspects of narrative characteristic of Hardy's work: his use of particular observers or focalisers, his employment of restricted narrators, and his taste for ellipsis, a tendency to omit direct representation of key moments in his stories, which appear only indirectly or in fragmented form in his discourse. If these narrative techniques can be labelled 'cinematic', I argue that it is also the case that films can create a 'Hardyesque feel' to their work by reproducing them (or their cinematic equivalents) on screen.

Roger Webster also explores the visual quality of Hardy's writing with particular reference to his interest in painting and the visual dynamics associated with Turner and the Impressionists. The danger, however, as Webster observes, is that whereas Hardy's use of 'painterly' techniques was radically experimental, producing new ways of seeing people and landscape, the use of 'painterly' material in film often succeeds only in stabilising a conventional image of Hardy and Wessex. Schlesinger's experimental angles of vision and mobile tracking, in fact, come closer to reproducing the effect of Hardy's 'moments of vision' than more deliberate allusions to painting.

Simon Gatrell begins by distinguishing between the material aspects of Wessex, which are relatively easy to reproduce, and Hardy's metaphorical landscapes, which film finds harder to handle. In close focus on scenes from Jack Gold's *The Return of the Native* and Phil Agland's *The Woodlanders* he shows how these directors respond to the challenge of Hardy's complex representation of the heath and the woodland within the bounds that Hardy set. Michael Winterbottom, however, deliberately rejects the paradigm of Wessex, and in switching Christminster from Oxford to Edinburgh and Casterbridge from Dorchester to Kingdom Come, he demonstrates more clearly than any that it is not the specific location, but 'the power of place to shape human lives, and the power of human beings to transform their own environment' that lies at the heart of Hardy's creation.

These general explorations of the problems, challenges, and opportunities of screening Hardy are followed by three historical essays on specific attempts to translate Hardy to film, firstly in the silent era, secondly to television (the successful BBC series of short stories in the seventies), and thirdly in the nineties. There is not a great deal that Peter Widdowson can say about the early silent films based explicitly upon Hardy's novels, since nothing appears to have survived of them apart from a few stills. It is significant, however, that Hardy himself took a keen interest in them, aware of their capacity to boost sales of the novels. Widdowson also discovers that D. W. Griffith's 1920 film *Way Down East*, ostensibly based upon a play by Lottie Blair Parker, shares several key plot elements with *Tess of the D'Urbervilles*, including a mock marriage (as in the serial versions of Hardy's novel), a home-administered baptism, and a real marriage to the idealistic son of a 'stern old puritan'. Widdowson detects a number of additional similarities between Griffith's film and Hardy's novel (the heroines of both are victims of prejudice, bigotry, and sexual double standards), all confirming his suspicion that Griffith deliberately pushed his film closer to Hardy's novel. At least one silent film to some extent based upon Hardy can therefore be said to survive.

For reasons about which one can only speculate (perhaps he was considered too serious and tragic a writer for the 'entertainment' business) Hardy's work was ignored by film-makers for nearly forty years, from the late 1920s to the late 1960s (apart from two attempts to film a short story). In the seventies, however, the BBC turned to some emerging playwrights of the calibre of Dennis Potter, David Mercer, and Ken Taylor for a series of six adaptations of Hardy's *Wessex Tales*. These are the subject of Roy Pierce-Jones's chapter, which considers their success in capturing some of the qualities of the original stories in stark comparison with a more recent (and fairly disastrous) attempt to turn 'The Melancholy Hussar' into a feature-length film.

The 1990s rediscovered Hardy as a source of film, according to Judith Mitchell, not so much because of a nostalgic desire to return to a more stable and straightforwardly narratable past but because he can be seen to share many postmodern anxieties and uncertainties:

As in the 1890s, men as well as women in the 1990s found themselves facing new versions of feminism and profound shifts in gender roles, and Winterbottom's adaptation of *Jude*, rather than harking back to a fantasy of historical stability or suggesting the possibility of easy solutions in the present, functions instead to reassure its audience that gender relations have always been problematic, and that bewilderment in the face of such changes is an understandable response.

The Claim too, in transporting *The Mayor of Casterbridge* to the American wild west, succeeds in capturing a sense of Hardy's exploration of masculinity in that novel. For the western as a genre is obsessed with masculinity and its relation to domesticity, representing 'men in flight from the domestic restraints of Victorian culture'. The (literally) fallen heroes of these and other adaptations of Hardy in the 1990s, Mitchell argues, reflect Hardy's complex and subversive attitude towards men's place in a binary gender system, and towards gender itself as a suspect determinant of identity.

The remaining essays in this volume focus on individual attempts to translate some of Hardy's best-known novels to the screen (there have significantly been no attempts to film the so-called 'minor' novels). Keith Wilson, author of the only full-length study of the many attempts to transfer Hardy to the stage, focuses here on the first modern feature film of a Hardy novel, John Schlesinger's *Far From the Madding Crowd* of 1967, which is ironically much closer to the original than Hardy's own stage adaptation of this novel. Wilson finds the characterisation of the two leads, Bathsheba and Sergeant Troy (Julie Christie and Terence Stamp), unconvincing, lacking the psychological depth that the novel provides for them through their past. While praising some of the visual qualities of this film, the dazzling set pieces such as the sword-play in Maiden Castle (not in the novel but authentic enough to the region), Wilson draws attention to some problematic details, which, as he recognises, are partly attributable to unresolvable differences between film and fiction.

Rosemarie Morgan identifies a different set of problems in Jack Gold's attempt to screen *The Return of the Native*, which results in a stagey version of the novel, theatrical in a pejorative sense. Morgan objects especially to the generic switch from tragedy to pastoral romance, which flattens all the dissonance of Hardy's novel. What should disturb and challenge its audience is submerged beneath the nostalgia of historical romance. Hardy's sensual and rebellious heroine is similarly reduced to mere prettiness.

Philip Allingham in chapter ten takes a close look at three versions of *The Mayor of Casterbridge*: the two produced for television and the more ambitious, less closely based feature film *The Claim*. Allingham focuses in particular on the way each of these adaptations deals with the difficult twenty-year interval between the first two chapters of the novel, when Henchard sells his wife, and the remaining action. There are problems here not only of continuity but of the complex relationship of past and present. Allingham also considers the way Robert Barnes, one of Hardy's most successful illustrators, handles this issue, for it seems clear that these illustrations formed an important bridge from the written word to its visualisation not only in the minds of Hardy's readers but in those of some of the directors too.

John Paul Riquelme celebrates the way in which Polanski's *Tess* manages to incorporate many of the dissonant elements in Hardy's original novel, itself 'a book of displacements and dislocation' both in style and narrative. Polanski's film goes beyond realism, beyond what Beckett calls 'the plane of the feasible', calling attention to its own cinematic techniques, the grain of its own voice. Among the dissonances Riquelme notes in the film are the grain of its leading actress's voice and the use of rack focus, especially in the confession scene, which prevent audiences from consuming the action as 'realistic', disturbing its relation to the events and objects depicted. He also draws attention to the way Polanski creates a simulacrum of Stonehenge and of Tess's boots, both of which occupy a 'genuinely illusory space' on screen.

Richard Nemesvari, in his analysis of London Weekend Television's version of *Tess of the D'Urbervilles*, which is in many respects more 'faithful' to the original than Polanski's *Tess*, returns to the question of genre, arguing in particular that its imposition upon the story of the limited conventions of television romance undercuts Hardy's complex mixture of melodrama and the grotesque. In the sympathetic portrayal of the villainous Alec D'Urberville Nemesvari finds echoes of the 'redeemed rapist' of modern soap opera. All the ambiguities surrounding Hardy's complex novel are thus flattened for a modern audience deemed incapable of coping with such difficult material.

In the final essay of the volume Robert Schweik compares two equally different versions of Hardy's final novel *Jude the Obscure*, the BBC version of 1971 and Michael Winterbottom's 1996 film. Schweik looks at five scenes as they appear in both versions; in nearly every case, the greater freedom with the original that Winterbottom allows himself enables him to produce a more recognisably Hardyan film. Literal fidelity is found to be less important than more significant aspects of film-making, of the way films can achieve sometimes shocking effects equivalent to those produced by the original novel.

Are there, then, any conclusions to be drawn from these detailed explorations of so many different attempts to transfer Hardy to the screen (apart from the fact that literary critics are notoriously difficult to please)? One thing is certain: anyone who had not realised it before should soon become aware of the complexity of Hardy's novels and the difficulty of translating them into a different medium. No other nineteenth-century writer, in my view, raises as many questions as he does, questions about genre (the astonishing mixture of the grim and the grotesque), about politics (his sensitivity to class issues combined with an absence of instant remedies), and about gender (his subversion not only of conventional bourgeois morality but of all suggested solutions to the problem of human sexuality).

It takes directors of the power and originality of Polanski and Winterbottom, I would argue, to engage fully with these questions, to have the confidence to depart radically from fidelity to the 'letter' of the original novels. Schlesinger too, I suggest, by being prepared to experiment with the conventions of cinema as Hardy did with the conventions of fiction, achieves similar effects in *Far From the Madding Crowd*. The gifted group of writers engaged by the BBC to transfer the Wessex Tales to television also succeed, I think, in producing through the medium of television effects comparable to those achieved by Hardy's novels. All these productions challenge their audiences as Hardy challenged his readers, forcing them out of conventional attitudes and responses. How these directors achieve this, finding cinematic equivalents for Hardy's complex literary effects, is the main subject of the essays that follow.

NOTES

1. Erica Sheen, 'Introduction', in Robert Giddings and Erica Sheen (eds.), *The Classic Novel: From Page to Screen* (Manchester: Manchester University Press, 2000), p.1.
2. James Naremore, 'Introduction: Film and the Reign of Adaptation', in James Naremore (ed.), *Film Adaptation* (London: Athlone Press, 2000), pp.1 and 15.
3. Dudley Andrew, 'Adaptation', *ibid.*, p.44.
4. Robert B. Ray, 'The Field of "Literature and Film"', *ibid.*, p.44.
5. Robert Stam, 'Beyond Fidelity: The Dialogics of Adaptation', *ibid.*, pp.57–9.
6. Peter Widdowson, 'Thomas Hardy at the End of Two Centuries: From Page to Screen', in Tim Dolin and Peter Widdowson (eds.), *Thomas Hardy and Contemporary Literary Studies* (Basingstoke: Palgrave Macmillan, 2004), p.178.
7. T. R. Wright, *Hardy and His Readers* (Basingstoke: Palgrave Macmillan, 2003).

1 'Hardy as a cinematic novelist': three aspects of narrative technique

Terry Wright

Narrative theory has generally been recognised as an area of common concern between film and fiction, for novels and films share what Harris Ross has called a 'vocation' to tell a story. From the perspective of their consumers too, it can be argued that 'spectators of film . . . and readers of novels share the same task, to create a coherent story from the information provided by the art work'.[1] In comparing some aspects of narrative technique to be found both in Hardy himself and in the films based upon his novels therefore, I hope to contribute something to the discussion of 'Hardy on Screen' which can appeal both to film and literary critics.

The three aspects of narration on which I wish to focus are firstly his use of particular observers or focalisers (the cinematic equivalent for which is the filtering of what is seen by the camera through the 'eyes' of a particular character), secondly the employment of restricted narrators so characteristic of Hardy's work (the way in which Hardy, even when supposedly employing an 'omniscient narrator', limits the narrator's knowledge to what is observable simply from the outside), and thirdly his use of ellipsis, the gaps and discontinuities in his narrative which force readers to supply what they cannot see. Both narratology and reader-response theory, I suggest, have made this a particularly fruitful way of comparing narrative technique in fiction and in film. All three devices, I will argue, are employed by Hardy and also by the directors of films based upon his novels in an attempt to give a 'Hardyesque' feel to their adaptations. Clearly I will need to make what Stanley Fish at an early stage of his career identified as one of the most difficult connections to establish between narratological description of the formal properties of the texts to reader-response analysis of the 'effect' these structures have upon readers and spectators,[2] but the attempt, I think, is worth making. It is at least a stage further forward than earlier impressionistic attempts to locate what was 'cinematic' about Hardy's work.

Earlier links between Hardy and cinema were far from complimentary about the comparison. Joseph Beach gave the title 'Movie' to his chapter on *The Mayor of Casterbridge* and *The Woodlanders* because of their supposed narrative 'technique of slapdash facility and looseness'. While demonstrating 'the vivid art of startling pictures full of movement, constantly shifting, and never failing in excitement and variety', Beach complained that Hardy tells his story only 'in outline, just enough so that the reader may keep abreast of the action, never lingeringly, so that he may get the relish, the intimate significance, the sense of being on the inside'. Hardy can therefore be accused of giving us 'hardly more than the scenario of a movie'.[3] John Wain was being more positive when he identified some of the devices central to *The Dynasts*, 'panoramic views dissolving into close-up, for instance', as 'cinematic'.[4] Joan Grundy included under the title 'Cinematic Arts' those optical effects which interested Hardy as much as they did the early film-makers: panorama, diorama, magic lantern shows.[5] But it was precisely his self-limitation to what could be seen (from the outside) that earned him David Lodge's classification as a

cinematic novelist, . . . one who . . . deliberately renounces some of the freedom of representation and report afforded by the verbal medium, who imagines and presents his materials in primarily visual terms, and whose visualisations correspond in some significant respect to the visual effects characteristic of film.[6]

Lodge claims that Hardy 'uses verbal description as a film director uses the lens of his camera' in ways that 'can be readily analysed in cinematic terms: long shot, close-up, wide angle, telephoto, zoom, etc.'. There is even a passage in *Far From the Madding Crowd* that anticipates the specialised vocabulary of film criticism, describing the way Bathsheba's many beauties 'struck upon all his [Boldwood's] senses at wide angles'.[7] This does not, however, make the work of adaptors any easier; Lodge argues that 'it is difficult for film adaptation to do justice to Hardy's novels precisely because effects that are unusual in written description are commonplace in film'.[8] Neil Sinyard has also called Hardy 'so intimidatingly visual as to make the camera seem almost redundant'.[9]

I want to challenge that view, considering examples of narrative technique in Hardy which critics such as Lodge and Sinyard have labelled cinematic alongside attempts to translate them onto screen, to find what Brian McFarlane has called 'cinematic equivalents' for these techniques. One key difference, as McFarlane points out, is that 'there is, in film, no such instantly apparent, instantly available commentary on the action' as is supplied by the 'omniscient' narrator of prose fiction.[10] I place scare quotes around 'omniscient' here because the narrator in prose fiction is rarely as omniscient as s/he is sometimes thought to be: there are degrees of knowledge which range from total to highly restricted. Many film critics, however, would deny that there is any such thing as a cinematic narrator. 'In watching films', David Bordwell argues, 'we are seldom aware of being told something by an entity resembling a human being'.[11] Others claim that it does make sense to talk of a 'cinematic narrator', programmed by the implied author to present certain information to the audience.[12] That narrator 'is not a human being',[13] of course, nor should s/he be identified solely with voice-over: 'voice-over', as Sarah Kozloff argues, 'is just one of many elements, including musical scoring, sound effects, editing' and camera-work, all of which contribute to cinematic narration.[14] The point is that stories get told in film, as they do in fiction, and the language developed by narrative theory to discuss the techniques employed in the process helps us to discuss them.

The failure, for example, to distinguish between the author, the implied author, the narrator, and the focaliser, a distinction commonplace in academic criticism, leads to some embarrassingly crude moments in the 1998 television production of *Tess of the D'Urbervilles*, which not only opens with a voice-over narrator pontificating about fate in a caricature west-country accent presumably designed to suggest Hardy himself, but later introduces a Hardy lookalike who happens to encounter Angel and Tess as they emerge from Wellbridge Manor after the confession scene. In the novel, as Richard Nemesvari explores in greater detail later in this volume, Hardy invents an unnamed character, 'a cottager of Wellbridge, who went out late that night for a doctor' and therefore observed the 'two lovers in the pastures, walking without converse, one behind the other'.[15] Hardy carefully embeds this character's story within his narrator's, adding a certain verisimilitude, a sense of these events having actually happened. In defence of the film, it could be argued on both critical and biographical grounds that these layers of narrative distance (author – implied author – narrator – focaliser) don't fully succeed in masking Hardy's personal involvement with Tess, the sense generated by the novel that she is a real person about whose fate he genuinely cares. But bringing the author so literally into the frame oversimplifies what the novel makes much more complex.

Such 'invocation of a hypothetical or unspecified observer', as Lodge remarks, 'is one of the signatures of Hardy's narrative style'.[16] As in the cinema, action in Hardy's fiction is often seen from a specific vantage point, a particular angle. Lodge gives the example of *The Return of the Native*, which opens with what he calls 'an emotionally loaded establishing shot of the *mise-en-scène*', Egdon Heath. 'Humanity appears on the scene', to quote the famous heading of chapter two, in the form of an initially unnamed old man with the appearance of 'a naval officer of some sort or another' (as in the cinema we are given merely visual information). The old man, later identified as Captain Vye, now becomes the focaliser, 'the "lens" through which we see', far ahead on the road on which he travels, 'a moving spot which appeared to be a vehicle'. Gradually Captain Vye approaches the van, which turns out to be 'a lurid red', the result of its belonging to the reddleman, Diggory Venn, who in turn becomes the focaliser for the curious 'pantomime of silhouettes' that ensues, involving a woman's figure on a barrow, outlined against the sky.[17] The narrative technique here resembles a shooting script even before it indulges in a close-up of Eustacia Vye's face.

Perhaps the most famous example of a particular observer of a key event in Hardy's fiction, which Polanski appears almost literally to have used as a shooting script for this part of his film of *Tess*, is Mrs Brooks, proprietor of The Herons. Having overheard 'fragments of the conversation' between Tess and Angel from her carefully specified position 'within the partly-closed door of her own sitting-room at the back of the passage', followed by the sound of the door to Tess's apartment closing, Mrs Brooks finds her curiosity to discover more irresistible. She peeps through the keyhole to the apartment, from which vantage point 'only a small space of the room inside was visible'. It is enough, however, for her to see Tess's face, bowed over the chair in front of which she is kneeling: 'her hands were clasped over her head, the skirts of her dressing-gown and the embroidery of her nightgown flowed upon the floor behind her, and her stockingless feet, from which the slippers had fallen, protruded upon the carpet'. As in the episode when Tess strikes Alec with a glove on his cheek when he harasses her on top of the threshing machine, the focus at this point on the detail of the garment and on the unprotected feet, serves synecdochally to register Tess's vulnerability. Mrs Brooks can only 'catch a portion' of the words Tess utters but she can see the 'pain' upon Tess's face, 'that her lips were bleeding from the clench of her teeth upon them, and that the long lashes of her closed eyes stuck in wet tags to her cheeks' (T, lvi, 380–1). Again, the close-up on these details of Tess's face registers the desperateness of her predicament.

In a characteristically sudden switch from the tragic to the comic, Hardy returns to Mrs Brooks, the observer of this scene. Frightened by 'a sudden rustle' from within, she beats a hasty retreat downstairs, taking refuge firstly in her parlour and then in the kitchen, from which she hears the floorboards creaking, another 'rustle of garments against the banisters, the opening and the closing of the front door, and the form of Tess passing to the gate on her way into the street'. Neither sight nor sound (the twin tracks of cinema) can provide sufficient information: she hears no 'word of farewell' but surmises that the D'Urbervilles 'might have quarrelled' or that 'Mr D'Urberville might still be asleep' until the dramatic revelation comes in the form of the red spot in the white kitchen ceiling, 'about the size of a wafer when she first observed it, but it speedily grew as large as the palm of her hand' before assuming 'the appearance of a gigantic ace of hearts' (T, lvi, 382). It is a marvellous example of Hardy's veering from realism to outrageous symbolism. Fate has dealt Tess a particularly dramatic hand; you could even say that she has finally succeeded in trumping Alec.

Realist cinema, of course, has its limits and Polanski, who chooses throughout *Tess* to play down the Gothic elements which feature both in the original novel and in many of his own earlier films, cannot expect an audience to accept a ceiling literally assuming the shape of a gigantic playing card. Fate has therefore to play a less symbolic game of chance with Tess. Polanski cannot resist adding a few cinematic elements, such as the man cutting the hedge outside the villa, possibly borrowed from Hitchcock's *North by Northwest*.[18] But the regular sound of the shears echoes the clock which ticks so loud throughout the confession scene, both standing in part at least for the encroaching of machines on the natural world. In most respects, however, Polanski follows Hardy's directions here very closely. The conversation between Angel and Tess is seen from Angel's point of view but from then on the action is mainly filtered through Mrs Brooks's eyes, as she peers through the keyhole to observe Tess's grief: the camera widens out to incorporate all the action and at one point catches the murder weapon hovering ominously over D'Urberville's breakfast ham but returns to the landlady's perspective for Tess's departure and the discovery of the bloodstain on the ceiling. What Polanski has picked up here, I would argue, is the cinematic potential of Hardy's writing, the same narrative technique (a necessity in film but not in fiction) of observing the action from a very particular place, providing the audience through intermediate filters and focalisers with vivid visual and aural stimuli. Hardy has to mediate these stimuli verbally, of course, but he focuses on the detailed sounds and images in a manner which Polanski can exploit to the full. He doesn't have to 'find' cinematic equivalents for what is in Hardy since the novel already provides them. Conversely, the scene in the film is recognisably 'Hardyesque', retaining key elements not only of the story (the supposed 'events') but of the discourse (the way the story is told), indirectly and in fragmented form from the perspective of an observer who is far from omniscient. The murder itself, like Tess's rape, is not directly described.

Not all of Hardy's 'specified observers'[19] can be translated so easily to the screen. Polanski can take aerial shots of Flintcombe Ash, capturing the bleakness of the scene in which 'the brown face' of the land looks up at 'the white face' of the sky, with 'the two girls crawling over the surface of the former like flies', but he can hardly ask his cameramen to adopt the perspective of the 'strange birds from behind the North Pole . . . gaunt spectral creatures with tragical eyes – eyes which had witnessed scenes of cataclysmal horror in inaccessible polar regions' and which peer down on the labouring girls in the hope of their 'disturbing the clods with their hackers so as to uncover something or other that these visitants relished as food' (T, xliii, 285–8). Here Hardy's focalisers are so exotically symbolic as to defy translation to screen. Similarly, when the young Jude peers in the direction of Christminster from the Brown House on the hill, noticing the 'halo or glow-fog overarching the place against the black heavens beyond it', we are told that, 'In the glow he seemed to see Phillotson promenading at ease, like the forms in Nebuchadnezzar's furnace'.[20] This is problematic for readers of the novel: 'Whose point of view are we receiving', asks Niemeyer, casting doubt on such a young boy's imagination being so biblically informed.[21] It is at least arguable that so precocious a student of the Bible as Jude would see the world in such apocalyptic terms but it is difficult to imagine how Michael Winterbottom could indicate this (unless perhaps in painterly terms, alluding to the work of John Martin). The film has necessarily to limit itself to a more mundane night-time view of Oxford.

The 'eye-witness', according to Robert Scholes and Robert Kellog, 'cannot see everything' and 'can know only one mind – his own'.[22] Written fiction, however, can employ an 'omniscient narrator', so called because of his or her ability to enter into all minds and see everything, including events where no subject is present. Hardy's narrators, however, rarely make use of their potential for omniscience, often restricting themselves to what can literally be seen. For Norman Page, as for Roger Webster in the following chapter of this book, both of whom draw on Hardy's enthusiasm for painting, it makes more sense to describe these narrators as pictorial rather than cinematic. But the point Page makes about the narrative technique of the opening paragraphs of *The Mayor of Casterbridge* contains many similarities to Lodge's analysis of *The Return of the Native*: the narrator is 'an interested but ignorant observer'[23] who cannot tell, for example, whether the man carrying the rush basket, who has been described in meticulous detail, 'was reading, or pretending to read, a ballad sheet which he kept before his eyes'. The suspicion is that he is only pretending in order 'to escape an intercourse that would have been irksome to him', but 'nobody but himself could have said precisely'. The woman, meanwhile, 'seemed to have no idea of taking his arm . . . and far from exhibiting surprise at his ignoring silence she appeared to receive it as a natural thing'.[24] This 'restriction to the observable' on Hardy's part, as Sheila Berger notes, is 'absolutely resistant to the privileges of an all-knowing, authoritative narrator'.[25] As in a film, readers are drawn into the novel by a detailed focus upon characters of whom they know nothing and about whom they can only speculate. They are led gradually into the action, learning with Elizabeth-Jane, who becomes the focaliser for the following scenes in Casterbridge, what has become of Henchard in the intervening years.

Both *The Woodlanders* and *Tess of the D'Urbervilles* begin with a similar combination of restricted narration and specified observers, illustrating what Terry Eagleton has called 'Hardy's cinematic technique of cutting . . . from a long, externalising shot, within which characters become objects against a landscape, to an angled camera or more slanted, subjective perspective'.[26] The opening sentence of *The Woodlanders* informs us that the 'rambler who . . . should trace the forsaken coach-road' from Bristol to the south shore of England would necessarily 'find himself during the later part of his journey in the vicinity of some extensive woodlands'. These, of course, will become the dwelling place of the protagonists in the novel but not before Hardy has followed an actual rambler, later identified as Barber Percomb, who will behold, through the uncurtained window of her cottage and lit by the fire, 'a girl seated on a willow chair' with a bill-hook in one hand and 'a leather glove, much too large for her, on the other'. Marty South's spar-making, as observed by the barber, who is mainly interested in her hair, is described in meticulous detail as is 'the palm of her right hand' whose 'red and blistering' injuries she later examines:

In her present beholder's mind the scene composed itself into an impression-picture of extremest type, wherein the girl's hair alone, as the focus of observation, was depicted with intensity and distinctness, while her face, shoulders, hands, and figure in general, were a blurred mass of important detail, lost in haze and obscurity.[27]

This passage has been cited by several critics to illustrate Hardy's interest in the Impressionists, an exhibition of whose work he had visited while writing this novel.[28] He found the phenomenological implications of their work fascinating, noting that 'we get only at the true nature of the impression that an object produces on us, the true thing in itself being still, as Kant shows, beyond our knowledge'.[29] The Impressionists tend also to be cited in studies of the development of new modes of narrative anticipating cinema. The novel, according to Keith Cohen, was remodelled in the 'impressionist era' by writers who were 'bored with the prevailing trend of an inflexibly omniscient-authoritative narrator'.[30] Hardy's narrators and focalisers are therefore part of a wider movement in fiction away from omniscience towards particular perspectives. They also change focus with the swiftness of a camera.

It is the word 'focus' in the passage above which connects it specifically with the camera rather than the painter. Because Barber Percomb is the observer of this scene he foregrounds Marty's hair as 'the focus of observation', leaving the rest of her body in the hazy background. Hardy provides the prose equivalent of a 'subjective shot' to tell us as much about the observer as about the object of his gaze. It is hardly surprising therefore that the opening sequences of Phil Agland's 1997 film of the novel follows the opening of the novel fairly closely. After trailing Barber Percomb along the coach-road into the woods, the camera follows him up to Marty's cottage. He doesn't actually peer through her window but does gaze closely at her while she works, her hair foregrounded by her position, Jodhi May facing away from camera to display her abundant hair in all its glory. Agland recognises the importance of reproducing Percomb's initial point of view as a way into the world of the woodlanders.

Tess of the D'Urbervilles, after the introductory encounter between Parson Tringham and Tess's father, also begins with some ramblers, firstly a generalised 'traveller from the coast, who, after plodding northward for a score of miles over calcareous downs and cornlands', is 'surprised and delighted to behold' in the Vale of Blackmoor 'a country differing absolutely from that which he has passed through': a picturesque part of the world 'constructed on a smaller and more delicate scale'. The narrator informs us that the district is of historic, no less than of topographical interest, citing as an example the 'May-Day dance' which 'was to be discerned on the afternoon under notice'. The passive mood of the verb here leaves somewhat ambiguous who is doing the observing, whether it is still the 'traveller' from the previous page. But the focus now falls on the dancers, described as a group, all in white dresses (though 'no two whites were alike amongst them') and all carrying 'a peeled willow-wand', a few 'middle-aged and even elderly women in the train' but 'the majority of the band being young'. Only after further observation of the similarities and differences between the women does the focus turn to Tess herself, with 'her mobile peony mouth and large innocent eyes'. She is such a striking figure, we are told, that 'strangers . . . would grow momentarily fascinated at her freshness'. The narrator then introduces Angel Clare and his brothers as particular examples of the 'idlers and pedestrians' who gather to observe the dancing (T, ii, 12–16). Angel then becomes the focaliser for what follows, being invited to choose a partner and attempting 'some discrimination' between the dancers but significantly failing to alight upon Tess until it is too late.

Polanski's film reproduces in cinematic form many of the strategies of this opening scene. After 'a long establishing shot of the landscape', the May-Day dancers appear, slowly making their way towards the camera, similarly undifferentiated from each other. All of Polanski's dancers seem young (in accordance with his well-documented taste) but Nastassja Kinski can only be distinguished from the crowd after a considerable time. As William Costanzo notes, Polanski reverses the order of the opening scenes in the novel, placing the encounter between Parson Tringham and Tess's father after the more general introduction to the beauty and customs of this part of Wessex.[31] Polanski begins the film following the pattern of Hardy's restricted rather than omniscient narrator, providing for his viewers a spectacle of picturesque interest which only gradually narrows its focus to the central character. In terms of narrative technique, in other words, Polanski reproduces in cinematic ways the manner in which Hardy's novel opens, gradually introducing his audience to a particularly striking character in her particularly beautiful environment. This mode of opening his stories is so characteristic of Hardy that when Irene Shubik was asked to produce a series of adaptations of his short stories for the BBC, as Roy Pierce-Jones notes in chapter six of this volume, she insisted that each should begin with a long shot of Wessex before cutting to its inhabitants. Compare also John Schlesinger's opening of *Far From the Madding Crowd* with a long pan over the seaside and its adjoining cliffs before settling on Gabriel Oak among his sheep.

The third aspect of narrative technique characteristic of Hardy which I want to consider in relation to its 'cinematic' quality is ellipsis, the omission of direct narration of events, of which we become aware as readers only indirectly. 'One of Hardy's most common narrative devices', as Paul Niemeyer explains, 'is *not* to show a significant action; instead he has a character *narrate* the event to a listener'.[32] Sometimes, most famously with Tess's rape and confession and with the murder of Alec, Hardy teases us by passing over a crucial event altogether. We come to the end of Phase the Fourth with a description of Tess bending forward, 'pressing her forehead against his [Angel's] temple', and are told that 'she entered on her story of her acquaintance with Alec D'Urberville and its results, murmuring the words without flinching, and with her eyelids drooping down'. The chapter ends here, so we turn the page eager with anticipation, to be confronted with the opening words of Phase the Fifth: 'Her narrative ended . . .' (T, xxxiv–v, 225–7). For a rival novelist such as George Moore this was outrageous: Hardy had missed a golden novelistic opportunity.[33] But this is how Hardy often operates, leaving gaps or blanks which the reader has to fill for him- or herself, luring us into the story, forcing us to engage imaginatively with his heroine.

Polanski, as Niemeyer shows, picks up on this; his film too is 'filled with ellipses' (if that doesn't sound too much of a contradiction), 'blank spaces' which the viewer is invited to 'fill in'.[34] The death of Prince, for example, is not shown but narrated by Tess, who mumbles something about the loss of the family horse to Alec on their first meeting. Her baptising of their child is similarly told by her to the vicar rather than shown directly as it is in the 1998 television version (which also has a particularly vivid enactment of the death of Prince). Polanski chooses, like Hardy himself, not to show the murder itself. In creating these ellipses, passing over key events with indirect rather than direct forms of narration, he remains true to the spirit of the original, as does John Schlesinger in his much-maligned version of *Far From the Madding Crowd*. Neil Sinyard, for example, complains bitterly about the scene at Weymouth (in the novel of course it is Bath to which Bathsheba pursues Troy and where she marries him) in which 'the sound of the sea drowns out a crucial conversation between Bathsheba and Troy'. Sinyard can find 'no discernible reason for this, other than an inability on screenwriter Frederic Raphael's part to imagine what they might be saying to each other'.[35] But this, I would argue, is genuinely 'Hardyesque' (in spite of being entirely invented). We are forced to imagine what the two lovers are saying to each other, just as in the novel itself we have to piece together what must have happened from the frequently interrupted and altogether incoherent narrative of Cainy Ball, who reports that the lovers 'went into a sort of a park place' and

sat there together for more than half an hour, talking moving things, and she once was crying a'most to death. And when they came out her eyes were shining, and she was as white as a lily; and they looked into one another's faces as far-gone friendly as a man and woman can be. (FMC, xxxiii, 231–2)

The close-up shots of the faces of the characters in the film (their words drowned out by the sea) are a cinematic equivalent of the verbal pictures Cain Ball provides of the external signs of their emotions in the novel.

Not everything in the film versions of Hardy's novels I have discussed can claim to be equally 'Hardyesque'. But in terms of the three aspects of narrative technique on which I have focused (the use of particular specified observers, of restricted narrators, and of ellipses) Polanski, Schlesinger, and Agland seem to me to have picked up characteristic patterns of narration in Hardy which it makes sense to label 'cinematic' since they anticipate modes of film narration. They do not follow the original slavishly; even in the scene at the Herons Polanski incorporates some of his own style of narration (for instance the man clipping the hedge). But they can be said to have made films of Hardy's novels which find ways of reproducing not only his stories (the raw events) but also his discourse (his mode of narration). It is not just, as Lodge argued, that Hardy is a cinematic novelist but that these examples of cinema, in some respects at least, are genuinely Hardyesque.

NOTES

1. Harris Ross, 'Introduction', in Harris Ross (ed.), *Film as Literature, Literature as Film* (New York: Greenwood Press, 1987), pp.55–7.
2. Stanley Fish, *Is There a Text in This Class?* (Cambridge, Mass.: Harvard University Press, 1980), pp.21–67.
3. Joseph Warren Beach, *The Technique of Thomas Hardy* (Chicago: University of Chicago Press, 1922), pp.134 and 146–7.
4. John Wain, 'Introduction' to Thomas Hardy, *The Dynasts* (London: Macmillan, 1965), p.x.
5. Joan Grundy, *Hardy and the Sister Arts* (New York: Harper and Row, 1979), pp.106–33.
6. David Lodge, 'Thomas Hardy as a Cinematic Novelist', in his *Working with Structuralism* (London: Routledge and Kegan Paul, 1981), pp.95–105 (p.96).
7. Thomas Hardy, *Far From the Madding Crowd*, ed. Suzanne B. Falck-Yi (Oxford: Oxford University Press, 1993), p.123. All future references in brackets in the text will be to this edition. This passage was discussed in an (as yet) unpublished paper by Stephen Regan at the Sixteenth Hardy International Conference in Dorchester in August 2004.
8. Lodge, *Working with Structuralism*, p.97.
9. Neil Sinyard, *Filming Literature: The Art of Screen Adaptation* (Beckenham: Croom Helm, 1986), p.48.
10. Brian McFarlane, *Novel to Film: An Introduction to the Theory of Adaptation* (Oxford: Clarendon Press, 1996), p.18.
11. David Bordwell, *Narration in the Fiction Film* (Madison: University of Wisconsin Press, 1985), p.61.
12. Seymour Chatman, 'The Cinematic Narrator', in Gerald Mast, Marshall Cohen, and Leo Braudy (eds.), *Film Theory and Criticism*, 4th edn (Oxford: Oxford University Press, 1992), p.478.
13. *Ibid.*, p.482.
14. Sarah Kozloff, *Invisible Storytellers: Voice-Over in American Fiction Film* (Berkeley: University of California Press, 1988), pp.43–4.
15. Thomas Hardy, *Tess of the D'Urbervilles*, ed. Tim Dolin (Harmondsworth: Penguin, 1998), p.233. All future references in brackets in the text will be to this edition.
16. Lodge, *Working with Structuralism*, p.98.
17. *Ibid.*, pp.99–100.
18. The suggestion of Hitchcock as the source for the hedgecutter was made by Tim Farmiloe at the Sixteenth International Hardy Conference, where I delivered a shortened version of this paper as part of a symposium on 'Hardy and Film'.
19. Lodge, *Working with Structuralism*, p.98.
20. Thomas Hardy, *Jude the Obscure*, ed. Dennis Taylor (Harmondsworth: Penguin, 1998), p.23.

21. Paul J. Niemeyer, *Seeing Hardy: Film and Television Adaptations of the Fiction of Thomas Hardy* (Jefferson, N. C.: McFarland, 2003), p.164.
22. Robert Scholes and Robert Kellog, *The Nature of Narrative* (Oxford: Oxford University Press, 1966), p.256.
23. Norman Page, 'Hardy's Pictorial Art in *The Mayor of Casterbridge*', *Etudes Anglaises* 12 (1972) 487–8.
24. Thomas Hardy, *The Mayor of Casterbridge*, ed. Keith Wilson (Harmondsworth: Penguin, 1997), pp.3–4.
25. Sheila Berger, *Thomas Hardy and Visual Structures: Framing, Disruption, Process* (New York: New York University Press, 1990), p.99.
26. Terry Eagleton, 'Flesh and Spirit in Thomas Hardy', in Tim Dolin and Peter Widdowson, eds., *Thomas Hardy and Contemporary Literary Studies* (Basingstoke: Palgrave Macmillan, 2004), p.14.
27. Thomas Hardy, *The Woodlanders*, ed. Patricia Ingham (Harmondsworth: Penguin, 1998), pp.5–11.
28. Cf. J. B. Bullen, *The Expressive Eye: Fiction and Perception in the Work of Thomas Hardy* (Oxford: Clarendon Press, 1986), pp.182–3.
29. Thomas Hardy, *The Life and Work of Thomas Hardy*, ed. Michael Millgate (Athens: University of Georgia Press, 1985), pp.261–2.
30. Keith Cohen, *Film and Fiction: The Dynamics of Exchange* (New Haven: Yale University Press, 1979), p.5.
31. William Costanzo, 'Polanski in Wessex: Filming *Tess of the D'Urbervilles*', *Literature/Film Quarterly* 9 (1981) 73.
32. Niemeyer, *Seeing Hardy*, p.135.
33. George Moore, *Conversations in Ebury Street* (London: Heinemann, 1936), p.81.
34. Niemeyer, *Seeing Hardy*, p.135.
35. Sinyard, *Filming Literature*, p.48.

2   From painting to cinema: visual elements in Hardy's fiction

Roger Webster

Hardy's novels contain a range of discourses which, to use a term Hardy favoured, foreground the visual potential of fictional narrative. More recent critical approaches have focused increasingly on this tendency, including Hardy's interest in and use of painting – both painterly techniques and direct references to specific painters or paintings embedded in the narration.[1] Visual perception figures at fundamental perceptual and epistemological levels in Hardy's writing; the emphasis on seeing and painting in his journals is complemented by a stress on eyes and visual dynamics in key scenes in his fiction. This emphasis on visual 'impression' has the effect of privileging visual perception whilst intensifying and condensing meaning in contrast to conventional ratiocinative narrative description; more than one critic has pointed to the way in which sharply realised visual scenes are followed by dense and sometimes awkward passages.[2] Hardy's visual imagination combines with innovative techniques he identified in the visual arts, especially in the paintings of Turner and the Impressionists, influencing his literary technique and his development of the novel. Criticism of Hardy's fiction has tended on the one hand to note a lack of formal narrative consistency, but on the other to identify the intensely visual or impressionistic aspect which sets the novels apart from the conventions of nineteenth-century classic realism. However, it is the shifts, fractures, and dislocations in narrative, as initially demonstrated by Hillis Miller,[3] and more specifically with regard to focalisation by Terry Wright in this volume, that provide the dynamic and arguably more modernist techniques which Hardy also found so stimulating in painting. Whereas Henry James and his followers pursued a tradition which privileged narrative consistency through form, Hardy's approach increasingly emphasises shifting perspective, a more kinetic approach to narrative which places his fiction closer to the experimental techniques which have much in common with the innovations associated with Impressionism and modernism in painting.

Critics have also commented on the connection between Hardy's visual techniques and film, as John Wain suggests: 'The cinema by-passes language and talks to us directly in images, so that these images take on symbolic force. And so does Thomas Hardy in *The Dynasts*.'[4] David Lodge argued subsequently that Hardy's fiction anticipates the advent of cinema:

Hardy uses verbal description as a film maker uses the lens of his camera – to select, highlight, distort, and enhance, creating a visualised world that is both recognisably 'real' and yet more vivid, intense and dramatically charged than our ordinary perception of the real world.[5]

This heightening of effect on the reader can be equivalent to that of cinema, as, for example, in *A Pair of Blue Eyes* (1873), of which there is to date no cinematic adaptation so a reading of the novel cannot be influenced retrospectively via the film. In the episode in which Knight clings perilously to the cliff, the rapid shifts in spatial perspective from close-up and zoom to long shot and macro lens view, followed by an evolutionary frieze, provide a sequence of visual juxtapositions which parallel the shifts in temporal perspective; these produce an effect similar to cinematic montage, most notably in the paragraph commencing, 'Time closed up like a fan before him.'[6] Hardy's emphasis here and more generally on perspective, landscape, light, and colour combine to produce what might be termed the kinetic or heightened realism of his narrative – character and plot being rendered powerfully through these effects rather than by internalised psychological analysis.

However, although the expectation might be that Hardy's innovative techniques would find equivalents in cinematic adaptations of his novels, this is not always the case, as in the three main feature films which I will consider: John Schlesinger's *Far From the Madding Crowd* (1967), Roman Polanski's *Tess* (1979), and Michael Winterbottom's *Jude* (1996). All three films explicitly display painterly qualities, but whereas Hardy's use of painting led to innovations in his narrative technique and can be seen as a parallel to the development of his increasingly profound exploration of social themes, in cinematic versions the opposite is more often the case – they tend more towards the picturesque and the production of stereotypical images with a 'Hardyesque' feel to them. These film versions generally present a safe, familiar version of Hardy's fiction accentuating the pastoral or striving for an authenticity which is validated by a sense of the painterly. I intend to show how Hardy's visual methods develop, especially with regard to painting, and how cinematic versions recognise and appropriate Hardy's painterly qualities – though in rather different ways from their literary deployment.

The intensely visual aspect of Hardy's fictional writing is evident in his first published novel, *Desperate Remedies* (1871); indeed contemporary reviews were critical of its heavy emphasis on visual elements as opposed to strength of plot. Very early in the novel, a strongly visualised scene perceived from the point of view of the heroine, Cytherea Graye, in which she is watching a group of masons together with her architect father at work on scaffolding surrounding a church spire, culminates with:

The picture thus presented to a spectator in the Town hall was curious and striking. It was an illuminated miniature, framed in by the dark margin of the window, the keen-edged shadiness of which emphasized by contrast the softness of the objects enclosed. (DR, i, 46)

This is the earliest published example of a device which Hardy uses and develops more fully throughout his fictional writing: framing the subject matter as if in a picture – in later works this narrowing of focus seems closer to a lens – and employing painterly techniques such as the *chiaroscuro* effect here. Hardy's journal comment in 1891, 'If I were a painter, I would paint a picture of a room as viewed by a mouse from a chink under the skirting',[7] reveals his preoccupation with perspective and angle of vision: the literary equivalents of pictorial framing or the cinematic lens. Immediately following this scene, Cytherea sees her father lose his footing and fall to his death, all happening as if in slow motion viewed through her eyes. The narrative provides a set of visual correlatives for Cytherea's emotional state of mind quite self-consciously, as she revives after fainting:

The next impression of which Cytherea had any consciousness was of being carried from a strange vehicle across the pavement to the steps of her own house by her brother and an older man. Recollection of what had passed evolved itself an instant later, and just as they entered the door – through which another and sadder burden had been carried but a few instants before – her eyes caught sight of the south-western sky, and, without heeding, saw white sunlight shining in shaft-like lines from a rift in slaty cloud. Emotions will attach themselves to scenes that are simultaneous – however foreign in essence these scenes may be – as chemical waters will crystallize on twigs and wires. Ever after that time any mental agony brought less vividly to Cytherea's mind the scene from the Town Hall windows than sunlight streaming in shaft-like lines. (DR, i, 47)

The passage implicitly and explicitly articulates Hardy's emphasis on visual perception and imagination: that light, colour, and certain scenes combined with a particular mode of regard are capable of rendering emotion and sensibility more readily than ratiocinative analysis. This intuitive approach to narrative composed around images, or what Hardy referred to as 'impressions', is based as much in conventions and innovations in the visual arts as in literature, and anticipates cinematic techniques.

The emphasis on the visual in *Desperate Remedies* is striking throughout the novel – Cytherea's character is expressed in a range of visual discourses, including comparisons to paintings:

And she had in turning looked over her shoulder at the other lady with a faint accent of reproach in her face. Those who remember Greuze's 'Head of Girl', have an idea of Cytherea's look askance at the turning . . . the action that tugs the hardest of all at an emotional beholder is this sweet method of turning which steals the bosom away and leaves the eyes behind. (DR, iv, 89)

This emphasis on the visual and the painterly acquires more developed and innovative forms in Hardy's later fiction – especially *Tess of the D'Urbervilles* (1891) and *Jude the Obscure* (1895). As well as the pronounced use of pictorial technique for descriptive purposes, what is also significant in the use of the painterly is the recognition of art as artifice: that fiction, like painting, is a constructed narrative employing conventions or devices and not a direct transcription of an assumed 'reality'. The initial framing device, rather than heightening the effect of realism or verisimilitude, works rather to draw attention to the conventions of art and therefore acts more as an intimation of metafiction or self-reflexivity – a recurrent theme in Hardy's writing, not least in the repeated use of mirrors which tends to disturb and distort rather than reflect, suggesting illusion and deception instead of a photographic accuracy or verisimilitude – or 'copyism', as Hardy termed it.[8]

Pastoral and rustic images normally suggest stasis and a timeless organic community; however, what seems uppermost in Hardy's deployment of visual techniques in fictional narrative is the transient and captured moment which implies a kinetic and dynamic movement and context – a narrative trajectory, often combined with a dislocating effect through the use of perspective. Hardy's ironic use of genre is manifested in the two early novels that most strongly reflect the pastoral convention, *Under the Greenwood Tree* (1872) and *Far From the Madding Crowd* (1874). These two novels are largely responsible for the apparent rustic clichés which have positioned a version of 'Hardy' in a simplified popular tradition – assisted by reviews such as Henry James's of *Far From the Madding Crowd* which asserted that 'the only things we believe in are the sheep and the dogs'.[9] Both novels again have strongly accentuated visual discourses, *Under the Greenwood Tree* being subtitled *A Rural Painting of the Dutch School*, and it is clear that Hardy had particular paintings in mind which influenced the novel's conception and its pastoral tone.

William Empson's definition of pastoral as 'putting the complex into the simple'[10] has some relevance to *Under the Greenwood Tree* in terms of its circumscribed location, plot, and overall lightness of comedy.

Significantly, the depiction of the rural landscape so central to Hardy's evocation of Wessex and novels of 'character and environment' is clearly influenced by painting as well as literary convention. Hardy was a frequent visitor to the National Gallery in London which, during the composition of *Under the Greenwood Tree*, had held exhibitions including a number of Dutch painters, and in 1871 had acquired Hobbema's now much reproduced work *The Avenue, Middelharnis*, dated 1689. In a journal entry several years later, Hardy noted,

The method of Boldini, the painter of 'The Morning Walk' in the French Gallery two or three years ago (a young lady beside an ugly blank wall on an ugly highway) – of Hobbema, in his view of a road with formal lopped trees and flat tame scenery – is that of infusing emotion into the baldest external objects either by the presence of a human figure among them, or by mark of some human connection with them . . . the beauty of association is entirely superior to the beauty of aspect. (*Life*, 120)

The Avenue, Middelharnis is almost certainly the painting by Hobbema that Hardy is describing. In several ways it offers a helpful illustration of Hardy's painterly and visual method which becomes more developed through the influence of Turner and the Impressionists in the 1880s and 1890s. The accentuation of foreground, middleground, and distance in the painting is pronounced, and is often taken as a model for the use of perspective; the vertical is also accentuated through the lopped trees – thus allowing for a range of visual perspectives from the viewer's position. The dominance of the receding line of the road – a recurrent motif in Hardy's fiction which has frequently been appropriated by Hardy's cinematographers – provides a set of physical intersections, a visual correlative for narrative trajectory and transition which, together with the distant figures, implies a suspended moment of interaction as well as movement and change. Thus the figures in the painting – however remote and anonymous – have the potential to become more foregrounded and to offer alternative perspectives. Combined with these optical and spatial effects, the emphasis on artifice – on the conventions of visual representation – is apparent throughout *Under the Greenwood Tree*. J. B. Bullen makes the point that whereas George Eliot's use of Dutch rural paintings in novels such as *Adam Bede* (1859) 'involves responses analogous to those which the general art-lover might experience before a picture, Hardy's often develops the comic potential latent in the difference between a scene in nature and its two-dimensional representation on a flat surface.'[11] One effect of Hardy's pictorialism is to distance the reader from the action, to view the scene as constructed fiction – more characteristic of the alienation-effects of modernism than of the conventions of nineteenth-century realism.

Hardy's interest in painting develops significantly during his novel-writing career, and the overall development in the range of fictional form and content is accompanied by frequent references to Turner and the Impressionists: Hardy was an inveterate gallery and exhibition visitor as his notebooks show.[12] In a series of journal entries in the winter of 1886 to 1887, at the time he was writing *The Woodlanders* (1887), the way in which Hardy's realisation of landscape is influenced by painterly techniques is evidenced:

December 7. Winter. The landscape has turned from a painting to an engraving . . . At the Society of British Artists . . . [t]he impressionist school is strong. It is even more suggestive in the direction of literature than in that of art . . . their principle is, as I understand it, that what you carry away with you from a scene is the true feature to grasp; or in other words, *what appeals to your own individual eye and heart in particular* amid much that does not so appeal, and which you therefore omit to record . . . [*January* 1887] I don't want to see landscapes, *i.e.*, scenic paintings of them, because I don't want to see the original realities – as optical effects that is. I want to see the deeper reality underlying the scenic, the expression of what are sometimes called abstract imaginings.

The 'simply natural' is interesting no longer. The much decried, mad, late-Turner rendering is now necessary to create my interest. The exact truth as to material fact ceases to be of importance in art. (*Life*, 184–5)

Hardy's views on the development of fiction parallel these on painting. In his three essays on fiction, published between 1888 and 1891, he rejects realism and formulaic conventions for a more impressionistic and visionary mode; the reader will, he states,

go with the professed critic so far as to inquire whether the story forms a regular structure of incident, accompanied by an equally regular development of char-acter – a composition based on faithful imagination, less the transcript than the similitude of material fact. But the appreciative, the perspicacious reader . . . will see what his author is aiming at, and by affording full scope to his own insight, catch the vision which the writer has in his eye, and is endeavouring to project upon the paper, even while it half eludes him.[13]

In the same essay, Hardy asserts that 'despite the claims of realism . . . the best fiction, like the highest artistic expression in other modes, is more true, so to put it, than history or nature can be'.[14] In a discussion on the idealised depiction of death in a 'well-known Capitoline marble' he sug-gests that there 'was always a jar somewhere, a jot or tittle of something foreign in the real death scene'.[15] 'The Science of Fiction' (1891) articu-lates his most explicit rejection of realism or 'copyism' and the move as he saw it represented by Zola to align 'storywriting to scientific processes'.[16] A passage which strikingly anticipates Virginia Woolf's attacks on real-ism in her essays 'Modern Fiction' (1919) and 'Mr Bennett and Mrs Brown' (1924)[17], admits both 'the desirability' and 'the impossibility of reproducing in its entirety the phantasmagoria of experience with infinite and atomic truth . . . creative fancy has accordingly to give more and more place to realism, that is, to an artificiality distilled from the fruits of closest observation'.[18]

The rejection of realism as 'copyism' is juxtaposed increasingly against a developing view of art as offering a distorted, fractured, or exaggerated image – 'To see in half and quarter views the whole picture'.[19] Other terms Hardy uses to signify this defamiliarising aesthetic are 'disproportioning', 'idiosyncrasy', and 'impression'. These combine with an emphasis on self-conscious or self-reflexive features – hence the problems that critics have encountered in attempting to position his novels within a traditional classic-realist paradigm. By 1890, Hardy came to formulate an aesthetic articulated in what he termed an author's 'idiosyncratic mode of regard': 'Art consists in so depicting the common events of life as to bring out the features which illustrate the author's idiosyncratic mode of regard; making old incidents and things seem as new' (*Life*, 225). These reflections are further amplified in a journal entry of July:

Reflections on Art. Art is a changing of the actual proportion and order of things, so as to bring out more forcibly than might otherwise be done that feature in them which appeals most strongly to the idiosyncrasy of the artist. The changing, or distortion, may be of two kinds: (1) The kind which increases the sense of vraisemblance: (2) That which diminishes it. (1) is high art: (2) is low art . . . Art is a disproportioning – (*i.e.* distorting, throwing out of proportion) – of realities, to show more clearly the features that matter in those realities, which, if merely copied or reported inventorially, might possibly be observed, but would more probably be overlooked. Hence 'realism' is not Art. (*Life*, 228–9)

Turner's paintings in particular offered Hardy a visual aesthetic which served his desire to move beyond realism:

Turner's water-colours: each is a landscape *plus* a man's soul . . . What he paints chiefly is *light as modified by objects*. He first recognises the impossibility of really reproducing on canvas all that is in a landscape; then he gives for that which cannot be reproduced a something else which shall have upon the spectator an approximate effect to that of the real. He said, in his maddest and greatest days: 'What pictorial drug can I dose a man with, which shall affect his eyes somewhat in the manner of this reality which I cannot carry to him?' – and set to make such strange mixtures as he was tending towards in 'Rain, Steam and Speed', 'The Burial of the Wilkie', 'Agrippina landing with the ashes of Germanicus', 'Approach to Venice', 'Snowstorm and a Steamboat', etc. Hence, one may say, Art is the secret of how to produce by a false thing the effect of a true. (*Life*, 216)

The importance of the parallels between painting and literature in Hardy's developing aesthetic suggests that his narrative method should be viewed in the context of modernism and innovations in the visual arts rather than in that of the traditions of literary classic realism. In particular Turner's abandonment of one-point perspective for a shifting, multiple representation combined with a concentration on a moment in time, a shift to a more synchronic than diachronic temporality or snapshot – techniques associated also with Impressionism – especially evident in Hardy's later novels from *The Woodlanders* (1887) onward. These spatial and temporal perspectives also combine with a heightened sense of art as device or artifice, a self-reflexive and proto-metafictional theme most evident in his final novel, *The Well-Beloved* (1897), which can be read as a ludic text that, as Hillis Miller has argued, is closer to Proust and Dostoyevsky and anticipates Borges and Fowles.[20] Just as the Impressionists drew attention to the texture of paint on the canvas, thus undermining the conventions of visual mimesis, so the thickening and multi-referential aspects of Hardy's language can at times draw attention to the textuality of fiction, fracturing realist conventions of an extra-linguistic reality. As Sheila Berger comments, Hardy

discourages belief in a consciously finished product either in the imagination or on the page. Hardy's submerged, even subversive, patterning in a series of visual structures – spontaneous and chaotic – ever-changing, disappearing, re-emerging through the novels and poems, is not like an architect's blueprint but like Coleridge's 'Kubla Khan'.[21]

Cinematic versions of Hardy's novels have drawn on the visual and painterly features of the novels, sometimes quite explicitly – as is the case with Winterbottom's *Jude*. Whereas Hardy's visual aesthetic becomes increasingly experimental, however, mainstream cinematic appropriations appear more preoccupied with assimilating and stabilising 'Hardy'; the finger on the aesthetic scales comes down more on the side of convention than experiment.

This is particularly evident in the cinematic treatments of *Tess of the D'Urbervilles* and *Jude the Obscure*, which have been the subject of more critical debate than any of Hardy's other novels. Without attempting to summarise the range of arguments, what can be adduced is that they have produced a rich 'critiography', as Peter Widdowson and others have shown,[22] which is itself highly illuminating in terms of literary history and sociology as well as revealing the complexity of Hardy's narratives. What emerges in critical trends that have become established around Hardy's fiction is a polarisation between an organicist, cohesive model of interpretation typified by Ian Gregor's study *The Great Web* (1974) and readings which view his fiction as a site of fractures, ambiguities, contradictions, and innovations, whether historical, sociological, or formalist in analysis. Approaching cinematic texts as re-readings or re-inscriptions of the literary text raises similar questions, making a kind of 'palimpsest' model appropriate, a metaphor which Hardy himself favoured[23] – and there is a similar process to be observed if we consider the three best-known feature film versions of Hardy's novels, John Schlesinger's *Far From the Madding Crowd*, Roman Polanski's *Tess*, and Michael Winterbottom's *Jude*.

Far From the Madding Crowd was Hardy's first major success, and Schlesinger's film is also the first surviving mainstream film version of a Hardy novel – both were responsible for constructing powerful images of rural life associated with Hardy's invention of 'Wessex'. Although *Far From the Madding Crowd* does not contain the more complex visual or painterly discourses of *Tess of the D'Urbervilles* or *Jude the Obscure*, the overall effect of the pastoral rural landscape that Schlesinger's film produces can be found in a paragraph which recalls *Under the Greenwood Tree*:

The rain had quite ceased, and the sun was shining through the green, brown, and yellow leaves, now sparkling and varnished by the raindrops to the brightness of similar effects in the landscapes of Ruysdael and Hobbema, and full of those infinite beauties that arise from the union of water and colour with high lights. The air was rendered so transparent by the heavy fall of rain that the autumn hues of the middle distance were as rich as those near at hand, and the remote fields intercepted by the angle of the tower appeared in the same plane as the tower itself.(FMC, lxvi, 342)

Hardy's treatment of landscape and nature in *Far From the Madding Crowd* ranges from this kind of depiction emphasising light, colour, and harmony to the scene where Bathsheba awakes having spent the night in the open following her viewing of Fanny Robin's corpse in her coffin and the discovery of her baby – the 'malignant' swamp with its fungi, rotting vegetation – 'a nursery of pestilences' (FMC, xliv, 329).

Landscape, nature, and their light and colour effects are used by Hardy as a projection or reflection of characters' states of mind, akin to his definition of 'impression' as partial and subjective: 'We don't always remember as we should that in getting at the truth, we get only at the true nature of the impression that an object, etc., produces on us, the true thing in itself being still, as Kant shows, beyond our knowledge' (*Life*, 247–8). Schlesinger's film tends to concentrate much more on the picturesque and pastoral to the point of cliché, combining this approach with a form of historical authenticity or verisimilitude which produces a safe, familiar version of Hardy. What is derived from the text is the use of colour, light, and shade to powerful effect, especially *chiaroscuro* as in the realisation of the scene above where Bathsheba's night outside is rendered primarily in colour contrasts rather than anything more sinister. Schlesinger also makes use of framing devices with doors and windows, often combining with 'half and quarter views'[24] of characters, together with radical juxtapositions of perspective – from dislocating aerial views to extreme close-up shots, providing a cinematic equivalent to the text's use of multiple perspective and shifting angles of vision. On several occasions the camera takes on the role of a character's angle of vision through a mobile, tracking technique – as when Troy enters Bathsheba's drawing room in a heightened emotional state having encountered Fanny Robin in the stables, his eyes apparently moving from Bathsheba to the mantel clock and then alighting on the domed musical carousel clock with its rotating soldier which he had given her the morning after their wedding night, but which now suggests a different turn in their relationship. Schlesinger's camera work accentuates moments of intensity – which might be considered as 'truths' or illusory – such as the scene in which Bathsheba's mockery of the corn merchants is repeated in slow-motion to reinforce Boldwood's initial infatuation, or Troy's swordplay both in his initial courting of Bathsheba and subsequently at the fairground as Dick Turpin. Though derived more from cinematic convention, these filmic epiphanies approximate to Hardy's intensely visualised moments and use of the term 'impression'.

Hardy said of Turner at the time he was beginning to work on *Tess of the D'Urbervilles*, 'What he paints chiefly is *light as modified by objects*' (*Life*, 216). His deployment of colour, light, and shade in *Tess of the D'Urbervilles* is highly developed; a striking feature is the use of an unusual lexicon which foregrounds the visual and painterly aspects of the narrative. Each phase of the literary text accentuates different colour spectra, using a variety of light and shade to express Tess's state. At times, it is as if this soft-focus Tess is, paradoxically, almost beyond language – at least beyond the discourses of class, gender, and religion which position and contain her:

Her affection for him was now the breath and life of Tess's being; it enveloped her as a photosphere, irradiated her into forgetfulness of her past sorrows, keeping back the gloomy spectres that would persist in their attempts to touch her – doubt, fear, moodiness, care, shame . . . She walked in brightness, but she knew that in the background those shapes of darkness were always spread. They might be receding, or they might be approaching, one or the other, a little every day. (T, xxi, 236–7)

The description with its emphasis on light and shade, combined with terms such as 'photosphere', or elsewhere 'polychrome' (T, xix, 161), 'aqueous light' (T, xx, 169), 'phosphorescence' (T, xx, 170), and 'pollen of radiance' (T, xxi, 235), has the effect of making Tess at certain phases indistinct and nebulous – a figure without boundary, 'conscious of neither time nor space' (T, xix, 162). Form is only present in the background; 'she was in a dream wherein familiar objects appeared as having light and shade and position, but no particular outline' (T, xxvii, 211), and 'moved about in a mental cloud of many-coloured idealities, which eclipsed all sinister contingencies by its brightness' (T, xxxiii, 254). In the later phase of the novel at Flintcomb-Ash farm, the colour spectrum is reversed and hard forms or outlines replace the softness of the light and colour effects – Tess is now surrounded by 'an achromatic chaos of things', 'a disordered medley of grays' (T, xliii, 335), with 'flints in bulbous, cusped, and phallic shapes' (T, xliii, 331), and the 'black angularities' of Alec D'Urberville's face (T, xlv, 352).

The correspondences with Turner's paintings are striking, especially his later works which Hardy so admired. Turner's abandonment of one-point perspective for a shifting, variegated representation of his subject matter – breaking with a unified classical mode where material detail and precision combine with a stable single-point centripetal perspective for a more fluid, centrifugal vision where colour and a sense of movement or kinesis such as in *Rain, Steam, and Speed – The Great Western Railway* (1844, see Illustration 1) are dominant – finds literary equivalents in *Tess* and *Jude*. His later paintings mark the beginnings of what we might think of as modern art, anticipating purely chromatic, non-figurative work in his paintings of the 1830s and 1840s such as *Landscape with Water* (c.1835–40) or *Norham Castle, sunrise* (c.1840–5). The lighting effects through which Tess's character is expressed in the literary text also feature powerfully through the work of the two cinematographers who worked on Polanski's *Tess*,[25] and although the film rarely achieves Hardy's levels of abstraction or 'idiosyncrasy', a term which Ruskin[26] as well as Hardy applied to Turner, the texture of colour, light, and shade in the cinematic text works very effectively in ways which parallel those in the novel, providing an emotional colour spectrum for Tess's predicament. The film's final scene where Tess is apprehended at Stonehenge recalls Turner's study of Stonehenge, originally published as an engraving in 1832, but the original watercolour was on public display in the Royal Academy in 1889, which Hardy would have viewed. The cinematic images do not contain the dramatic cloudscape and lightning of Turner's painting, but the overall effect is highly Turneresque with its aqueous tones and the final sunrise.

Illustration 1. Joseph Mallord William Turner, *Rain, Steam, and Speed – The Great Western Railway* (National Gallery, London).

Although there are no direct references to Turner in *Jude the Obscure*, the subject matter has much in common with his later paintings: the clash of modernity and tradition, the significance of Gothic and classical styles, the impact of the machine – especially transport and the railway; a novel, as Hardy stated, that is 'all contrasts' (*Life*, 272). Certainly in Winterbottom's painterly film, Turneresque allusions are used to considerable effect, most notably the first train journey that Jude takes, which is reminiscent of *Rain, Steam, and Speed*, admired by Hardy. The film's overall feel in terms of colour, light, and shade is close to the novel. Hardy employs a much reduced colour spectrum as compared with the idealised sections of *Tess* and earlier novels, indeed *Jude* might almost be thought of as a black-and-white novel such is the emphasis on *chiaroscuro* and the overall bleak and sombre tones which predominate. The limited number of pictorial references tends to accentuate this effect, such as that to Sebastiano del Piombo's *The Raising of Lazarus* to describe his ailing aunt Drusilla's countenance (J, III, ix, 210). The film draws on these visual and painterly qualities to considerable effect, the brief first section at Marygreen being in monochrome only in which Winterbottom employs a range of camera perspectives from the exaggerated perspective of the

Illustration 2. Edouard Manet, *A Bar at the Folies-Bergère* (The Samuel Courtauld Trust, Courtauld Institute of Art Gallery, London).

ploughed field, evocative of the novel's 'The fresh harrow-lines seemed to stretch like the channellings in a piece of new corduroy' (J, I, ii, 33), to a moment rendered as if through young Jude's eyes as he walks to the school, to an aerial perspective of the beginning of Phillotson's journey to Christminster culminating in the panoramic view of Christminster. This scene is rendered as if 'miraged' as in the novel, owing more, as Hardy's narrator describes Jude's recollection, to 'the painter's imagination' (J, I, iii, 42). The cinematic image of Christminster, still in monochrome, is as of a conventional realist watercolour with its one-point perspective and distant steeples – the illusory stasis a sharp contrast to the preceding juxtapositions. As Paul Niemeyer remarks, '[Winterbottom] uses his locations to create a sense of barrenness and dislocation. If anything, this *seems* like what a film of *Jude the Obscure should* look like.'[27]

Perhaps the most striking painterly parallel between novel and film revolves around the dislocating use of mirrors, which I would suggest is derived from Edouard Manet's last major work painted in 1881, *A Bar at the Folies-Bergère* (see Illustration 2). Although the possibility of direct influence must remain speculative, it was frequently exhibited between

1882 and 1900 at the salon in Paris which Hardy visited in the 1880s. The scene in the novel which corresponds to Manet's painting is that when Jude returns to Christminster to discover Arabella working in a tavern:

At the back of the barmaids rose bevel-edged mirrors, with glass shelves running along their front, on which stood precious liquids that Jude did not know the name of, in bottles of topaz, sapphire, ruby and amethyst. The moment was enlivened by the entrance of some customers into the next compartment, and the starting of the mechanical tell-tale of monies received, which emitted a ting-ting every time a coin was put in.

The barmaid attending to this compartment was invisible to Jude's direct glance, though a reflection of her back in the glass behind her occasionally caught his eyes. He had only observed this listlessly, when she turned her face for a moment to the glass to set her hair tidy. Then he was amazed to discover that the face was Arabella's. (J, IV, xxv, 199)

There are obvious striking similarities between the novel scene and the painting. The physical appearance of the barmaid in Manet's painting could well pass for Arabella: both are dressed in black and white and wearing flowers in their bosoms; the colours of the liqueurs are similar. But the main corresponding feature is the complexity in their visual relations: what is reflection and what is not? Does the mirror reveal more indirectly than the unreflected image? Manet was working within the established conventions of realist painting, but pushing them to their limits with this work; as with Turner's later works, the unitary perspective of the viewer is fragmented and problematised – and there is also the self-reflexive dimension, which raises fundamental questions about representation and the viewer. Certainly it reveals Jude's dislocation and the impossibility of fixing Arabella's duplicitous identity as he watches her flirting with a stranger, ironically telling him that she has left her husband in Australia. The innovative uses of perspective and narrative point of view reveal that Arabella's reflection is in a sense her true self, though her true self is multiple and fractured – arguably more equipped to survive in a modern and mobile environment than Jude is. Manet's painting has been described as a defining point in Parisian culture representing the relations between production and consumption: the scene presented in the mirror reveals a world of commodification and transaction of desire which parallels the scene Jude observes in the mirror. The interplay of distorted perspectives resists attempts to unify or organicise, in much the same way that the novel overall resists the kind of resolution to be found in Hardy's earlier fiction.

Winterbottom's film makes much use of painterly techniques, many of the interior and portrait scenes reminiscent in their colouring and composition of Italian and Dutch classical art: the first scene in colour of Jude working with stonemasons in a church, and some of the landscapes suggestive of English Victorian landscapes – such as the winter scene when Jude first leaves Arabella to visit his aunt. Winterbottom also evokes a *fin-de-siècle* atmosphere reminiscent of Manet in the tavern scenes with Kate Winslet's cigarette-smoking Sue. When Jude discovers Arabella working as a barmaid, the parallels are striking: the use of reflected figures in mirrors and the uncertainty of where the bar is, blurred images and frosted glass, coloured bottles on shelves, recall both Hardy's scene and Manet's painting. Although the narrative line in the film is rather more explicit, culminating with Jude and Arabella in bed again in Christminster, the sharp contrast with more traditionally rendered scenes is a powerful visual correlative for the transactional and consumerist culture which engulfs Jude – ironically his drink from Arabella is 'on the house'.

Hardy's developing interest in painting and the visual arts not only provided an alternative aesthetic which informed his views on and writing of fiction, but also means that his novels can be read as more innovative and experimental and thus situated closer to modernism than has often been appreciated. It is certainly the case that Hardy's writing accentuates the visual in ways which anticipate the advent of cinema, and which lend themselves to cinematic adaptation, perhaps more so than many of his contemporary novelists. Cinematic treatments inevitably colour the ways in which we read Hardy's fiction. Walter Benjamin's thesis that film is a medium which demystifies the 'aura' of static high art forms, painting in particular, is somewhat problematic if applied to film versions of Hardy's novels. On the one hand they reach a much wider audience, as Hardy himself anticipated when consulted about an early film version of *Tess of the D'Urbervilles*, but on the other hand arguably they do more to create an aura of English pastoral and period drama than produce 'a tremendous shattering of tradition'[28] – an effect which the novels themselves and Turner's paintings unquestionably achieve.

NOTES

1. See Sheila Berger, *Thomas Hardy and Visual Structures: Framing, Disruption, Process* (New York: New York University Press, 1990); J. B. Bullen, *The Expressive Eye: Fiction and Perception in the Work of Thomas Hardy* (Oxford: Clarendon Press, 1986); Joan Grundy, *Hardy and the Sister Arts* (London: Macmillan, 1979); Roger Webster, 'Visual Imagination in the Novels of Thomas Hardy' (unpublished PhD thesis, University of London, 1979).
2. See for example John Peck, 'Hardy and Joyce: A Basis for Comparison', *Ariel* 12 (1971) 71–86.
3. J. Hillis Miller, *Thomas Hardy: Distance and Desire* (Cambridge, Mass.: Harvard University Press, 1970).

4. Thomas Hardy, *The Dynasts* (1904–8), Introduction by John Wain (London: Macmillan, 1965), p.xiii.
5. David Lodge, 'Thomas Hardy as Cinematic Novelist', in Lance St John Butler (ed.), *Thomas Hardy After Fifty Years* (London: Macmillan, 1977), p.80.
6. Thomas Hardy, *A Pair of Blue Eyes* (London: Macmillan, 1975), pp.240–1. I have used the paperback version of the Macmillan New Wessex Edition for all Hardy's novels referred to in this chapter.
7. Florence Emily Hardy, *The Life of Thomas Hardy 1840–1928* (London: Macmillan, 1962), p.235. Subsequent references to the *Life* in brackets in the text are to this edition.
8. Thomas Hardy, 'The Science of Fiction' (1891), in Peter Widdowson (ed.), *Thomas Hardy: Selected Poetry and Non-Fictional Prose* (London: Macmillan, 1997), pp.262–3.
9. Quoted in Laurence Lerner and John Holmstrom (eds.), *Thomas Hardy and His Readers: A Selection of Contemporary Reviews* (London: Bodley Head, 1968), p.30. Henry James reviewed *Far From the Madding Crowd* in *The Nation*, New York, 24 December 1874.
10. William Empson, *Some Versions of Pastoral* (London: Chatto and Windus, 1986), p.22. First published 1935.
11. Bullen, *Expressive Eye*, p.47.
12. In addition to Hardy's journal and notebook entries which were published in Florence Emily Hardy, *The Life of Thomas Hardy 1840–1928*, see also Richard H. Taylor (ed.), *The Personal Notebooks of Thomas Hardy* (London: Macmillan, 1978), which includes 'The Schools of Painting Notebook', pp.103–14.
13. Thomas Hardy, 'The Profitable Reading of Fiction' (1888), in Widdowson (ed.), *Thomas Hardy*, p.247.
14. *Ibid.*
15. *Ibid.* The jar of 'Keelwell's Marmalade' on Sorrow's grave (T, xiv, 133) is a good example of this.
16. Hardy, 'The Science of Fiction', in Widdowson (ed.), *Thomas Hardy*, p.262.
17. In these essays Virginia Woolf criticises John Galsworthy, H. G. Wells, and particularly Arnold Bennett as 'materialists' who in their attention to detailed description and 'solidity' lose the essence of life's 'impressions'. See Virginia Woolf, 'Modern Fiction', in David Lodge (ed.), *20th-Century Literary Criticism: A Reader* (London: Longman, 1972), pp.88–9.
18. Hardy, 'The Science of Fiction', in Widdowson (ed.), *Thomas Hardy*, p.262.
19. *Ibid.*, p.264.
20. See J. Hillis Miller, Introduction to The New Wessex Edition of Thomas Hardy, *The Well-Beloved* (London: Macmillan, 1975), pp.16–18.
21. Berger, *Thomas Hardy*, p.35.
22. Peter Widdowson, *Hardy in History* (London: Routledge, 1989), pp.11–16.
23. For example, see *Life*, 'What has been written cannot be blotted. Each new style of novel must be the old with added ideas' p.218; or FMC p.273, 'man, even to himself, is a palimpsest, having an ostensible writing, and another beneath the lines'. See also J. Hillis Miller's introduction to *The Well-Beloved* above, pp.15–16, on Proust's comments on the novel in which he identifies the repetitive plot symmetries in Hardy's novels.
24. Hardy, 'The Science of Fiction', in Widdowson (ed.), *Thomas Hardy*, p.264.

25. The Directors of Photography were Geoffrey Unsworth and Ghislain Cloquet; Unsworth died during the making of the film.
26. See John Ruskin, *Modern Painters* (London: George Allen, 1898), vol. IV, p.259. First published 1856.
27. Paul J. Niemeyer, *Seeing Hardy: Film and Television Adaptations of the Fiction of Thomas Hardy* (Jefferson, N. C.: McFarland, 2003), p.172.
28. Walter Benjamin, 'The Work of Art in the Age of Mechanical Reproduction' (1933), in *Illuminations* (London: Fontana, 1973), p.219.

3   Wessex on film

Simon Gatrell

At the simplest, Hardy's Wessex is a fictional region of England, with fictional names for most of its places; however, his work and the regional name he resuscitated have proved so popular that now there is English Wessex as well as Hardy's Wessex, which latter has come to mean a nineteenth-century quintessentially rural space. For most viewers of adaptations of his novels it is enough that countryside with cows or sheep predominates, that the people wear period costume, and speak with accents that are more or less south-western. But all the film-makers who have addressed Hardy's fiction have felt the pressure of Hardy's Wessex – and in particular of the local-historian mode of Hardy's later years, in which places, customs, music, history were exactly so and no other, and if they were not he provided a note explaining the divergence.

Despite this pressure, it has proved impossible for any film-maker to shoot any scene in the place that Hardy intended. There are various reasons for this – historical (the place has changed too much to be convincingly Victorian), circumstantial (the film had to be made out of England for legal reasons, or it had to be made out of Wessex for financial reasons), or aesthetic (the film offers a deconstruction of Wessex). However almost all the films do make an attempt to provide settings that approximate to what Hardy described, whether in Brittany or Cheshire or Dorset.

There are a number of straightforward devices that film-makers can employ to convince an audience that what they are seeing is indeed Hardy's Wessex. The application of Hardy's fictional name to the place shown is one: presenting an image of Shaftesbury and calling it Casterbridge, or Corfe Castle and calling it Casterbridge, or Cerne Abbas and calling it Casterbridge, or Buxton and calling it Casterbridge. Only a handful of viewers would be aware both that Hardy based Casterbridge on Dorchester and that what was on the screen was not Dorchester; and not many of those would care, perhaps. Naturally enough this Wessex-naming occurs in every film, but the practice has been unevenly applied. Of the two versions of *Far From the Madding Crowd*, for instance, Schlesinger's is very sparing with Wessex names – just Weatherbury and Casterbridge, and the latter only once; whereas Renton's spatters them all over the place, even down to the dragging of Newmill Pond (which we never actually see in the novel), or Fanny's lodging at Mrs Twills in North Street in Melchester. Schlesinger's film is shot entirely within the boundaries of Hardy's Wessex, and more than any other (perhaps because it was the first adaptation of the modern era) attempts to take account of the fact that Wessex for Hardy was a cumulative idea – fourteen novels, forty-odd stories, and many poems all contributing something to the culture, history, density of the place – by including allusions to other novels: Frank Troy rides with a reddleman across a heath, and they pass men burdened with bundles of furze; Boldwood introduces a steam threshing-machine to the remote arable districts of Wessex, though he does not invite any women to work on it (and also he apparently has not heard of the seed-drill that Farfrae some fifteen or twenty years earlier had recommended to Casterbridge[1] – where indeed a younger Boldwood was on the commission to enquire into Henchard's bankruptcy); there is also present on Boldwood's farm the horse-drawn reaping-machine that Hardy describes so eloquently in *Tess of the D'Urbervilles*; some of the misery of the hiring fair in Casterbridge is borrowed straight from Hardy's important essay 'The Dorsetshire Labourer', as is the idea of house-ridding (which also turns up in *Tess of the D'Urbervilles*) – the shepherd Samways's family and all their possessions on a cart outside an inn. Since Schlesinger is so assiduous in suggesting to the informed viewer his awareness of the wider context into which the ideas of *Far From the Madding Crowd* might be fitted, perhaps he saw no particular need to reinforce the authenticity of the environment with widespread use of Hardy's names.

Renton's adaptation, on the other hand, starts with a Wessex handicap; the environment of the film is even to a casual eye north-of-England. The scale is too large for Dorset, the slopes are too steep; the distances are too great, the drystone walls and split stone roofs are pervasive; there are barely any hedgerows. It is easy enough to find out that the settings are in the neighbourhood of Macclesfield and Buxton on the borders of the Peak District, and perhaps the economic concerns of Granada, the Manchester-based television company, dictated this decision. Hence the proliferation of Wessex names, continually reassuring disconcerted viewers that it is, in spite of the evidence of their eyes, Wessex they are seeing.

All the adaptations recognise that some kind of regional accent is essential for most of the characters, but there is very little speech in any that would decently pass for Dorset, and when there is, what the characters are given to say is often patronisingly humorous, as for instance

Joseph Poorgrass and Cainy Ball driving home from Casterbridge to Weatherbury near the beginning of Schlesinger's *Far From the Madding Crowd*. It is depressing to hear Nastassja Kinski's Tess wavering between German and mummerset, or Alan Bates as Henchard widening his accent to match his wig. The least offensive solution is to have the important characters who are expected to speak with an accent merely broaden a few vowels and emphasise a little their Rs, and leave the rest to the imagination. All of the workfolk use some basic Wessex grammar, but there is a ration of about one Wessex dialect word per film.

Much more successful is the use of traditional music and dance. Dance was a great thing for Hardy, and it becomes a great indicator of Wessex for film-makers, who invent scenes like the three-handed reel that develops to Gabriel Oak's flute-playing at Casterbridge in Schlesinger's *Far From the Madding Crowd* – an addition which is justified by the stony gaze of the shepherd Samways, who has just been hired by Boldwood at the starvation rate of seven shillings a week, staring at the folly of those who can dance in the face of such dealings.

Hardy everywhere shows the potential dance has to stimulate erotic attraction, and the film-makers see this too. The scene wherein Eustacia and Damon dance at East Egdon, for instance, achieves a very powerful sexual charge, as do Elizabeth-Jane and Donald at the celebrations in Casterbridge – but it is in *Tess of the D'Urbervilles* that Hardy exploits this aspect of dance to its full, through the intensely eroticised and chaotic dance in the hay-trusser's barn at Chaseborough:

Of the rushing couples there could barely be discerned more than the high lights – the indistinctness shaping them to satyrs clasping nymphs – a multiplicity of Pans whirling a multiplicity of Syrinxes; Lotis attempting to elude Priapus, and always failing.[2]

Ian Sharp's LWT account of the scene interprets Hardy's description in a naturalistic way, the dancers, some stripped to their underclothing, performing manoeuvres more like 1940s jitterbugging, communicating very forcibly that what they perform is no structured set dance, but a rhythmical riot. In Polanski's *Tess* the dancers are considerably more restrained, and remain fully clothed. Sharp comes much closer to realising the combination of sexual charge and ominous anarchy that Hardy generates as prelude to Tess's imminent violation. Indeed this scene represents vividly the fundamental difference between the two versions: in keeping with the passivity pervading Polanski's film, Nastassja Kinski waits for her friend so far away from the dance as to be entirely dissociated from it, while Justine Waddell's energetically active Tess sits almost within the barn (and is evidently entertained by the orgiastic gyrations she so intently watches).

Work is an essential element of Wessex. In the course of his writing Hardy explored a very large range of rural occupations, and on occasion considered the machinery that was replacing the hand culture and craft that predominate in his work. Directors too delight to show sheep-dipping or shearing, spar-making, milking cows, harvesting, and sowing, though they offer only a very intermittent sense that the labour could be hard – in the versions of *Tess of the D'Urbervilles*, in Renton's account of Fanny Robin, in Marty South. They also dwell with interest on the early machines, horse-drawn reapers, or steam-driven threshers. It is Renton's *Far From the Madding Crowd* that shows most clearly the large number of labourers required for efficient haymaking and harvesting by hand, and by implication how many livelihoods will be lost when Oak-introduced machines take over part of the work.

All the foregoing material aspects of Wessex (and others, such as dress, or social customs and rituals) are relatively easy to produce or reproduce in the *mise-en-scène*. Film-makers are faced with greater complexity when they wish to communicate the inward elements of Wessex. In all of Hardy's work the characters have an intimate and powerful relationship with the places they live and work in; to a greater or lesser degree their lives are shaped by their environments. Many writers have some such understanding, but none embodies it with such intensity and consistency. In this respect, finding satisfactory fields and cows is not sufficient. It is easy enough to recognise, for example, that in *The Woodlanders* humans are often seen in terms of trees, and trees often have human characteristics, but finding a way to communicate this interpenetration on the screen is another matter. As almost every theorist on film adaptations has noted, film finds simile and metaphor hard. Hardy can write that the smoke rising from the chimney of Marty South's cottage is like another tree-trunk, but it is difficult (though perhaps not impossible) to make that verbal comparison resonate visually. It is one of many similar details in *The Woodlanders* that Phil Agland does not try to incorporate into his filmed account of the novel.

Indeed, in terms of place, *The Woodlanders* and *The Return of the Native* offer more particular problems for the film-maker, since they are both set primarily in a single isolated environment with very powerful and complex metaphorical qualities that Hardy keeps at all times at the forefront of the reader's consciousness. How might it be possible to bring to the screen all that Hardy ascribes to Egdon Heath, or the relationships he creates between it and Eustacia, Clym, or Thomasin? The simple answer is that it is not possible; but if the adaptation is to carry any conviction as a version of the novel, then it has to pay some particular attention to the heath. A closer look at a couple of scenes from either film will suggest some possible solutions to such difficulties.

The celebrated first chapter is not the only place in *The Return of the Native* where Hardy gives life, almost consciousness, to the environment in which the action takes place, but it is the most prominent, and it is quite unsuited to film. A director and screenwriter might ignore it perhaps, or try to incorporate some of its strength and discursiveness in later scenes. Gold's version of the novel has been almost universally derided, and not without reason – many of the compression decisions made in the screenplay seem wrong-headed, the dialogue is often wooden, and the actors mostly make it worse, even a seasoned professional like Joan Plowright (as Mrs Yeobright). However, he decided to take on the first chapter of the novel, and to use the opening credits of the film to make the audience aware of the essential fabric of his heath, and of one character's relation to it.

The first title reads 'Thomas Hardy's The Return of the Native', which appears over a long shot of an upland landscape, golden brown in autumn, dissected by a stream, with a patch of green on one hilltop; the country is wild and unpopulated (it is in fact a fragment of Exmoor National Park, which is not Dorset heathland, but then neither is Egdon, being itself half-imaginary). It is brightly lit, though, which seems against the grain of Hardy's opening chapter. The shot then fades to the back of a full-length hooded cloak in blue, billowing out with the speed of its wearer striding uphill through dead bracken, as other credits move across the screen. Then there is a cut to the same cloak walking along a rocky path alongside a small river rushing in spate down falls, after which it fades to a man in an old coat and hat digging clay in a patch of grass beside the same small river, and the blue cloak walking past without breaking stride or turning to acknowledge the other human presence; then it fades again to the underbelly of a ram in a pen being anointed with some red substance that the previous shot might imply is recently dug clay, the shot panning to the right to show a small flock of ewes in an adjoining pen, and beyond them the blue cloak walking uphill. Now it fades to a close-up of a man carrying a burden of furze-branches who walks across the shot, revealing behind him the blue-cloaked figure walking away into a furzy valley that sharply recalls Hardy's accounts of Egdon – all this to the accompaniment of an urgently romantic waltz, which refers more to the cloak than the country. The next fade is half-revelatory – a side-on shot of the figure in the blue cloak striding against a now misty sky along a grassy slope; it was always a woman's cloak, but now the skirt of a dress and a profile framed by the hood make the wearer's gender clear for the first time. After this the fade is to the same figure still moving with long steps and great vitality up a steep hillside covered with golden bracken and some small winter-bare trees – the waltz theme drives her on; then another fade to a close-up of her back as she climbs the hillside, bathed in sunshine again now, despite the wintry vegetation. Again there is a fade, this time to a long shot, the blue figure melting into the blue sky as she reaches the top of the hill, the shot zooming in over the hillside towards her; and then a climactic fade to close-up from a different angle (and surely a different setting) as her hands throw back her hood and reveal the exquisitely beautiful face of Catherine Zeta Jones (who enacts Eustacia Vye). At the same time we hear her voice-over: 'Deliver my heart from this fearful lonely place, send me a great love from somewhere, or else I shall die, truly I shall die'; as this continues, there is a fade to what is soon evidently an aerial shot, at first revealing that she is standing on one of the hills that was in the opening shot of the credits, and then fading to a different angle as the shot pulls away still further and the figure diminishes and merges into the brown hillside on the opposite side of the valley. At the same time the voice-over melts into a soprano vocalise that spirals with ultimate sentimentality into silence. Finally there is a fade into darkness with specks of flickering light, the tune of a folk-ballad ('Earl Marshall') played on folk instruments and the caption: 'Egdon Heath 1842'.

This opening works quite hard and effectively. Primarily it prepares the viewer for a narrative of romantic intensity – through the music, through the tantalising focus on the figure's back, through the figure's isolation from even potential human contact, through the dramatic flourish of revelation of the darkly beautiful face that turns in the general direction of the camera with slightly parted lips that might suggest passion or anguish, through the character's plea for a surpassing love to save her from inevitable death; it tells a viewer where the emphasis of this reading of Hardy's novel will fall. But the opening also attempts to address some other important aspects of Hardy's text. The country itself is established as significant, and as uncultivated and apparently uninhabited; it might even be said that visually it does offer a landscape of 'chastened sublimity' such as Hardy describes, though the tonal quality of the music runs rather counter to such a conception. But the sequence does more: it suggests some important aspects of Eustacia's relationship with the landscape. She calls the place 'fearful and lonely', but the context suggests paradoxically that her plea for a lover who will take her away from the place is made to the place itself. The camera has stressed Eustacia's isolation in the environment and from those who are able to exploit its resources, not only by her obliviousness to the people but because her back is turned in rejection of all the viewer can see; however, towards the end of her pilgrimage through the heath she is twice seen to fade into the environment – once into the sky, once into the earth – moments which imply an unconscious and unacknowledged harmony with the fearful and lonely place; and they also diminish the scale of the human in relation to the landscape, as the opening chapter of the novel does. This unconscious harmony between Eustacia and the heath is felt throughout the novel, pulling against her conscious hatred of it.

The successive scenes of the digging and application of reddle must appear rather mysterious to an uninitiated viewer, and indeed they are rather artificial, but they are as good an explanation of what Diggory Venn does, why he is red-skinned, as could be managed without a verbal account. The furze-gatherer is irreproachable, and represents the only Egdon trade. Eustacia's dramatic disregard for the two workfolk she passes accurately reflects not only her self-isolation, but also her class-disdain for those socially beneath her. The final fade, out of credits into the film proper, denotes both place and time, and the contrast between the floridly scored but repetitive waltz of Eustacia's romantic heart and the edgy fiddle-and-accordion, and equally repetitive folk tune, effects a class-transition as well as a thematic one.

There is not much in the rest of the film that will stand up so well to detailed scrutiny; especially (and sadly) laughable is the scene in which the newly returned Clym Yeobright declares his love for the heath and leaves his mother and cousin in their trap to walk home by himself. The film-makers mostly invent the sequence. Their excellent intention is to create a parallel with the opening credits: the scene is very much shorter though, and includes two moments of unconscious comedy, the first when Clym pauses before his walk to take in deep breaths of heath-air, in a Pythonesque parody of urban man reaching countryside at last; the second when Eustacia appears to him out of a suddenly gathered mist, stroking a white horse, like a latter-day virgin with a unicorn, is then obscured, and has disappeared seconds later when the mist thins again. The scene is too brief to establish visually any harmony between Clym and the country he walks through; what it rather confirms is the accuracy of Hardy's claim in the novel's first chapter that 'a person on a heath in raiment of modern cut and colours has more or less an anomalous look'.[3] In spite of Clym's avowal of love for Egdon, his figure in its elegantly cut grey morning-suit does appear anomalous in the landscape he walks through, and the visual alienation can be seen deliberately to anticipate Clym's fundamental misunderstanding of the lives of those who dwell and work on the heath.

Phil Agland's *The Woodlanders* is also mostly shot in the region, though as always not in the places that Hardy describes. With this novel, however, the history of Hardy's revisions to its environment offers particular support to the idea that the specifics of Wessex location in relation to England are merely a surface matter – that what matters is the fictional environment itself. To put it simply, over a 25-year period of revision

Hardy shifted the Hintocks miles eastward (for the most part by altering names and distances and directions), while descriptions of the places
themselves remained essentially unchanged.[4] Even so, in the 1912 preface to the novel Hardy wrote that he had no precise idea where to find
Little Hintock. The best he could do was to say that it was somewhere
in Blackmore Vale. The tenor of this note is similar to one he wrote the
same year for *The Return of the Native*:

> To prevent disappointment to searchers for scenery it should be added that though
> the action of the narrative is supposed to proceed in the central and most secluded
> part of the heaths united into one whole, as above described, certain topographical
> features resembling those delineated really lie on the margin of the waste, several
> miles to the westward of the centre. In some other respects also there has been a
> bringing together of scattered characteristics. (RN, author's postscript, 444)

Such warnings by Hardy could certainly be used to justify, almost to
authorise, the decisions made by Gold and Agland (and any other director) to use places that embody the essential qualities of the original, but
are quite far removed in space.

Agland's chosen settings are good at suggesting a community isolated
by woodlands and orchards, and dependent upon them; but they cannot (and do not try to) match the intensifying effect of Hardy's descriptive writing, which makes Little Hintock seem at times as if it is in the
depths of a temperate rainforest, surrounded by a belt many miles deep
of cider-apple orchards. Like the novel, the film gives a strong sense of
woodland industries and crafts (including both a sawpit with top and
bottom sawyer and a steam-engine-driven flat-bed saw not mentioned by
Hardy), and music, dance, and folk-ritual have their usual place. And
though, as already suggested, the film cannot hope to give the full effect
of Hardy's metaphors, there is a sharp intelligence at work on the fun-
damentally important interrelationship of the characters and the natural
world around them. I want to take as example the two passages in the
novel where the pain inherent in the division of Giles and Grace is felt at
its most intense.

At first viewing, the presentation in the film of the scene in chapter
twenty-eight of the novel in which Grace watches first her husband ride
away from her on a white horse towards Felice Charmond at Middleton
Abbey, and then Giles climb up the same hill towards her with his horse-
drawn cider-press, is a disappointment to anyone familiar with the novel.
Hardy's account is deliberately Keatsian: the landscape is overflowing
with fruition, Giles is autumn's very brother, and Grace herself thinks
how bountiful nature is that takes away a man with the right hand and
provides another with the left – until the reality of her married state sweeps
such pagan thoughts away. The bare bones of the scene survive in the film:

there is a hillside along and down which Edred slowly disappears, but it is bare and grassy, and the path along which the horse picks its way is much too narrow for a cider-press; so, as the white horse vanishes towards the bottom left of the frame, the long shot remains virtually static, and at the top right, on a track hitherto unperceived, Giles appears leading his horse. The first of Hardy's ironies is thus excluded – Giles has not passed Edred on the way. But the radical difference is in the landscape itself; we are offered in the film a very beautiful image of Giles, his horse and his press against a woodland, but the wood appears to be in spring, April perhaps, not September – ash trees are still bare; and instead of the warmth of the splendid sunset Hardy describes, the light is decidedly cold as Giles draws up to Grace. The ensuing dialogue is altered, so that they break down the reserve between them through the identification of the variety of apples on Giles's waggon, rather than through discussion of the novel's further irony that Giles gave Grace the horse on which her husband is betraying her. Almost at once, in both novel and film, they are driven apart emotionally through a piece of conventional propriety. In the novel Grace (as a married woman) objects to Giles caressing a flower she wears between her breasts (with sensuous metonymical force); in the film, with much less metaphorical charge, she simply rejects Giles's offer to walk her home, because she is a married woman.

The effect of the two versions is quite different. It is possible that there was time-pressure and financial pressure on the film-makers which forced them to shoot at a specific season and place, but if so they have chosen to utilise the situation to make a different statement from Hardy's, but one equally powerful. The relative barrenness of the landscape, the coolness of the light, the drabness of the clothes both wear, are designed to underline the perpetual futility of the relationship between Giles and Grace, even now that Grace is being set aside by her husband. What Hardy, on the other hand, sets out to show in the scene is the fruitful potential now present in their relationship, a potential frustrated by social convention.

But Agland recognises that he must somewhere display that potential, and use Hardy's terms in doing so. Thus, in the second crucial scene later in the film, he again alters the environment Hardy provides. The moment comes when Giles and Grace kiss passionately for the only time, where-upon Grace's father arrives to tell her that she cannot after all be divorced from her husband. In the novel the encounter takes place in the middle of anonymous woodland, Grace walking after Giles as he is on his way home; the reader's focus is on the kiss and the dialogue between them. In the film it takes place in a richly blossoming orchard, where Giles is grafting an apple-tree; the new growth thus implied, and the strong phallic sug-gestion of the scion inserted into the bark of the stock (a reminiscence of the flower in Grace's bosom), anticipate the embrace and kiss that follow, and make the arrival of Melbury with his news of failure the more painful. The effect achieved by the tonal reversal in these two scenes in the film is to delay presentation of the fertile potential between Grace and Giles until the last possible moment, and in a production which romps through Hardy's rapid plot in an hour and a half this is perhaps only sensible.

Though Renton's *Far From the Madding Crowd* was shot quite outside Wessex, and Polanski's *Tess* was filmed quite outside England, in both there is a considerable effort to find places that come close to what Hardy describes. When Michael Winterbottom filmed *Jude* hundreds of miles beyond Wessex, he did so deliberately. He rejected that aspect of Wessex that tied Christminster to Oxford, Melchester to Salisbury, Shaston to Shaftesbury, and instead offered the visual impressions he had drawn from Hardy's narrative. His most powerfully effective change was to base Christminster not on Oxford, or anywhere remotely resembling it, but on the ponderous and dark neoclassicism of regency Edinburgh. And to enforce the deliberateness of the transfer, both the socialist orator that Sue goes to listen to and the undergraduate who demands the creed in Latin from Jude have Scottish accents. The architecture and shape of Marygreen is thoroughly northern. Jude works for a while at some obscure industrial concern that might be a mine, but certainly does not fit with the popular conception of Wessex. And yet the threatening and sombre university city is called Christminster, the film is subdivided by captions repeating Hardy's own book-divisions – 'At Melchester', 'At Aldbrickham and elsewhere', and so on – and most characters with regional accents are from the south-west. The consequence might be ambiguity or confusion, but it is not, and this is because Winterbottom has understood an essential relationship between *Tess of the D'Urbervilles* and *Jude the Obscure*. *Tess of the D'Urbervilles* is the novel in which Wessex first reached its completed state as a region, in which the central character walks across what seems like half of it. *Jude the Obscure* in this respect is a counter-text; the Wessex skeleton remains – the place-names, the dialect – but Hardy uses this framework to suggest that much of the material culture that had given body to Wessex in his earlier work is irrelevant at the end of the century. It is no coincidence that Jude characteristically travels by train rather than on foot. Winterbottom just goes a step further than Hardy: if Jude and Sue can travel across Wessex by train, they can travel across Britain with as little difficulty. What is important is not that Christminster should repeat the topography of Oxford, but that the viewer should be amazed that Jude could conceive so deep an affection for a place so obviously inimical. Winterbottom retains the name Christminster because Hardy has endowed the word with so much associative significance, but its yoke to Oxford has been broken.

When he went on from *Jude* to make *The Claim*, a film based on the plot of *The Mayor of Casterbridge*, Winterbottom took his deconstruction of the idea of Wessex to the furthest possible point that would include its survival.

There is not much need to rehearse in detail the qualities of Casterbridge. Hardy provides it with a history from the Romans onwards, a history that the nineteenth-century citizens are continually knocking up against. It is a place shaped by generation upon generation of inhabitants, showing all its pasts in its architecture and its street pattern. The full title of the novel addresses itself to the life of the town with irony: the mayor is Henchard, but Casterbridge has had a mayor for hundreds of years; the life and death of the mayor is the history of the town; there are three mayors while the novel proceeds. At the same time the town is intimately connected with the surrounding agricultural countryside, socially and economically. The names of the places from which carriers' carts come to Casterbridge – 'Mellstock, Weatherbury, the Hintocks, Sherton-Abbas, Kingsbere, Overcombe' – lay down a Wessex interconnectedness amongst Hardy's novels.

Neither of the two made-for-television versions of the novel, one with Alan Bates as Henchard, the other with Ciaran Hines, is shot in Dorchester. The former was filmed in Corfe Castle, the latter in Cerne Abbas, both places sufficiently stony and with substantial histories of their own, though anyone aware of the identity between Casterbridge and Dorchester would miss many elements of the town as Hardy describes it. For *The Claim* Winterbottom removed the narrative from Wessex altogether, to California's Sierra Nevada mountains in the years after the 1849 gold rush, from Casterbridge to a town called Kingdom Come. In doing so he avoided the problem of representing Casterbridge, but in fact Casterbridge remains in the film as a ghost, as the negative image of what Winterbottom has created, as everything Kingdom Come is not.

Kingdom Come is less than twenty years old, built with gold drawn from a mine, which Dillon had accepted eighteen years earlier in exchange for his wife and child. Dillon is no elected officer temporarily supervising the affairs of Kingdom Come; he is owner, absolute monarch. He lays claim to it often and no one disputes his claim (is this the Claim, really?), and he gives the best part of it away to Lucia/Lucetta in compensation for not marrying her, as part of the expiation of his sin in selling his wife for the gold that financed the town in the first place. The town is extremely impermanent; half of it consists of tents, though you only see them in passing, and the main buildings are all leggy, wooden, constructed on stilts against the snow, quite tall but appearing fragile – though the interior scenes, especially in the saloon and whorehouse, are as solid as those in

Illustration 3. Kingdom Come is set on fire in *The Claim*, United Artists, 2000.

the Three Mariners or Peter's Finger; there are aerial walkways, also built to circumvent the snow, which are in extreme contrast with Casterbridge's firmly terrestrial Walks. At the end of the film Dillon torches the whole place (see Illustration 3), and we have understood by then that the point of Kingdom Come is that it has no history and is completely disposable. This material obliteration is a more effective last testament than Henchard's, the terms of whose will are already being set aside as they are being read.

In Hardy's vision Casterbridge's close relationship with the agricultural landscape surrounding it is as important as its fabric and history, and this intimacy with its environment Kingdom Come shares, though the environment is the opposite of fertile: from every corner of every struc-ture, snow and rock are all there is to see. Where surrounding Wessex has been laboured over, has been tamed for millennia, is on an intimate scale, is green and brown and blue, and has supported the lives of count-less men and women, the high Sierra (though actually, by a further irony, the Canadian Rockies) is black and white, on a vast scale, and hardly marked by human occupation; and though presumably native Ameri-cans had hunted in the mountains for many hundreds of years before the gold rush, the film offers no sense of that. The snow is permanent, it seems, unfruitful, sterile, full of danger. In Casterbridge life is harsh for the underclass of the town, but they do not have to face it in such arid conditions. And yet in spite of this carefully designed otherness, even in the first scene of *The Claim* there is an echo of Casterbridge: a coach driving along the snow-covered street of Kingdom Come pushes aside a herd of cattle that blocks the road. In chapter twenty-nine of the novel Hardy wrote:

The head of stock driven into and out of the town at this season to be sold by the local auctioneer was very large; and all these horned beasts, in travelling to and fro, sent women and children to shelter as nothing else could do.[5]

The environment of *The Claim* is directly attached to that of *The Mayor of Casterbridge* in other ways – as for instance in the relationship between Dillon's cabin in the back hills and the furmity-seller's tent at Weydon fair – both containers of the central character's secret past, but continuing Winterbottom's ironic reversal in their relative permanence as structures.

What the film suggests is that Hardy's human narrative has vitality when separated from the weight of cultural history that surrounds it; but it also shows, as clearly as Hardy does, that the fates of the significant characters are intimately bound up with their environment; it doesn't matter that it is snow and mountain, tent and timber-frame, innocent of tradition or long-established custom. Wessex in itself is unimportant, even irrelevant, Winterbottom claims; but Hardy's account, found everywhere in his work, of the power of place to shape human lives, and the power of humans to transform their environment, for long or for short spaces of time, is confirmed.

NOTES

1. I take it that this anachronism was suggested by Poorgrass's song 'I sowed the seeds of love', since the film moves directly from Boldwood hand-broadcasting the seed to his first attempt to force Bathsheba to marry him at the end of the six-year waiting period after Troy's disappearance.
2. Thomas Hardy, *Tess of the D'Urbervilles*, ed. Juliet Grindle and Simon Gatrell (Oxford: Oxford University Press, 1988), ch. 10, pp.66–7.
3. Thomas Hardy, *The Return of the Native*, ed. Simon Gatrell (Oxford: Oxford University Press, 1990), ch. 1, p.6. Subsequent references in brackets in the text are to this edition.
4. Fuller details can be found in my *Thomas Hardy's Vision of Wessex* (Basingstoke: Palgrave, 2003), pp.136–9, and on the website associated with the book (www.english.uga.edu/Wessex).
5. Thomas Hardy, *The Mayor of Casterbridge*, ed. Dale Kramer (Oxford: Oxford University Press, 1987), p.205.

4   The silent era: Thomas Hardy goes
way down east

Peter Widdowson

To be invited to write the essay on silent film versions of Thomas Hardy's
fiction is, it transpires, to draw the short straw. This is for one simple
but incontrovertible reason: of the five films known to have been made of
his novels between 1913 and 1929, all prints are, in the words of movie
databases, 'presumed lost'. In other words, there is nothing to write about.
What, then, is one to do – except compose the ultimate postmodern essay:
depthless, contentless, a meta-essay that can only circle round its absent
centre and navel-gaze its own inability to be written? I confess there were
moments when I thought of producing a spoof piece which claimed to
have found a silent film version of Hardy's famously 'lost' first novel,
The Poor Man and the Lady, but faced with the Borgesian intricacies of
trying to invent an earnest discussion of the way the film adapted and
visualised a text which did not exist, I shied away (it remains a tempting
idea, though). And then I had a stroke of luck – the nature and results of
which will comprise the bulk of the later part of this essay.

But first, let me briefly clear the ground regarding those lost silent films
that we know about. As Paul J. Niemeyer's book *Seeing Hardy: Film and
Television Adaptations of the Fiction of Thomas Hardy* does this fairly exhaus-
tively – especially in his 'Appendix A: The "Lost" Hardy Adaptations,
1913–1953' – there is little point in repeating much of his research here.
But it is worth establishing that there were four silent films made during
Hardy's lifetime and one the year after he died: a Famous Players Film
Company (USA) version of *Tess of the D'Urbervilles* in 1913 (all details
appear in the 'Filmography' at the end of the present volume); a Turner
Films Ltd (UK) *Far From the Madding Crowd* in 1915; a Progress Film
Company (UK) *The Mayor of Casterbridge* in 1921; a Metro-Goldwyn-
Mayer (USA) *Tess* in 1924; and a British International Pictures (UK)
Under the Greenwood Tree in 1929. Given how recent was the provenance
of the new technological art form, it is to Hardy's credit that in his seventies and eighties he could react with the considerable aplomb his letters
reveal to the overtures made to him to adapt his work for the cinema – perhaps merely confirming the now long-running critical notion that Hardy

was a 'filmic' writer *avant la lettre*, that he had an instinctive and prescient sympathy with the form. More prosaically, it suggests his business sense: as early as 22 February 1911, he writes to Sir Frederick Macmillan for advice on an enquiry seeking to make a film of *Tess*: 'I should imagine that an exhibition of successive scenes from *Tess* . . . could do no harm to the book, & might possibly advertise it among a new class';[1] and on 12 March, on accepting the offer of 'ten per cent on the gross turnover', he comments to Macmillan: 'I confess that my chief thought was whether it would affect the book-sales' (*Letters*, IV, 142–3).

The film under discussion was the Famous Players' *Tess* of 1913, starring Minnie Maddern Fiske, and Hardy attended a private view of it in October, but his only recorded comments about it are tantalisingly (and typically) close to his own chest. The first is in a letter to Sir George Douglas of 23 October: 'It was a curious production, & I was interested in it as a scientific toy; but I can say nothing as to its relation to, or rendering of, the story' (*Letters*, IV, 312); the second, to Edward Clodd on 10 December, mentions that the film is already on release in London: 'You would be amused to see an Americanized Wessex Dairy. However, it *doesn't* matter to me or to the book how they represent it' (*Letters*, IV, 327–8). Despite Hardy's own emphasis here, there is some disingenuousness, as we shall see, in his suggestion of indifference as to how the film-makers treat his novel.

The Turner Film Company production in 1915 of *Far From the Madding Crowd*, adapted and directed by Larry Trimble and starring Florence Turner, is one of the better documented of Hardy's silent films. Hardy signed the agreement in June 1915, the London trade and press premiere was on 16 November that year, and general release was on 28 February 1916. A manuscript draft of the synopsis which Hardy may have written for the premiere souvenir programme (to be discussed in more detail by Keith Wilson in chapter seven) is in the Dorset County Museum, as is a copy of the programme itself – extensively illustrated with stills from what it calls the 'picture play'. The day after the premiere, when a reviewer was praising the 'Wessex' authenticity of the film,[2] Hardy wrote to Macmillan: 'I am glad to hear that Far from the Madding Crowd comes out so well' (*Letters*, V [1985], 133). However, a letter of 9 October 1920, when he was being pressed to renew the film rights to the novel by a director who had bought them off the now defunct Turner Film Company, contains the ambiguous comment: 'As it seems to have been a failure . . .', where 'it' could refer to either the film or the company (*Letters*, VI [1987], 42). But this did not stop Hardy from responding quite positively to approaches to turn his work into film. Back in November 1915, despite earlier misgivings, he reflects to Macmillan: '"The Dynasts" is still more interesting as a possible film' (*Letters*, V, 133; he returns to this idea on 24 October 1919: *ibid.*, 335) – hence pre-empting John Wain's later critical judgment that devices in the epic drama are 'cinematic' and that its text is, in effect, 'a shooting-script'.[3] February 1918 sees him entertaining the possibility of a British Actors' Film Company version of *Jude the Obscure*, although the film appears never to have been made (*Letters*, V, 254), and in another letter to Macmillan, on 24 October 1919, he scans his fictional *oeuvre* to see which novels it would be possible or appropriate for a British company to buy the rights to: 'there are plenty that the Master Films Co. might have . . . Anyhow, The Mayor of Casterbridge, The Trumpet Major, and (if they want sensation) Desperate Remedies, would film very well, I should think, so that if you are willing to offer them either [sic] of these I would agree' (*Letters*, V, 335).

On 19 February 1921, Hardy was wondering whether to insert the words 'No alteration or adaptation being such as to burlesque or otherwise misrepresent the general character of the novel' into the agreement with the Progress Film Company of Shoreham, Sussex, to film *The Mayor of Casterbridge* (*Letters*, VI, 72). Nevertheless, he checked out the scenario for the film as requested by its director and screenwriter, Sidney Morgan, commenting on 22 March: 'Will see to the dialect of the titles [sub-titles in a silent film] &c. The general arrangement seems as good as is compatible with presentation by cinemas.' He also recommended Hermann Lea's photographic guide-book, *Thomas Hardy's Wessex* (1913), 'for guidance' (*Letters*, VI, 78). The film was also the occasion of the 81-year-old Hardy's gently ironic observation to Florence Henniker on 2 July 1921:

This morning we have had an odd experience. The film-makers are here doing scenes for "The Mayor of C." & they asked us to come & see the process. The result is that I have been talking to The Mayor, Mrs Henchard, Eliz. Jane, & the rest, in the flesh . . . It is a strange business to be engaged in. (*Letters*, VI, 93)

The final film involving Hardy was the 1924 Metro-Goldwyn-Mayer Corporation adaptation of *Tess of the D'Urbervilles*, directed by Marshall Neilan, starring Blanche Sweet, Conrad Nagel as Angel, and Stuart Holmes as Alec. On 13 September 1922, he was again worried by the phrasing of the agreement with the company, especially 'the right "to adapt and change the said work and the title thereof" – under which the Corporation would have power to distort or burlesque the novel, to the possible injury of the book here in England as elsewhere' (*Letters*, VI, 152). Nevertheless, on 25 October 1922, a letter from Florence Emily Hardy to a representative of Goldwyn Pictures in London indicates that Hardy saw it as 'a great advantage' that the film was being shot on location in England (the 1913 *Tess*, 'being American made, having failed to carry

Illustration 4. Tess (Blanche Sweet) and Angel (Conrad Nagel) are surprised at Stonehenge in *Tess of the D'Urbervilles*, MGM, 1924.

conviction over here'), and that he would again help with 'hints' about 'characters, places, &c' (*Letters*, VI, 163). There is no further reference to it in the letters and nothing to suggest Hardy ever saw it. A typescript copy of the screenplay, however, indicates that while the plot keeps closely to Hardy's, the time-setting of the action has been moved from the nineteenth century to the early 1920s (featuring motor-cars and telephones). The hats worn by the police arresting Tess at Stonehenge, for example (see Illustration 4), suggest 1920s Chicago rather than late-Victorian Britain. Two alternative endings – one happy, one tragic – were shot. The former (in typescript) has Tess in gaol with 'Guard hoisting black flag', but with the penultimate title reading: 'She's free. It's the repreive [sic] from the Home Secretary –', whereupon Tess and Angel embrace. The screenplay ends with the final title, 'Some day . . . their day . . .', and fades on the smiling couple in a canoe on a lake. The other ending (in a shorter, handwritten script) omits the above business, merely retaining the titles: 'It is not the end, it's only a brief goodbye. I shall be waiting for you where those who love are never parted', 'Some day, you and I –', '– Someday –', but closes by repeating 'Someday – you and I' (rather than 'Some day . . . their day . . .') before 'The End' comes up.[4] Apparently, exhibitors could opt to show either ending, although later re-releases included only the tragic one.[5] With nice irony, one is reminded of Hardy's own strategy for the ending of *The Return of the Native*.[6]

Hardy's attitude to the filming of his fiction, therefore, appears to have been ambivalent: on the one hand, he was instinctively and/or financially drawn to it; on the other, he was artistically anxious about what would be done to his work when he lost control of it to another medium. The latter attitude becomes clearer, despite his posture of indifference noted earlier, if I quote a couple of other letters from 1913 when the first version of *Tess of the D'Urbervilles* was in production. On 8 April, he wrote that he could see no objection to a film of the novel being made, as long as 'the producers are clearly given to understand that it must be done seriously, and that the story must not be vulgarized or treated lightly, so that all possibility of a farcical view of the tragedy is prevented' (*Letters*, IV, 265). And on 6 September, writing to Macmillan about the rights agreement, he worries about the phrase 'all details as to the manner of producing' being left to the film company: 'Does this cover a power to tamper with the story to any extent . . .? e.g. changing it from a tragedy to a story in which everything ends happily', he asks. The film, in fact, appears to have had Tess imprisoned rather than hanged: 'Safe at least from the world that had tempted and cursed her, Tess spends the remaining years of her life with her broken heart and shattered hopes, a martyr to a man's wrong.'[7] Hardy then goes on to suggest that it should be 'understood that the representations on the films must not depart from the story as related in the novel' (*Letters*, IV, 302). It is, perhaps, one of 'life's little ironies' – one I am not sure Hardy himself would have savoured – that the only extant silent film made in his lifetime which may be seen as a version of one of his novels controverts many of his wishes as laid out above. D. W. Griffith's *Way Down East* of 1920,[8] I want to argue, is a re-working, albeit heavily disguised, of *Tess of the D'Urbervilles*.

While searching movie databases in vain for silent films of Thomas Hardy, my eye fortuitously happened on a plot summary of Griffith's famous movie, and I thought: 'that looks familiar'. Let's be clear however: this 'Simple Story of Plain People' (the film's sub-title) is set in New England *c.*1920; has principal characters called Anna Moore, David Bartlett, and Lennox Sanderson; contains excruciating scenes of farcical comedy alongside the genuinely powerful main drama; has a spectacular and celebrated climax in which Lillian Gish (Anna) falls into a frozen river in a blizzard, is swept towards a waterfall on an ice-floe as the pack-ice breaks up (there are movie legends about how Gish got through this ordeal, filmed 'for real' on the Connecticut River), and is rescued on the very brink of the falls by Richard Barthelmess (David) who has pursued Anna by jumping from floe to floe as they surge down the river. And the film 'ends happily' with three weddings (but no funeral).

But by way of making my case, let me rehearse the plot of *Way Down East*. Anna Moore is a beautiful but poor country girl, who is persuaded by her mother to visit rich relatives in the city (Boston) in order to improve their lot. There she meets Lennox Sanderson (Lowell Sherman), a lustful metropolitan roué and cad who 'depends for his living upon a rich father'.[9] He is desperate to have his wicked way with Anna, but she holds out for honour and matrimony. Lennox therefore concocts a fake wedding (as in Hardy's own 'bowdlerised' serialisations of *Tess* for the *Graphic* and *Harper's Bazaar*), and thereafter beds his 'bride'. Soon after making her pregnant and losing interest in her, he tells Anna about the true status of the wedding and deserts her. The pregnant Anna wanders hopelessly until her sickly baby is born in an inhospitable lodging-house and she realises that she must baptise it herself before it dies. This she does in a moving scene which, as I will show, clearly echoes *Tess*. The baby subsequently dies, and Anna resumes her wandering, ending up in the pastoral haven of Bartlett Village, where she finds work on the farm of Squire Bartlett, 'a stern old puritan, who lives according to his own conception of the Scriptures, particularly the "Thou Shalt Nots"', and who immediately suspects the exhausted Anna of being a 'loose woman'. His dreamy, idealistic son, David, who 'though of plain stock, has been tutored by poets and visions wide as the world', begins to fall in love with Anna – 'Knowing only Anna's blameless life among them, David thrilled with the thought that she is the virginal white flower of his dreams' – and she with him: 'At last, the great overwhelming love – only to be halted by the stark ghosts of her past.' Lennox, who has an estate nearby, returns to haunt her, and later her past is revealed to old Squire Bartlett, who banishes her from his house. Finally Anna, about to plunge into the blizzard raging outside, denounces Lennox: 'I was an ignorant girl betrayed through a mock marriage . . . HE is the man who betrayed me!' David attacks Lennox, and then races out into the storm to rescue Anna, as described above. After the rescue, Lennox offers to marry her – 'Come, Anna, I know I didn't do the right thing. I'm willing to marry you now if you want me' – but the offer is rejected and David claims her as his bride.

Now a couple of things have to be acknowledged here: the plot deviates from *Tess*'s in significant ways (especially the ending); there are extraneous, often 'comic', characters and business introduced; and the theme of poor innocent country maiden seduced by wealthy/upper-class cad need by no means derive from *Tess* since it was stock material in Victorian melodrama – although no one to my knowledge has ever suggested that Hardy's plot is anything other than his own invention. Nevertheless, the similarities between film and novel, in terms of plot, characterisation, and moral stance, are surely sufficiently close to justify my proposing *Way*

Down East as a version of the *Tess* story. This is coincidentally reinforced by comparing it with the screenplay for the MGM film only four years later – which at times suggests that Marshall Neilan may have recognised the allusiveness of the earlier film. But first we need to consider the source-text that we know Griffith did indeed adapt.

In 1920, Griffith paid the huge sum of $175,000 (more than the entire cost of his classic 1915 movie, *The Birth of a Nation*) to a theatre producer, William A. Brady, for the screen rights to what most commentators describe as an already outdated and old-fashioned stage melodrama, *Way Down East: A Pastoral Drama in Four Acts* by Lottie Blair Parker (aka Charlotte [Blair] Parker and Mrs Harry Doel Parker). She is listed, with the play, in Davis and Joyce's *Drama by Women to 1900: A Bibliography of American and British Writers*,[10] but little beyond the most basic facts seems to be known about her. All I have been able to discover is that she was an American writer and performer (born 1858, Oswego, N. Y.; died 5 July 1937, Great Neck, N. Y.), who wrote three plays between 1896 and 1906, the most successful being *Way Down East*, which, according to one source, was one of America's 'most popular plays' at the time and 'barnstormed across the US for ten years'.[11] First written in 1896 under the title *Annie Laurie* and filed for copyright as *Way Down East* in August 1897 when it first opened in Rhode Island,[12] it was also produced in the very early spring of 1898 at the Manhattan Theatre, New York, Davis and Joyce noting: 'prod. at Manhattan Theatre, Jan. 19, 1898', while the Internet Broadway Database gives the date of first performance as '7 February 1898', with its closing date 'unknown', but noting that it was revived at the Academy of Music on 14 December 1903 and again on 21 August 1905.[13] It was produced on all these occasions by William A. Brady, who had commissioned Joseph R. Grismer to 'elaborate' the play. The final version, copyrighted in 1899 (under Lottie Blair Parker's name only), is the 'book' to which Griffith bought the film rights in 1920, although Grismer had also rewritten the play as a novel in 1900.

The publishing history and accessibility of the play itself is no less uncertain. The only copy I could initially trace was one listed in the Library of Congress catalogue with '[n.p.]' before the date, '1899'; but Davis and Joyce list it as: 'NY: priv. pr., 1898'. The supposition must then be that the play was 'n.[ever] p.[ublished]', but 'priv.[ately] pr.[inted]', either in an acting edition for the 1897/8 productions or just following them. There is no record, either, despite its popularity, that the play ever transferred to Britain, and it is certainly difficult to get hold of a printed copy in this country now: indeed, the only copy the British Library could identify – and hence the only one I have been able to read – is a microfiche of a poor quality typescript in the University of Cambridge Library (the microfiche itself deriving from the New York Public Library).

The typescript is undated, apart from a manuscript note on the title/cast-list page which says that the play was 'elaborated by Joseph R. Grismer', and that it was 'Produced at the Manhattan Theater, NY., 7 February, 1898'.

There were several reasons why it seemed essential for me to read the play – pre-eminently because it might turn out to be the mediating link between Griffith's film and *Tess of the D'Urbervilles*. Given that the play was written/performed only five or six years after the furore surrounding the publication of Hardy's novel and its subsequent wide popularity, my preconceived questions before I read the play were: how much more obviously would Lottie Blair Parker's 'pastoral drama' be an 'adaptation' of *Tess* than even Griffith's film was, and what then had Griffith done to the play in making *Way Down East*? How wrong could I be about the first question (the second, as I shall show, remains substantive). Except for a few basic plot données which could have derived from any melodrama, Parker's play turns out to be quite unlike Hardy's novel, being a run-of-the-mill piece of American 'cornball' comedy (indeed, dreadfully corny at times) with some melodrama along the way involving the Anna Moore/Lennox Sanderson/David Bartlett trio. The setting is ineluctably New England pastoral, the dialogue is of the stereotypical rural redneck variety ('You ain't got a spare piece of pie layin' around the pantry, have ye?' [1, 9]),[14] the characterisation of the three characters mentioned above is as flat as a pancake, and the plot . . . ? Well, let me consider the plot in relation to the second question about what D. W. Griffith did to his raw material in making the film of *Way Down East*. For two major points emerge from all this: first, that Griffith shows consummate skill as a filmmaker; and second, more provocatively, that he seems to have created a film which is much closer to *Tess of the D'Urbervilles* than his ostensible source. Did Griffith then *know* the novel? Did he know what he was doing? Did he make the allusions intentionally and consciously?

Several of Griffith's transformations of Parker's 'pastoral drama' are striking in this context. One of these concerns the character of Kate, Squire Bartlett's niece, who vies with Anna Moore for the role of heroine – certainly in the more predominant lighter sections of the play. She is sparky and pretty, and most of the men are smitten by her – including the susceptible Lennox – but she ends up marrying The Professor, a stereotypically absent-minded fool (whom Griffith puzzlingly retains in his own 'comic' scenes). There is a Kate character in the film, too – a kind of Mercy Chant figure whom David/Angel's parents hope he will one day marry, but whom he cannot love, especially when idealistically besotted by Anna/Tess – however, what is noteworthy is how minor, plain, and backgrounded Kate becomes as Griffith centres the action and the drama on Anna. An even more pointed instance of Griffith's creativity is his restructuring of the original play. The bulk of the play's first act is made up of the corny comedy mentioned above, with Anna arriving at the farm about halfway through; and while there are hints of a 'dark' past and some unspecified relationship with Lennox Sanderson, the details are not disclosed until the end of Act 3, and Anna, in a scene which Griffith retains in the film and Lillian Gish plays brilliantly, denounces Lennox for the cad he has been to her. This means, of course, that all the events of the past – Anna's visit to Boston, her meeting with Lennox, the mock marriage, the baptism and death of the baby – are all merely *reported* by one or other of the characters rather than being represented on stage. Conversely, Anna's arrival at the farm in the film occurs over halfway through it, and all the major events noted above (and, we may note, those resembling *Tess* mostly closely) have been previously and highly effectively acted out.

I might add a couple of further points of detail here to support my suspicion that Griffith was pushing his film closer to Hardy's novel. The characterisation of the three main figures is fleshed out considerably: Lillian Gish's extraordinarily emotive face conveying Anna's progress from sweet and innocent country maiden at the mercy of a city slicker to infatuated new bride, to betrayed wife, to tragically bereft mother, to distraught victim of her newly revealed past and apparent disgrace; David's dreamy idealism and infatuation with his own image of Anna is emphasised, as is Lennox's careless lecherousness and ersatz gentility. Furthermore, while the play makes no mention of Anna and her mother's poverty prior to the mother's death, nor of the fact that it is her mother who urges her to visit rich relatives, the action of the film opens with this: 'Sore need of money drives the mother to appeal to . . . their rich relatives in Boston . . . "Oh Mother, I hate to ask them for money" . . . "All right, Mother, I'll go".' Equally, the developing love-affair between Anna and David has powerful verbal and other echoes of that between Tess and Angel. Griffith is at pains to convey the lush and fertile environment of the Bartlett farm and its surroundings, where flowers and trees blossom, cows graze, baby birds are born, and spring points to 'awakening'; and later, in a summer visualised by butter- and hay-making, Anna and David's love-affair takes place 'By the river and the distant music of the falls – Around them the sweet scent of summer fields' – all of which, of course, is inescapably reminiscent of the famous descriptive passages at Talbothays and the Vale of the Great Dairies. Furthermore, Anna's past-haunted rejection of David's proposal of marriage – 'Please! Please don't! I can never be ANY MAN'S WIFE!' is not a million miles from Tess's repeated rejections of Angel: '"I cannot be your wife – I cannot be!" . . . "I feel I cannot – never, never!"'.[15]

Illustration 5. Anna (Lillian Gish) baptises her baby in *Way Down East*, United Artists, 1921.

Even more striking, perhaps, is Griffith's treatment of the baptism scene. While he may have picked up a hint from Anna's line in the play, 'I left the place where I had known nothing but *sorrow*' (1, 13; my emphasis), the play itself has nothing about the baby's baptism or its name – indeed, one character goes so far as to say: 'HER child that died without an honest name' (3, 12). On the other hand, the scene in the film is extended and very moving (again wonderfully acted by Lillian Gish). Furthermore, from Anna's return home pregnant to her mother (in the play, her mother dies before Anna loses the baby) – when she confesses her plight, she cries '"Mother! MOTHER!"', just as Tess does at the same moment ('"O mother, my mother!" cried the agonized girl' [T, xiii, 82]) – to the baptism scene itself, it closely tracks the novel. Anna's landlady tells her that 'The baby without a name' (*Tess* refers to it as 'a nameless child' [T, xiv, 91]) 'without being baptized, . . . will never see God' (Tess thinks: 'Her darling was about to die, and no salvation' [T, xiv, 93]), and Anna, the film tells us, 'Helpless and alone in the dreadful hours of the night, and stricken with a terrible fear for her baby's soul . . . herself performs the sacred rite' (see Illustration 5). She sprinkles water on the baby's head, as does Tess, and pronounces: 'In the name of the Father, and of the

Son, – and of the Holy Ghost. I baptize thee "TRUST LENNOX"', while Tess says: 'SORROW, I baptize thee in the name of the Father, and of the Son, and of the Holy Ghost' (T, xiv, 94) – where even the capitalised names seem to echo each other.

As I was about to complete the present essay, I happened on a 1985 article by Sarah R. Kozloff – the only piece to my knowledge that makes any connection at all between film and novel, but one confirming both my impression that no one hitherto (nor since Kozloff's essay, I may add) seems to have seen the similarities, and my supposition that Griffith knew *Tess of the D'Urbervilles* and was consciously invoking it. She points out that Hardy sold the rights for an American dramatisation (written by Lorimar Stoddard) in which the actress Minnie Maddern Fiske played the title role in March 1897, although it remains unclear whether Griffith saw a performance. However, Kozloff establishes convincingly that he *did* see the Famous Players film of 1913, in which the 48-year-old Fiske starred as Tess, and thought her performance 'wonderful'. Kozloff also presents convincing evidence that Griffith probably knew Hardy's novel at first hand, and believes he was 'personally responsible for incorporating elements from [*Tess*] into the story line of [Parker's] play'.[16] What then might be the reason for this strategy of Griffith's? While the film of *Way Down East* was popular and commercially successful (it grossed $4.5 million in the 1920s); is wonderfully directed, acted, and shot; and its finale universally admired as a bravura classic of early cinema, it also has a more serious burden – to which its somewhat portentous opening titles should alert us:

Since the beginning of time man has been polygamous . . . Not by laws – our Statutes are now overburdened by ignored laws – but within the heart of man, the truth must bloom that his greatest happiness lies in his *purity* and constancy. Today *Woman* brought up from childhood to expect ONE CONSTANT MATE possibly suffers more than at any other point in the history of mankind, because not yet has the man-animal reached this high standard – except perhaps in theory [my italics].

If there is anything in this story that brings home to men the suffering caused by our selfishness, perhaps it will not be in vain.

And as the action opens, the title introduces the main character: 'We call her "Anna" – we might have called her "Woman" – for is not hers the story'. Later, reflecting on the type of man Lennox is as he sets up the mock marriage in order to seduce Anna, we are told: 'Sanderson belongs to a class which, if it cannot get what it wants in one way, it will go to any length to get it in another.' And towards the end, as Lennox tries to force Anna to leave the Bartlett farm because she is too close for his own comfort, the following exchange occurs: 'Anna: "Suppose they find out about YOUR past life!". Sanderson: "Oh, its different with a MAN! He's supposed to sow his wild oats"'.

Are we then in the presence of a proto-feminist movie, one which points up the sexual double standard and its reinforcement by class position? Certainly, 'the man-animal' seems to be the villain of the piece, and 'Woman' in her 'purity' the heroine – 'for is not hers the story'? My emphasising and juxtaposing of those two words above is, of course, immediately to summon up the famous sub-title of Hardy's novel: 'A Pure Woman Faithfully Presented by Thomas Hardy'. Tess, like Anna, is the victim of prejudice, inequality, injustice, and bigotry ('Thou Shalt Nots' – Tess's sign-painter and Squire Bartlett have much in common). Neither was Hardy a fan of repressive 'Statutes'and 'laws' which crush the human spirit ('The letter killeth', as Jude and Sue were to find out). It is my suggestion – and here I part company with Sarah Kozloff, who wants to argue (unconvincingly) that 'Griffith's film demonstrates that he either missed or ignored Hardy's thematic concerns'[17] – that, on the contrary, he steered the film away from his source-play and towards the novel in order to have that earlier and darker work as a kind of intertext which reinforced his own attempt to 'Faithfully Present' a telling 'her-story'. Of course, there remain the spectacular climax on the ice-floes ('tampering with the story'), the triple wedding ('happy ending'), and the 'burlesque'/'farcical' comic scenes (are they retained in a sadly mis-taken attempt to emulate Hardy's much admired 'rustic chorus'?). But given the force and artistry with which Griffith portrays how 'the Woman Pays', Hardy might *not*, after all, have thought it yet another of 'life's little ironies' that the only surviving film produced in his lifetime, and which he didn't even know was being made, was an 'Americanized' *Tess of the D'Urbervilles* called *Way Down East* (not even *West*). One thing is certain: he'd have loved Lillian Gish.

NOTES

I wish to express my gratitude to Nicky Clyne and Lilian Swindall of the Dorset County Museum, and to the Learning Centre staff at the University of Gloucestershire, all of whose efficiency and patience made my recondite searches possible.

1. Richard Little Purdy and Michael Millgate (eds.), *The Collected Letters of Thomas Hardy*, 7 vols. (Oxford: Clarendon Press, 1984), vol. IV, p.140. All further references to this edition will appear in brackets in the text.
2. Anon., 'A Wessex Film', *The Times*, 17 Nov. 1915, p.5. Quoted in Paul J. Niemeyer, *Seeing Hardy: Film and Television Adaptations of the Fiction of Thomas Hardy* (Jefferson, N. C.: McFarland, 2003), Appendix A, p.250.

3. John Wain, 'Introduction' to *The Dynasts* (London: Macmillan, 1965), pp.ix–xiv.

4. Typescript in Dorset County Museum (ref: H.1997.679. I), '"Tess of the d'Urbervilles" Production No. 193 . . . Copyrighted MCMXXIV by Metro-Goldwyn Pictures Corp.', p.27. The handwritten version, with slightly different headnotes, is also in DCM (ref: H.1997.679. II).

5. See Niemeyer, *Seeing Hardy*, Appendix A, p.253.

6. For details of the footnote Hardy added to the Wessex Edition of 1912 explaining that readers could choose between the endings, see chapter eight, note 7.

7. From a promotional synopsis of the film in *Moving Picture World*, 13 September 1913. Quoted in Sarah R. Kozloff, 'Where Wessex Meets New England: Griffith's *Way Down East* & Hardy's *Tess of the d'Urbervilles*', *Literature/Film Quarterly* 13 (1985) 35–41, 38.

8. Produced and directed by D. W. Griffith, *Way Down East* was previewed in August 1920, opened in New York on 3 September 1920, then toured as a road-show, and went on general release with United Artists on 21 August 1921. It starred Lillian Gish, Richard Barthelmess, and Lowell Sherman; the screenplay was by Anthony Paul Kelly, based on the play *Way Down East* by Lottie Blair Parker and adapted variously by Joseph R. Grismer and William A. Brady. Cinematography was by G. W. Bitzer and Hendrick Sartov; art direction by Charles O. Sessel and Clifford Pember; and original music score (recorded 1928) by Louis Silvers and William Frederick Peters. A shortened version was re-released in 1931 with synchronised music and sound effects. Fully restored by David Shepard for the Museum of Modern Art, New York, in 1985 at 145 minutes running time. Currently available in the UK as a Eureka video and DVD.

9. All quotations from the film are taken from the title-boards with which a silent movie communicates its 'sound'. They will not be referenced hereafter.

10. Gwenn Davis and Beverly A. Joyce (compilers), *Drama by Women to 1900: A Bibliography of American and British Writers* (London: Mansell, 1992), p.118.

11. Tim Dirks, review of *Way Down East* at http://www.filmsite.org/wayd.html, 25/08/2004.

12. See Kozloff, 'Where Wessex Meets New England', p.36.

13. 'Lottie Blair Parker' at http://www.ibdb.com/person.asp?ID=7377 + 5804/ 5805/5806, all 25/06/2004.

14. All references to Lottie Blair Parker's play *Way Down East* are to the microfiche copy described in the present essay. They appear in brackets in the text, giving act and page number as in the original typescript, thus: (1, 9).

15. Thomas Hardy, *Tess of the D'Urbervilles*, ed. and with notes by Tim Dolin, intro. Margaret R. Higonnet, Penguin Classics edn ([1891] Harmondsworth: Penguin Books, 1998), Chapter xxvii, p.171. All further references will be to this edition and will appear in brackets in the text.

16. Kozloff, 'Where Wessex Meets New England', pp.38, 39. I am also beholden to Kozloff's research for points of detail about the complicated relationship between Lottie Blair Parker's play and Griffith's film.

17. *Ibid.*, p.39.

5   Screening the short stories: from the 1950s to the 1990s

Roy Pierce-Jones

The most recurrent problems with adapting literary texts for the screen seem to concern issues relating to fidelity to the text.[1] The grand ambition for so many film-makers seems to be to transfer tried and tested novels to the screen, even when they are almost always criticised for reducing these sometimes 'hallowed' literary texts into mere ghosts of their former glory. All too often what is yearned for is a mere visualisation rather than a new work of the imagination, inspired by the written word. Little consideration seems to have been given to adapting more manageable short-story formats. These concentrated narratives or literary miniatures lend themselves to filmic form and there have been many screen transfers to support such a viewpoint, including: Jean Renoir's treatment of Maupassant's *Une Partie de campagne* in 1936; Carol Reed's realisation of Graham Greene's *The Third Man* in 1949; John Houston's haunting version of James Joyce's *The Dead* in 1987; and Robert Altman's intertwining mosaic of several short stories by Raymond Carver in *Short Cuts*, released in 1993.

Whilst the novels of Dickens, in particular, remained popular with film-makers throughout the post-war years, his short stories were ignored for cinematic adaptation. Hardy proved even less popular with film-makers, since even his novels were unfilmed till late in the 1960s. The only exception was a very low budget Children's Film Foundation production, aimed at the popular children's Saturday matinée market, called *The Secret Cave* (based on 'Our Exploits at West Poley') in 1953. What made Hardy more popular from the 1960s onwards, both on film and television screens, needs to be considered. What does seem clear is that Hardy, that most 'cinematic writer' as he has become labelled by David Lodge and others, was not a popular writer with either the American or the British film markets between the 1930s and the late 1960s. Most of this chapter will concentrate on how Hardy's short stories have fared when they have been adapted for television audiences, since only one of his short stories, *The Melancholy Hussar*, has been turned into a feature film in 1998 and received a very limited cinema release in Britain under the title *The Scarlet Tunic*. What this chapter will be mainly concerned with is the conditions under which Hardy's short stories came to be adapted for a television audience.

The importance of drama to the early television schedules is evident. John Caughie describes how in Christmas week 1938 the very limited transmission of twenty-two hours of television included fourteen hours of drama.[2] The audience for these pre-war plays and adaptations was hardly representative of the nation at this time. Television sets were very expensive and restricted to the London area, and viewers' tastes reflected a theatre-going metropolitan audience (many of the plays were broadcast live from the West End of London). These audiences were very used to listening to similar fare on the radio and in particular to long stretches of dialogue, without the need to consider the visual impact of these dramas. The limitation of technology also impacted on the form these screen dramas took. Most of the actors were employed on the English stage during the week and so the tradition of Sunday dramas became established very early on in television. Whilst Britain could be described as a largely secular country by the late 1930s, there remained a huge church-led and establishment-backed core of society who decided what was appropriate for Sunday broadcasting. This, together with the paternalistic influence of the BBC's first Director General, John Reith, meant that a somewhat constrained, conservative attitude to television existed in the United Kingdom. Among any number of 'literary' names whose work was adapted during this period, Hardy's name was conspicuously absent. It would require the opening-up of television as a greater populist medium and a recognition that there was now a far more open or 'permissive' society before Hardy's work was to reach the television screens by the late 1960s.

A number of significant factors emerged during the 1950s that would bring about these major changes in television for the future. These included practical improvements such as the increase in transmission; steadily growing sales of television licences, due to the introduction of television rentals; and the explosion in interest generated by the coronation in 1953. The technical improvements meant that the BBC began to use 35mm film from 1954 onwards, though the sense of 'event' drama via live transmissions continued throughout the decade. The aesthetics of cinema films now became influential too, as British television moved away from the 'illustrated radio' approach of previous years. As television grew in popularity, so cinema audiences went into a decline; this resulted in people moving from one visual industry into another and bringing with them very different attitudes about producing dramas both in terms of their technical approaches and in terms of their content.

Between 1955 and the early sixties some important developments continued to impact upon these changes. The introduction of ITV in

September 1955 meant that the BBC faced competition for the first time in their television history. The availability of this network of regional companies spread very quickly and it became clear, very early on, that this commercial network was not as beholden to the BBC's middle-class Reithian values. ITV's drama output was much more broad-based in its appeal, with a good deal of American imported programmes beginning to fill the increasing schedule hours now on television. Not only did ITV look across the Atlantic for its programmes, they also attracted various writers, actors, directors, and producers to become involved during this period of expansion. What became clear, at about this time, was that the adaptation of literary classics was not seen as an essential part of their scheduling. The BBC, therefore, was left to continue with their rather safe and solid productions of literary classics. The Sunday slot for these serialised dramas continued to be popular throughout the 1960s, with certain key texts and key writers being returned to again and again. These dramatisations were timed for a Sunday tea-time family audience. Whilst Dickens's *Oliver Twist* could be softened and made more palatable for these audiences, Hardy's work could not.

An important figure who emerged in television drama during the 1950s and 1960s was Sydney Newman, the Canadian producer who became Drama Supervisor for ITV's *Armchair Theatre* series in 1958. Newman was much more concerned with developing new voices for contemporary British screen dramas than he was with working on literary adaptations or costume dramas. This engagement with modern drama was very much in keeping with the significant changes taking place in Britain during this time. A new wave of actors, writers, and directors was emerging both in the theatre and in British cinema. In the novel too there was a marked trend towards social realism. These new writers, directors, producers, and actors would be greatly influenced by such developments when they came to adapt the work of Hardy from the 1960s onwards. Issues of race, sex, class, and realism were now being aired on a regular basis on television, and Newman, together with other producers at ABC and Granada in particular, were recruiting young men and women into television with a real passion for the medium and its possibilities. As Tony Garnett recalls: 'What emerged at that time came out of a different climate. There was an optimism in the air, particularly on the Left: the privations of the post-war years, and the conformity of the 1950's, were giving way to a new energy and openness.'[3]

Newman's tenure at ITV lasted till 1963, when he replaced Michael Barry as Head of Drama at the BBC. Whilst Newman had been promoting new work on *Armchair Theatre* and gaining huge audiences on Sunday nights over on ITV, Barry had continued to produce literary adaptations and adaptations of stage classics by the likes of Chekhov and

Brecht on BBC television. The result, in the main, was that 'the "Sunday Night Theatre" series was almost completely overshadowed by "Armchair Theatre" during this period'.[4] Irene Shubik remembers Newman saying at her interview with him for a production assistant post at ITV that he 'didn't want to do any costume crap'.[5] Shubik followed Newman to the BBC, where he was pursuing a similar agenda of producing exciting, innovative modern television drama. The most famous strand was *The Wednesday Play*, which began in 1964. Writers were nurtured by producers at *The Wednesday Play*, and later at *Play for Today* (1970 onwards), and given considerable freedom to develop their writing talents. Among this group of writers were Dennis Potter, David Mercer, Douglas Livingstone, Rhys Adrian, William Trevor, and Ken Taylor, the six writers who were to adapt Hardy's *Wessex Tales* for the BBC in 1973 for Irene Shubik, the producer of the series.

Shubik had been an influential co-producer on *The Wednesday Play* since 1967, when she was appointed by Sydney Newman, her old boss at ITV. She remained with the single drama division through the 1970s too, when BBC's drama flagship changed to *Play for Today* in 1970. Many of the same actors, cameramen, writers, and so on who had worked on the *Wednesday Play* continued to work for Shubik on *Play for Today*. In 1973, Shubik was asked to produce a series of six fifty-minute screen adaptations from Thomas Hardy's short stories, as a joint production between the BBC and Time-Life. She chose the stories herself and allocated each one to the writers she had already worked with on *The Wednesday Play* or *Play for Today* slots. Two considerations guided her choice of Hardy's short stories, 'Would they work dramatically on the screen? Would they provide the viewer with sufficient variety? – for Hardy, like many great writers, can be repetitive'.[6]

Three of the stories come from Hardy's *Wessex Tales*, published in 1888 ('The Withered Arm', 'Fellow-Townsmen', and 'An Imaginative Woman'). Two stories came from Hardy's collection *Life's Little Ironies*, published in 1894 ('A Tragedy of Two Ambitions' and 'The Melancholy Hussar'). The sixth story came from the 1891 collection *A Group of Noble Dames* ('Barbara of the House of Grebe'). The contemporary appeal of these particular stories was very striking for Shubik:

He presents them in many dimensions, viewing them with a profoundly ironic and very modern eye. His attitudes to women, religion and class could be those of now. Even in those most melodramatic tales of witchcraft and horror, 'The Withered Arm' and 'Barbara of the House of Grebe', no characters behave other than believably in terms of modern psychology.[7]

Hardy's time had apparently arrived for he was being looked upon here as a contemporary writer.

The series was to be aired on BBC2, which had started to define itself as a more mature, challenging upmarket station than its sister channel, BBC1, which now had to battle for ratings with the clearly populist ITV channel. Whilst Sydney Newman still had little personal interest in literary adaptations and costume dramas, he recognised that there was a demand for it and appointed Shaun Sutton as Head of Serials. The success of *The Forsyte Saga*, first shown on BBC2 in 1967, then later repeated on BBC1 one year later, made it very clear that literary adaptations could make a huge impact as 'event' television. The Galsworthy adaptation managed to establish a number of important points. Firstly, a middle-class market could be baited and won over with 'quality' television that could include classic serial dramas as well as documentaries, current affairs, and foreign cinema. Audiences had to invest in the new 625-lines technology to watch *The Forsyte Saga* on BBC2, and though it was a studio-based, black-and-white serial, the introduction of colour-television technology was also appealing to this aspiring market. By the time the serial was shown on BBC1, its viewing figures had reached 18 million. However popular the cosy, traditional Sunday tea-time serial had been, the BBC had never had such a success with a literary adaptation. Although it was screened on a Sunday evening,[8] the content was far more adult than would have been allowed previously. The rape of Irene by Soames seemed much more graphic to TV audiences in 1967 than it had been back in 1949, when it was filmed by MGM as *That Forsyte Woman*. The success of the Galsworthy paved the way for far more adaptations of literary texts that dealt with these adult themes, often displaying quite provocative or graphic scenes. BBC2 became the channel that offered Dostoevsky, Tolstoy, Balzac, and Zola, rather than Dickens and Austen, which continued to be produced by BBC1. It was on BBC2 that Hardy's 'The Distracted Preacher' was shown in 1969. This long-lost tape has a script by John Hale and was produced and directed by Brandon Acton-Bond, whose previous credits for the BBC had included a number of Francis Durbridge plays and more traditional theatrical screen transfers, such as *She Stoops to Conquer* in 1966.

Irene Shubik cast some excellent actors for her series in 1973. Experienced actors such as Claire Bloom, Billie Whitelaw, Paul Rogers, and Norman Redway were cast opposite younger actors such as John Hurt, David Troughton, Ben Cross, Susan Fleetwood, and Ben Kingsley. The directors too had impressive credentials to their names. Desmond Davis was already a fine film director, and Gavin Miller, Mike Newell, and David Jones would each direct successful feature films in future years for the cinema. The cinematographers too were either very experienced like Ken Westbury and adventurous like Peter Hall, or they were young and promising cameramen such as Brian Tufano and Peter Bartlett, who would go on to film such landmark television dramas as *Edna the Inebriate Woman* or significant British feature films such as *Trainspotting* and *Billy Elliot*.

There may have been room for a good deal of individual creative input from such a talented collection of actors, writers, and directors, but Shubik did manage to bring a unifying style to the series. She insisted that each dramatisation began with a long shot of Wessex and any human character would be seen from afar, dwarfed by the landscape. At the end of each film, the camera would pull away from the characters, and once more the final image would be of the landscape.[9] The costume team unified the visual style of each episode too, and the music of Joseph Horovitz was a constant in each dramatisation. His slow, lyrical theme is played in the background as the credits for the series unfold before the individual credits for each particular episode.

The design for these opening credits manages to combine both literary motifs and suggestions of dark forebodings, synonymous with Hardy. A photograph transforms into an image of fallen trees, which then fades to some partly folded handwritten parchment paper that is partly covered by a linen garment. This fades to a lock of hair and a portrait in a chained locket, indicating remembrance. This in turn fades to hands entwined in stone, with flowers falling about them, before some rather ominous images of cloudy skies rise above trees just as Horovitz's piano introduction comes to a halt: *Wessex Tales* then appears in italic capital letters across the screen. Such televisuals created a seamless set of associated thematic motifs and concerns. Nature, death, memory, transience, fate: all are themes that are treated by Hardy in these stories. The screen dissolves are particularly effective, as they capture something of that (filmic?) quality in Hardy, whereby his descriptions can almost suggest a gliding from one location to another and from one state of mind to another. Time too is established here as being relentless, whilst human life is always transitory.

Only three of these short story adaptations have survived in the vaults, and they have never been shown since 1975. There seems little chance now that they will gain a release on video or on DVD, since the series is not complete, which is a pity, as each of the surviving films is of interest. 'A Tragedy of Two Ambitions', in particular, has survived very well in terms of the acting styles, direction, and the fine script by Dennis Potter.

In the course of his prolific writing career, Potter adapted several literary texts for television that spanned from Angus Wilson's *Late Call* in 1964 to F. Scott Fitzgerald's *Tender is the Night* in 1985. Potter had strong opinions on 'classic serial' adaptations, as he referred to them in his critical television reviews. He took particular umbrage against the BBC's twenty-part adaptation of Tolstoy's *War and Peace*, which made him wonder 'why are we doing all this? The adaptor must make his peace (a sort of armed truce) with his subject before he puts pen to paper, otherwise we shall go on being fobbed off with such failures as *War and Peace*, which is almost as good as *'Crossroads'*.'[10] He told the author Angela Carter, 'If you're tackling something of that stature (Hardy), you feel some presence looking over your shoulder.'[11] The brevity of the short-story format certainly allows Potter to stay faithful to the structure and to the idiom of Hardy's tale. Any alteration of certain scene sequences drives the story on and there are no major omissions in his dramatisation.

Potter was no stranger to the subject of social and class mobility. He was born to a working-class family in the Forest of Dean in the 1930s and distanced himself from his family and his rural community when he entered Oxford in 1956, having gained a scholarship to read Philosophy, Politics, and Economics. He returned again and again in his work to try to untangle the mixed emotions he felt as a consequence of this class shift. 'Only those who were born and nourished in a small, relatively isolated community can know how strongly the day-to-day shapes of the past merge into and appear to dominate the seemingly more uncertain contours of the present',[12] he wrote in 1962. One can imagine Hardy agreeing with such sentiments. Both as a journalist and as a playwright, he spent a good deal of time trying to understand what price had to be paid for what some may have considered a class betrayal. In two of his most significant plays of the 1960s, *Stand Up, Nigel Barton* (1965) and *Vote, Vote, Vote for Nigel Barton* (1967), he traces with considerable autobiographical candour the emotional complexities of the relationship between father and son.

In Hardy's story 'A Tragedy of Two Ambitions', the father is a feckless, greedy, drunken figure, seemingly without any redeeming features as a human being, yet both Potter's script and Paul Rogers's performance allow us to be drawn to the freedom that such an amoral lifestyle brings with it. Here is an example of the 'lifeforce', untouched by the constraints of nineteenth-century morality or any codes of Christian conduct. Both his sons by contrast seem to have lived lives that are constrained and overtly disciplined, particularly in the case of the elder brother Joshua, played with tight-lipped intensity by John Hurt. Their whole existence, as Hardy notes at the start of his story, seems to have been restricted from the very start:

The sun dropped lower and vanished, the shouts of the village children ceased to resound, darkness cloaked the student's bedroom . . . None knew of the fevered youthful ambitions that throbbed in two breasts within the quiet creeper-covered walls of the millwright's house.[13]

Potter's script emphasises the freedom that Joshua Harlborough the father enjoys, compared to his elder son in particular. John Hurt's character preaches a sermon that alerts everyone that they must all face torment, despair, and grief, yet there is never a glimmer of recrimination when we are confronted by the father. Potter allows us to witness a man left free to roam where he likes, to sleep in the hedgerows, to take up with loose women, to live off his family's hard-won money and to waste most of it on drink. Hardy has the younger son Cornelius, on returning home from Canada, mention that a man had been sent to prison for seven days for breaking windows in that town and that he is sure that he is their father. Potter makes more of this by showing us the incident. Just as the audience has been given a P. O. V. from above the quadrangle at the Theological College, when the father visits 'Josh', as he calls him, to extract money from him, so we are given another aerial shot of the drunken father, as he staggers home, the worse for wear. Filmed as if part of a nightmare by Michael Tuchner, the father, to the musical accompaniment of the oboe (suggesting mischief), smashes the window to a bookshop and howls to the heavens above 'Oh it's nice to be home', then laughs as if he is taunting the gods.

The next scene, before his fall into the weir, pokes further fun at the church, for his return is at Easter – the time of the resurrection. He chides his sons in the woods with his claim that his ambition is to 'lower people's wicked pride'. Contemporary audiences, of course, had become accustomed to such an anti-heroic character, who represented chaos and disorder. But with the death of their father on their consciences, the sons lose the moral highground too. When the younger brother asks, 'Do you think human hearts are iron cased safes?' and then insists, 'It will out', the elder brother refuses to agree, though Potter makes it clear, as Hardy does, that his religious faith has been severely shaken. 'I see him every night', says Cornelius. Both admit to contemplating suicide, but hang on to the forlorn hope that they will be united one day. Such a dark comedy clearly fitted in with contemporary tastes that mistrusted the moral certainties of the more edifying Victorian texts.

The second of the three remaining examples of the *Wessex Tales* is 'Barbara of the House of Grebe', adapted by another key writer from post-war working-class roots, who had considerable experience of writing for *The Wednesday Play* and *Play for Today*. David Mercer had, by 1973, an impressive list of credits that included writing for the RSC and for major British films such as *Morgan! A Suitable Case for Treatment* (1965). Like Potter, he understood class displacement, but he was also attracted to identifying that friction between anarchic vitality and the more disciplined, though often sterile demands of society. Mercer tended to subvert naturalism in his portrayals of class conflict. Such subversion frequently led to stylistically complex examinations of anguished minds. It was an inspired choice to ask him to write the treatment for this most Gothic of short stories by Hardy. Two important influences are apparent in terms of the visual language for this particular film. The director, David Jones, was clearly working in the wake of the Hammer House of Horror films and the Gothic and horror pictures that had been produced in Britain by directors such as Roger Corman in *Tomb of Ligeia* (1964), Robert Wise in *The Haunting* (1964), and Jack Clayton's *The Innocents* (1961).

The styles of performance lack a unified approach in this adaptation. There is an unfortunate clash of acting styles when one looks at, for example, the performance of Leslie Sands, an elderly actor much admired by Mercer,[14] as Sir John Grebe, and the very controlled still performance from Ben Kingsley, as Lord Uplandtowers. Although still primarily a stage actor in 1973, Kingsley understood that acting for the camera was about reduction and not enlargement of performance. The other major criticism is that certain scenes appear very melodramatic now, whilst others are underplayed to good effect. James's camera is also not really used to full filmic effect. The emotional turmoil of Joanna McCallum, as Barbara, is never fully explored by the director. Far too many scenes are of 'talking heads', which would certainly never be allowed in any of Roger Corman's Gothic films, for example. There are one or two effective uses of flashback and the silent meal-time scene is reminiscent of *Citizen Kane*, where Orson Welles shows the disintegration of a marriage through the characters' silence. Again the use of personal musical codas works to the advantage of this particular story and also unifies the series. In this episode Barbara's character is presented by a mournful clarinet, which is particularly haunting when she is seen writing and thinking of her first love. Overall there is something missing in this adaptation that really reflects on the choices made by the director. The genre cries out for visual atmosphere to be explored. Other film-makers have treated Wessex itself as a vital 'character' in their films, but here the country house, where most of the story unfolds, is left unexplored.

The final *Wessex Tale* that survives is fascinating, since we can compare this 48-minute television adaptation with a full-length feature film version of the same story, released in 1998. *The Melancholy Hussar*, directed by Mike Newell, and written by a somewhat less famous, but very experienced and accomplished writer, Ken Taylor, provides ample proof that screen adaptation is not solely reliant on being able to visualise every image that a writer, such as Hardy, may come up with. The greatest compliment that we can give to this television adaptation is that we feel we have come into contact with Hardy's characters and their situation in a very real sense. Their understanding of Hardy's story is obvious and they decide on a number of visual and aural motifs and codas to accentuate our understanding of the text and to achieve a rhythm and cinematic scope to this short film for television. Newell understands how vital the *mise-en-scène* is in such a film and he treats the audience to a controlled and effective piece of film-making by choosing with care not only his shots, but what is placed within these frames. For example, time is central to this story. Newell and his writer not only include, references to meetings and rendezvous in the script, but we are constantly aware of chimes and ticking clocks, of bugles calling the last post, and lights fading all too soon. The fate of this eighteen-year-old woman seems predestined throughout, as she waits for those who do not arrive. Life's desires are only dreamt of, not realised. She tells the Hussar that their plan to escape together is only a dream, but when he says 'Only you can make it so', she immediately replies 'I can not say no'. 'If we do nothing, the dream is gone', says the Hussar. Whilst Hardy himself does not employ this exact dialogue, it is absolutely in keeping with their emotional attachment to one another and with the feeling of being trapped. Hardy has Phyllis say that she was trapped 'in her father's house [which] was growing irksome and painful in the extreme; his parental affection seemed to be quite dried up'. She is not a native of the village and is missing her mother, whilst her father is now engrossed in Mesmerism. She inherits the young Hussar's 'passionate longing for his country, and mother, and home'.

Ken Taylor's scripts recognise the subtle nuances in Hardy's writing, which indicate that this is not a conventional love story, it is a tale of mutual need, whose outcome for both literary and television audiences is sensed as being inevitable. Just as we know that Tess or Bathsheba's attraction to particular men will end badly, so Taylor manages to indicate the inevitable sense of tragedy by using a degree of Brechtian distancing as we see their story unfold. The execution of the Hussars at the end of the film and Phyllis's reaction to it exemplify this. The camera keeps the men in longshot with the stretch of the sea that cruelly divides them from their homelands as their final backdrop. Shots are heard and we immediately cut to two unidentified graves, which fades to them with grass now growing over them. The camera then pans to the wall, above which we see another grave, this time with a headstone dedicated to Phyllis Grove, who went on to live as a spinster till she was eighty-seven. Another view of the graves appears and the credits roll. This displays the same simple economy of Hardy's own final paragraph:

Their graves were dug at the back of the little church, near the wall. There is no memorial to mark the spot, but Phyllis pointed it out to me. While she lived she used to keep their mounds neat: but now they are overgrown with nettles, and sunk nearly flat. The older villagers, however, who know of the episode from their parents, still recollect the place where the soldiers lie. Phyllis lies near.[15]

The series was well received, though audience figures were not high as it was only screened on BBC2 in 1973 (later repeated in 1975). It was shown in America as part of *Masterpiece Theatre*, as was the next Hardy short-story television adaptation – 'The Day After the Fair', which again came from the BBC in 1987. Adapted from a stage play by Frank Harvey, this proved a popular adaptation of Hardy's story 'On the Western Circuit'. The adaptation lasted one hour thirty-five minutes and was directed by Anthony Simmons, with a script by Gillian Freeman. One thing does need mentioning here, since Paul Niemeyer is right to alert us to the fact that until the mid-1990s American television screened such dramas as Hardy's adaptations almost as a cultural conduit. British television was seen as a symbol of quality television that emphasised the 'art' rather than the 'entertainment' aspect of these programmes. Now cable companies in America are developing more and more new work in conjunction with British television companies. The tussle between populism and middle-brow/high culture that fuelled developments in literary adaptations for British television seems to have been resurrected.[16]

The only other adaptation of Hardy's short stories during the 1980s was another film version of *Our Exploits at West Poley* by the Children's Film and Television Foundation in 1985. It gained a very limited cinema release, since the outlets for children's cinema features had by now disappeared, compared with its heyday in the 1940s and 1950s. It was shown on television in 1990 and was seen as notable only for an early screen appearance by future film star Sean Bean in a minor role as Scarface. The rest of the cast included stalwarts such as Brenda Fricker and Frank Mills, whilst the Man Who Has Failed was played by Anthony Bate, an excellent choice for this enigmatic character. But it is a pedestrian affair on the whole. Roger Ebbatson has pointed to this as being a tale in which 'the drama instigated by the diversion of the stream and the interplay and rivalry of the two villages does not mask for the reader the underlying sense of a bourgeois pathos of loss and removal from pleasure and innocence'.[17] Any such insights, however, are sadly lacking in this film.

Stuart St Paul's feature film of 'The Melancholy Hussar', released as *The Scarlet Tunic* in 1998, is similarly unimpressive. An additional problem on this occasion was that Indynk Films relied on individual investors making up the budget for the film. In exchange for this, they could appear as 'supporting artists'. The result of this is that the film always looks unconvincing when we witness small crowd scenes, such as those at the tavern or at the army camp. But this is only the start of the problems one has with this very poor screen adaptation.

Stuart St Paul and his screenwriter Colin Clement seem to have had little faith in Hardy's short story and therefore made changes to its structure, radically altering and embellishing certain characters and situations. Love interests extend beyond the relationship between the Hussar and the doctor's daughter. A sadistic army captain, played by Simon Callow, is introduced to the tale and the scene where he whips our young Gallic hero, played by Jean-Marc Barr, is almost hissable as a piece of melodrama. The innocence and purity that Mary Larkin brought to the part of Phyllis in the BBC version is not replicated here. Her name is changed, for some peculiar reason, to Frances, and is played by one of Britain's finest actresses – Emma Fielding. Miss Fielding is capable of subtle and nuanced playing and is a particularly fine Shakespearian actress, but simplicity and naivety do not really come easily to her in this adaptation. The cameo performances from respected actors such as Jack Shepherd, John Sessions, and Lynda Bellingham do not blend together in a believable or cohesive way either.

This production, from start to finish, looks as though it has been devised and shot without any real understanding of the purpose of this story. St Paul must have been excited at the prospect of filming this costume drama, since a good many literary adaptations made during the 1990s had brought healthy box-office profits.[18] This film failed even to get a video release in Britain until 2004. As the director and his company, Indynk Films Limited, didn't have a proper distribution deal either in Britain or the USA, the director was forced to hawk his film from the back of his car to cinemas that formed a small independent cinema chain in Britain.[19] The film got a late video release in the USA, after it had been screened on a cable channel under the generic title 'Romance Classics'.

The success of the televised adaptations of Hardy's short stories, I suggest, is not simply a matter of their greater fidelity to the original texts. The 1973 series managed both to remain faithful to Hardy and to explore contemporary parallels with the post-war years in Britain, as television became an important popular medium for adapted literary texts. The poor quality of the few examples we have of Hardy's short stories being adapted for the cinema screen might suggest that they are inappropriate for the big screen. But it may simply be that the right directors have not yet addressed themselves to this material.

NOTES

1. Brian McFarlane, *Novel to Film: An Introduction to the Theory of Adaptation* (Oxford: Clarendon Press, 1996), pp.13–15. Building on Roland Barthes's work, McFarlane argues that fidelity to the text demands cardinal functions to be retained if one is looking for a 'faithful' adaptation. These key narrative moments can be altered by catalysers, which allows for some alteration in form or detail, but still retains the fundamental functions of the narrative.

2. Cited by Lez Cooke in *British Television Drama: A History* (London: BFI, 2003), p.8.
3. Tony Garnett, 'Contexts', in Jonathan Bignell, Stephen Lacey, and Madeleine Macmurraugh-Kavanagh (eds.), *British Television Drama: Past, Present and Future* (Basingstoke: Palgrave, 2000), p.11.
4. *Ibid.*, p.52.
5. Irene Shubik, 'Television Drama Series: A Producer's View', in Bignell, Lacey, and Macmurraugh-Kavanagh (eds.), *British Television Drama*, p.42.
6. Irene Shubik's introduction to *Thomas Hardy's Tales from Wessex* (London: Pan, 1973).
7. *Ibid.*
8. Newspapers relished announcing the news that churches throughout the country were having to change their service times to try to prevent losing so many members of their congregation who were stopping at home to watch the programme. There is no real evidence to support this.
9. Irene Shubik, *Play for Today: The Evolution of Television Drama* (Manchester: Manchester University Press, 2001), p.88.
10. W. Stephen Gilbert, *The Life and Work of Dennis Potter* (London: Hodder and Stoughton, 1995), p.223.
11. *Ibid.*, p.228.
12. Dennis Potter, *The Changing Forest: Life in the Forest of Dean Today* (London: Secker and Warburg, 1962), p.7.
13. *Ibid.*, p.98.
14. Leslie Sands gave an acclaimed performance in David Mercer's West End hit *After Haggerty* in 1970 at the Criterion Theatre.
15. Hardy's description of their wedded relationship is far fuller than the television adaptation depicts, but the economy of this scene does show how film can 'cut to the chase' when time dictates the content.
16. Paul J. Niemeyer, *Seeing Hardy: Film and Television Adaptations of the Fiction of Thomas Hardy* (Jefferson, N. C.: McFarland, 2003), pp.206–10.
17. Roger Ebbatson, *Hardy: The Margin of the Unexpressed* (Sheffield: Sheffield Academic Press, 1993), p.65.
18. Most of these adaptations were from the novels of Jane Austen. Whilst Ang Lee's film of *Sense and Sensibility* grossed millions in profit, Stuart St Paul's *Scarlet Tunic* grossed little over £35,000 at the UK box office. It never gained a theatrical release in the USA.
19. Telephone interview with Emma Fielding, October 2003.

6   All fall down: Hardy's heroes on the 1990s cinema screen

Judith Mitchell

In 1949 Albert J. Guerard complained that Hardy's male protagonists suffer from an 'almost pathological unaggressiveness'. These 'impotent spectator[s]', writes Guerard, 'drift as sleepwalkers through scenes in which other men, and women particularly, love and hate with passion'.[1] Guerard's remarks have turned out to be prophetic, in that the Hardy Industry during the last half of the twentieth century focused mainly on Hardy's heroines, an altogether more vibrant group of fictional characters whose vitality and variety have made them suitable subjects for feminist analysis, and who have been represented in film adaptations by big-name stars such as Julie Christie (as Bathsheba in Schlesinger's *Far From the Madding Crowd*), Nastassja Kinski (as Polanski's *Tess* and as Elena in Winterbottom's *The Claim*), Catherine Zeta Jones (as Eustacia in Gold's *Return of the Native*), and Kate Winslet (as Sue in Winterbottom's *Jude*). His heroes, on the other hand, have mostly been played by talented but lesser-known actors (Peter Firth as Angel Clare, Ray Stevenson as Clym Yeobright, and Christopher Eccleston as Jude, for example).[2] In this chapter I will examine Hardy's notions of masculinity and two of his male protagonists (Jude Fawley and Michael Henchard) as they are represented in 1990s film-length adaptations and in the novels on which these adaptations are based. I have chosen to focus on adaptations made in the 1990s because this was a decade of prolific adaptations of nineteenth-century novels (of Austen and Dickens, for example, as well as Hardy); I have chosen film-length adaptations as opposed to television mini-series because the former tend to give rise to the more interesting forms of 'commentary' and 'analogy', as opposed to 'transposition', to use Geoffrey Wagner's terms;[3] and I have chosen to comment on Michael Winterbottom's adaptations in detail because Jude Fawley and Michael Henchard embody two of Hardy's most searching explorations of masculinity. Guerard called them Hardy's 'only two men of more than average interest and vitality';[4] more recently, Tim Dolin has referred to these troubled protagonists as 'victim[s] of [their] masculinity'.[5]

The 1990s revival of nineteenth-century novels in film has been theorised in the context of a number of cultural effects and affects. Raymond Bellour suggests that film in general satisfies a 'demand for narrativity' that much modern and postmodern fiction no longer provides.[6] Dianne Sadoff and John Kucich attribute late postmodernism's 'obsession' with the Victorians to its construction of its own cultural identity as 'post-Victorian', with the Victorians functioning as postmodernism's 'historical "other"'.[7] Then there is the classic adaptation's 'gentrification effect', the spectator's acquisition and demonstration of what Pierre Bourdieu calls 'cultural capital' as a result of viewing such films.[8] And finally, Anne Friedberg elucidates the capacity of the nostalgia film to turn the past into a 'safe, familiar place'.[9] Thus Esther Sonnet reads the 'proliferation of historical costume dramas in the "post-feminist" 1990s . . . as not simply . . . the *absence* of contemporary concerns but a rather more disturbing "longing" for a "return" to a specifically pre-feminist past, and to the sureties of a social order grounded in a stability of gender-fixed positions, . . . a past in which tightly defined gender roles are the bedrock of domestic, political and social order'.[10]

Film adaptations of Hardy, like those of other classics, generally satisfy filmgoers' desires for both narrativity and 'gentrification', simply by virtue of their status as representations of nineteenth-century novels. As for their capacity to satisfy a longing for a return to stable gender roles in the context of a safe, familiar past, however (something Austen adaptations, for example, can generally be counted on to do), most adaptations of Hardy fail abysmally. We cannot look to Hardy to provide us with a reassuring past in which gender roles are comfortably resolved, because for him they never were. Like the postmoderns, Hardy constructed himself to some degree as 'post-Victorian', in that he assiduously resisted the gender norms and classifications of his time. The present in his texts is frequently represented as hazardous, repressive, and unsatisfactory, and in its tenuous hope for the future it constitutes our own past only uneasily. Jude's statement (to which I will return) that he and Sue had ideas that were 'fifty years too soon' (J, VI, x, 423)[11] now resonates ironically, especially as it situates this more promising future for gender relations in the period just before the ideologically repressive 1950s.

Patricia Ingham, who reads Hardy's novels in terms of their narrative syntax, outlines two common narrative 'sentences' in which heroines of nineteenth-century novels were typically immersed: that in which the heroine is chastened, ultimately choosing the right husband, and that in which she redeems her faults through 'shame, guilt, self-hatred, good works or forms of self-immolation and/or death or exile'.[12] As a group, Hardy's male characters also tend to be subjected to a recurring syntax, an even starker narrative 'sentence' – one that reads simply, 'He failed.' The two-suitor plot abounds in Hardy's fiction, for instance, but the masculinity embodied in these Girardian rivalries[13] is consistently portrayed in terms of losing, rather than winning. The eventual outcome is frequently the loss of the female object of rivalry, by not only one but both rivals: Henry Knight and Stephen Smith both lose Elfride; Bishop Helmsdale and Swithin St Cleeve both lose Lady Constantine; Clym and Wildeve both lose Eustacia; Henchard and Farfrae both lose Lucetta; Winterborne and Fitzpiers both (at least figuratively) lose Grace; Alec and Angel both lose Tess; Jude and Phillotson both lose Sue; and even in the absence of such rivalry the older and younger Pierstons both lose all of the Avices. It is not only the poor man who does not get the lady; often, indeed, no one gets her. In 'Candour in English Fiction' Hardy famously disparaged 'the false colouring best expressed by the regulation finish that "they married and were happy ever after"',[14] and the happy marriage, a conventional sign of successful closure in the nineteenth-century novel, is signally absent from his fiction. Even in novels in which there is a clear 'winner', such as *Desperate Remedies*, *A Laodicean*, or *Far From the Madding Crowd*, the female 'prize' frequently undergoes a process of modification (usually a version of Ingham's 'chastening') in the course of the contest, so that the winner's victory is significantly muted. Only in the pastoral fantasy of *Under the Greenwood Tree*, in which Dick Dewy remains blissfully unaware of his rival, is the enjoyment of the hero's victory untrammelled – for the hero himself, at least, though not for the knowing reader.

Material success, too, eludes most of Hardy's heroes, and 'Our Exploits at West Poley' (1883), Hardy's 'Story for Boys', provides us with a paradigmatic figure of this kind of masculine failure. 'The Man who had Failed' haunts the text, reappearing at all the key moments. Significantly, he has no name apart from this self-designation (it is what he 'calls himself' (115)).[15] Significant, too, is the perfect tense: his failure has already occurred; it has become a fixed part of his identity. He can speak from a position of freedom, as he has opted out of the 'normal' struggle for success (he 'has been all over the world, and tried all sorts of lives, but he has never got rich, and . . . has retired to [West Poley] for quietness' (115)). He is thereby absolved from further effort, and his advice is regarded by the townspeople as 'worth attending to', even though it is fairly banal (he cautions the boys to adhere to 'quiet perseverance in clearly defined courses' as opposed to 'erratic exploits that may do much harm' (163)).[16] The authority of this overtly emblematic figure of failure paradoxically derives from failure itself; Leonard, the narrator of the story, reports that he was not old enough at the time to realise that 'the losers in the world's battle are often the very men who . . . have the clearest perceptions of what constitutes success; while the successful men are frequently blinded to the same by the tumult of their own progress' (115).

It is not surprising that Hardy's narratives of embattled masculinity and its failures resonate with postmodern audiences. Like Hardy, such audiences view gender as a vexed category, and its new plurality of expression is experienced – much as we can imagine Hardy might have experienced it – as both liberatory (in theory) and anxiety-producing (in practice). At the *fin-de-siècle, fin-de-millennium* turn of the twentieth century, a cultural moment in which, according to Michael Bracewell, 'veracity has become synonymous with confusion and dysfunctionalism',[17] Hardy's narratives of failed manhood appeal to our sense of contemporary reality. And the ways in which his heroes fail are noteworthy as well, as Hardy is not interested in standard configurations of masculinity so much as in characters who fall short of such configurations in oblique and complex ways, thereby revealing the inadequacy of such gender norms. Few conventionally 'virile' or 'gentlemanly' heroes inhabit his works; 'Our Exploits' – significantly intended as a story for and about boys becoming men – is uncharacteristic in its clear mapping of this conventional binary (although even here the Man who had Failed positions himself outside it). Steve, the hero of the story who grows up to be 'the largest gentleman farmer of those parts' (163), initially exhibits a kind of raw virility '(a Carlylean "Doughtiness – the courage and faculty to do"' (114)) but succeeds in the end, Leonard conjectures, by adopting the sober restraint advocated by the Man who had Failed.

That this traditional polarity between forcefulness and restraint continues to inflect current models of masculinity there is no doubt, as witnessed by the large numbers of action heroes in contemporary cinema, in perpetual tension with 'new' models of gentler masculinity. Susan Jeffords contends that the 1990s produced 'a changed image of U.S. masculinity, . . . an image that suggests that the hard-bodied male action heroes of the eighties have given way to a "kinder, gentler" U.S. manhood, one that is sensitive, generous, caring, and perhaps most importantly, capable of change'.[18] Real men, of course, like Hardy's heroes, fit neatly into neither of these familiar configurations; but 'doughty' virility and manly gentleness remain the defining terms of normative masculinity. To a large extent, popular paradigms of successful manhood have not changed significantly since Hardy's radical questioning of them. The film-length adaptations of Hardy's work made in the 1990s question them too, albeit not so radically. Gold's *Return of the Native* (1994), Agland's *Woodlanders* (1997), and St Paul's *Scarlet Tunic* (1998), as well as Winterbottom's *Jude* (1996) and *The Claim* (2000), portray a variety of masculine failures, a group that gives rise to a remarkably consistent iconography, that of the (literally) fallen hero. The function of these icons of failure, I will argue, is primarily one of consolation. Peter Widdowson contends that the 'softened' film representations of Hardy 'speak only to fictions of the present in a consoling way',[19] and one way these films console their viewers is by enhancing the unheroic in their heroes. They thereby literalise late-twentieth-century anxieties about gender, confirming the postmodern viewer's sense that masculinity itself is a fiction, contradictory and impossible to perform, but one that continues to be privileged as the accepted site of male success. In *Jude* and *The Claim* Michael Winterbottom explores Hardy's bleak awareness of this dilemma as it is represented in *Jude the Obscure* and *The Mayor of Casterbridge*.

Jude

Winterbottom's *Jude* has elicited disapproval from its literary audience, largely because of its casting of Kate Winslet as Sue and its omission of Jude's death. The most exacting member of this audience, however, can have no objection to Winterbottom's opening scene of Jude in the field with the birds. Several familiar Hardy motifs are immediately apparent: the diminished human figure; the corduroy-like appearance of the fields; the camera pulling up and back as the farmer beats Jude, which constitutes a kind of narratorial commentary on the episode. Filmically, this opening scene carries a good deal of weight. The beating foreshadows the violence that will attend Jude's career, and the scene is filmed in black and white, a specular effect that Winterbottom subsequently alludes to in all the scenes of Jude's bewilderment at the various crises that follow. And, as the film's scenes of crisis revert to subdued colours, the character of Jude, I will argue, reverts to childhood.

Film theorists have recently begun to explore the function of male film stars as erotic objects of the gaze,[20] but Christopher Eccleston (who delivers a brilliant performance as Jude) exhibits a virtual absence of erotic appeal under Winterbottom's direction. We are constantly treated to unappealing shots of him: displaying his rear view awkwardly to the camera, wearing tattered combination underwear, lying in bed in a foetal position. Kenneth MacKinnon notes that views of male backs can indicate a 'capacity for privacy'[21] and that male buttocks are usually erotic, but Eccleston's back view is made to appear ignominious rather than erotic, often because of Winterbottom's extreme camera angles (such as our prolonged view from below of Jude ascending the ladder when he is working as a stonemason). The many low-angle close-ups of Eccleston weeping in a helpless, childlike, and slightly repulsive fashion also detract from his

Illustration 6. Jude (Christopher Eccleston) is comforted by Arabella (Rachel Griffiths) in *Jude*, Polygram/Revolution/BBC, 1996.

erotic appeal; they enhance his vulnerability, but Winterbottom's camera negates the potential eroticism of this vulnerability by its uncomfortably close focus. A particularly telling instance of such childlike grief is that in which an agonised Jude is comforted after Sue's wedding by a motherly Arabella, in a kind of grotesque bedroom Pietà (see Illustration 6). A protracted extra-diegetic spectacle, this scene has the effect of marking the moment, but not erotically. Jude's foetal position and grotesque drunken grimace, filmed from the foot of the bed as the camera slowly zooms in on the couple, emphasise his weakness in relation to both alcohol and Arabella, and render him anything but attractive.[22] Winterbottom's film 'unmans' Jude by casting him as a child, pathetically dependent on women and unable to make sense of his environment or to care for the next generation.

Indeed, the relationship between Jude and Sue in the film, despite the sex scene complete with 1990s full-frontal nudity, is portrayed as that of two children. In scenes that do not appear in the novel, Winterbottom has Jude and Sue playing on the beach and riding bicycles in the country, and immediately before their discovery of the dead children we see Sue and Jude chasing each other up the stairs. On the one hand, the film gives us the impression of Jude's and Sue's combined inadequacy, of change happening more quickly than they can handle, despite Jude's assertion that their ideas are 'fifty years too soon' (J, VI, x, 423). In his emphasis on the childlike nature of his characters, it almost seems as if Winterbottom is alluding to Hardy's earlier title, 'The Simpletons'. On the other hand, this additional, apparently innocuous material plays an important part in muting the bleak ideological emphasis of the novel. The beach and bicycle scenes, reiterated as they are recalled by Jude in flashback near the end of the film, represent Jude's and Sue's years of happiness in a way significantly eschewed by Hardy (Christine Brooke-Rose notes the novel's 'remarkable occultation' of this period, of which Hardy's narrator merely remarks, 'that the twain were happy – between their times of sadness – was indubitable').[23] Winterbottom's extra-diegetic literalisation of the lovers' delight, rendered in stock 1990s romantic imagery, tends to counteract an important aspect of the novel's exploration of masculinity. Tim Dolin notes that Hardy's novel 'invokes and finds untenable' conventional narratives of masculine achievement (spirituality, vocation, education, and marriage), and thus succeeds in 'making "man" a question';[24] but the film's focus on the lovers' enjoyment of each other reinstalls the 'marriage' narrative as a possible site of male success. The film's ending reinforces this ideological shift. In its closing sequence, a frustrated Jude cries, 'We are man and wife, if ever two people were on this earth' (a nearly direct quotation from Part VI, iii, eight chapters short of Hardy's ending), after which the camera zooms back on his solitary figure standing in the snow. Such a conclusion leaves open a possibility never entertained by Hardy's text, the possibility of reconciliation between the two lovers, thus covertly reinstating hope in the heterosexual love story – a story in which contemporary mainstream audiences undoubtedly retain a certain amount of faith, however muted.[25]

Indeed, critics have noted that Winterbottom's film generally 'softens' the harshness of the novel: we do not see Sue distraught in the children's grave (even though this is surely a highly cinematic moment); Phillotson is not physically assaulted by the townspeople; Jude never makes his last fatal visit to Sue in the rain; and he does not die cursing the day he was born. I would argue, however, that the violence of Hardy's text is not so much diminished by Winterbottom's adaptation as displaced to the *mise-en-scène*. The audience is visually and aurally assaulted by the close-ups of train wheels taken with a camera mounted on the tracks or on the underside of a railway carriage, for instance, as the characters fly from place to place – an aggressive reminder of the rootlessness precipitated by industrialisation, and the railroad in particular, at the end of the nineteenth century. Also, in a striking sequence that Winterbottom adds to his source material, little Juey is terrorised by a violent magic-lantern show, which functions as a sort of *mise-en-abîme* (a story within the story, repeating key elements of the larger narrative), at least for the literary audience: the threatening ghosts, the confused action, the recurring skeletons can be seen to represent, in miniature, life as it is experienced by the characters in Hardy's novel. We experience this scene mostly from little Juey's point of view (a standard suture established by a shot-reverse shot), a perspective we continue to share as the insane laughter on the sound track morphs into cries of pain just before the jarring jump cut to Juey's terrified view of Sue in childbirth. At first we are given a close-up of her anguished face, but then the camera pulls back at the level of the child's gaze to focus on her bloody vagina. The violence of this scene, which is well in excess of anything in Hardy's novel, is also in excess of the expectations of 1990s viewers, who are used to witnessing childbirth scenes but not usually so graphically. The straight-on camera angle, the blood, the heightened colour, the brilliant lighting, and the isolation of Sue in the visual field (reminiscent of Bergman's stark tableaux in *Cries and Whispers*)[26] combine to create a shocking visual effect, for us as well as for Juey. In fact, we are doubly shocked: first by the bloody spectacle itself, and then by the realisation (when the shot reverses to Juey crouching in the doorway) that the spectacle is also being witnessed by a child. In a genre that purports to function as a guarantee of taste, this scene amounts to a kind of assault on the audience, one that nicely parallels Hardy's assault on his readers' sense of novel-reading decorum. In addition, of course, the scene performs the thematic function of adding plausibility to Juey's motive for the murder-suicide.

Apart from its affective and thematic effects, the childbirth scene also works structurally, to ensure that much of the violence and horror of the filmic narrative rests with the male child rather than the man. In a paradigmatic role-reversal, little Juey is made to bear the weight of the death and despair that occur in the film, while helpless tears are given to the adult Jude, whose death as scripted by Hardy is elided. This represents a shrewd decision by Winterbottom as the film audience, through sharing Juey's perspective, gets to experience some of the novel's futility without the risk of bathos inherent in Jude's recitation of Job's curse on his deathbed. The casting of Ross Colvin Turnbull, too, is salutary; while the film is compelled to literalise the children (thereby forfeiting their anti-realist effect in the novel), at least Winterbottom's Juey is not conventionally 'cute' but rather oddly pathetic, a fitting 1990s analogue for Little Father Time. The parallels between Jude and Juey, in fact (visually emphasised in a shot of Juey in bed in a foetal position, see Illustration 7), point to one of the key determinants of masculinity in Winterbottom's adaptation.

Illustration 7. Juey (Ross Colvin Turnbull) adopts a foetal position similar to that of his father in *Jude*, Polygram/Revolution/BBC, 1996.

Judith Kegan Gardiner suggests that 'a developmental, age-inflected
theory of gender . . . could oppose the challenge of "being a man" not to
being a woman or a male homosexual but to being a boy',[27] and this is
what Jude remains in Winterbottom's adaptation. Hardy's boy Jude 'did
not want to be a man' (I, ii, 13), and near the end of the film Winterbottom's adult Jude voices his perplexity as to 'what is good for man',[28]
remarking, 'the further I get the less sure I am of anything'.

Manhood in Winterbottom's film, as in Hardy's novel, proves difficult
or impossible to attain. Jude as a New Man is represented as unformed
and uncertain, particularly in relation to the New Woman, who is crudely
signified in the film by Kate Winslet's ability to ride a bicycle, smoke
cigarettes, and drink like a man (much to the disappointment of the literary audience, for many of whom Winslet constitutes a casting mistake).[29]
But for a general audience, Winterbottom's choice may in fact be highly
effective, in that Winslet has the capacity to represent the New Woman of
the 1890s in 1990s terms (when asked what she likes about the characters
she has played, for instance, Winslet is reported to have described them as
'ballsy').[30] Masculinity in the film, as in Hardy's novel, resides primarily
in the female characters: Sue and Arabella, in both the novel and the film,
are more active and decisive (Sue intellectually and Arabella sexually)

than the more passive Jude. Susan Jeffords's analysis of the gentler masculinity represented in many 1990s popular films applies to *Jude* only uneasily; like Hardy's novel, Winterbottom's film refuses to represent this gentler masculinity as a comfortable solution to the complex problems of gender relations and modernity. This refusal of conventional masculinity is partly achieved through the film's flirtation with the grotesque, as I have suggested, and in this respect Winterbottom achieves a satisfyingly postmodern result.

Frances Mascia-Lees and Patricia Sharpe contend that 1990s popular culture in America was characterised by a discourse of 'self-help', which promised empowerment through an acknowledgment of weakness,[31] but *Jude* acknowledges its protagonist's weakness to no avail. As in the 1890s, men as well as women in the 1990s found themselves facing new versions of feminism and profound shifts in gender roles, and Winterbottom's adaptation of *Jude*, rather than harking back to a fantasy of historical stability or suggesting the possibility of easy solutions in the present, functions instead to reassure its audience that gender relations have always been problematic, and that bewilderment in the face of such changes is an understandable response. For once, Hardy's predictions seem overly optimistic: a hundred years after Jude's proclamation that his and Sue's ideas were 'fifty years too soon', gender relations continued to be perilous, marriage frequently disastrous, and masculinity difficult if not impossible to achieve. Winterbottom's film, by means of the sweeping liberties it takes with Hardy's novel, preserves the spirit of its original in the masochistic viewing pleasure it offers its audience as they witness its main character's failure to live up to the oppressive demands of middle-class masculinity.

The Claim

Four years after *Jude*, Winterbottom directed *The Claim*, set in roughly the same time period as Hardy's publication of *The Mayor of Casterbridge*, but involving a very different kind of costume drama, that of a traditional western. The website for the movie refers to 'the Hardy influence' as 'more . . . an inspiration than an adaptation',[32] and the film's literary audience, at least initially, vociferously rejected its status as an adaptation of Hardy's novel.[33] But *The Claim*, like Amy Heckerling's *Clueless*, conforms perfectly to Geoffrey Wagner's definition of an 'analogy', a film that represents 'a fairly considerable departure [from its source text] for the purpose of making another work of art', with no attempt to reproduce the original.[34] For my purposes, it is interesting that Hardy's *Mayor* so spontaneously inspired a western (Frank Cottrell Boyce, the screenwriter for

The Claim, reports, 'it was just absolutely obvious, one of those ideas that takes two seconds to come up with').[35] From the point of view of gender, Winterbottom's choice of the western genre for the relocation of Hardy's plot is entirely appropriate. Lee Clark Mitchell theorises the western as a genre obsessed with masculinity; Jane Tompkins contends that the western 'answers the domestic novel',[36] representing men in flight from the domestic restraints of Victorian culture. Hardy's *Mayor of Casterbridge* is similarly obsessed with masculinity and its relation to domesticity, and in many ways it also represents Hardy's dissatisfaction with the domestic novel (which he famously castigates in 'Candour in English Fiction' as 'a literature of quackery').[37] According to Mitchell, the western, set in a geographically defined fictional space that purports to be removed from cultural constraints, signifies a nostalgic escape from middle-class obligations, a time of precorporate capitalist individualism, sexual liberty, and intense male bonding.[38] Violence in the western is in many ways the measure of the man, and I will focus on Winterbottom's filmic analogy to *The Mayor of Casterbridge* with this in mind.

Like *Jude*, *The Claim* opens with a suitably Hardyan scene, in which small dark human figures are dwarfed by the backdrop of the immense snow-covered mountains. And as in *Jude*, this black-on-white motif signifies hardship; most of the action takes place in this austere, forbidding landscape, relieved only by the indoor scenes that mainly feature the saloon or the sickroom. In other words, the *mise-en-scène* itself is violent, as in many westerns, not just visually but also aurally as the sound track amplifies the noises of footsteps, creaking horse harnesses, and most of all the wind, which creates a remote and slightly ominous undertone throughout the film. But the scene's violence is not restricted to the landscape. As the camera zooms in on the struggling black figures, the first interaction we witness is an altercation between two men over the possession of firearms in 'Mr Dillon's Town', followed by a fight over an insult to Hope Burn, Dillon's daughter. Clearly an analogue for Casterbridge, Kingdom Come is a rough frontier settlement that 'belongs' to Mr Dillon, who built the gold-rush community and who functions as its lawgiver, much as Michael Henchard functions in Casterbridge. The violence of the frontier culture, we may note, obviates the need for a Mixen Lane, as the whole town represents an anti-bourgeois space removed from 'civilisation'. Hardy's Roman ruins, too, have become redundant, as the town is in the process of making its own history (little mention being made of the landscape's indigenous occupants); and by the same token, there is no need for a skimmity-ride, as a form of rough justice is already the norm. Abel Whittle's public exposure is replaced by a scene of Dillon horsewhipping a man on his bare back in the snow as the punishment for a crime; the audience shares the perspective of a horrified Hope, who later learns from Dalglish (the railroad engineer and Farfrae figure) that the whipping has likely prevented the man from being lynched, a comment that lets us know that underneath Dillon's taciturn exterior he is a decent man, just as in Hardy's text Abel Whittle lets both Elizabeth-Jane and the reader know about Henchard's covert kindness to his mother. Finally, Dillon's fiery demolition of the town and solitary death are prefigured in the image of the pack horse bursting into flame and galloping away after the railway crew's nitroglycerine explodes.

Like Henchard, Dillon sells his wife and child, an episode rendered exclusively through Dillon's flashbacks to a shrieking blizzard and the muted visibility of a whiteout as he and his young family struggle towards the safety of a miner's shack twenty years earlier. But Dillon's relation to domesticity is portrayed as more straightforward than Henchard's, simply because of the film's setting in the already anti-bourgeois wild west. In lieu of Henchard's engagement to Lucetta, Dillon is living with Lucia when the film begins. Their relationship is frankly sexual, giving rise to the only erotic scenes in the film; Henchard's misogyny has become redundant in a setting in which most women pose no threat of domesticity. When Lucia seduces Dalglish, therefore, their liaison takes the form not of a marriage but of a one-night stand. Domestic entanglements are not so complicated in the film adaptation, because Winterbottom has chosen to stage the action in a space in which masculinity is measured by other means. Hope is thus Dillon's biological daughter in the film, and the Newson story has been elided, thereby forfeiting the novel's rich complexity as to questions of paternity.

The Claim also forfeits, I will argue, some salient aspects of the novel's ideological implications. In particular, the inherently conservative western genre fails to do justice to Hardy's searching exploration of masculine gender norms. As in Hardy's text, the main conflict in the film is between two different concepts of masculinity: that of Dillon, the old-fashioned autocratic man of action, and that of Dalglish, the harbinger of the railroad, technology, and respectability. And as in *The Mayor of Casterbridge*, the younger, more bourgeois man walks away with the respect of the town and the hand of the daughter at the end. The spoils go to the man who exhibits a civilised self-control, and again the western (which Mitchell discusses in relation to its 'performance of restraint')[39] is an appropriate vehicle for such a message. In a typical western shootout scene, real men refrain from violence until other means have been exhausted, and Dalglish shoots one of Dillon's men only in order to prevent more violence, thus proving his manhood (earlier in the film he has been dismissed as 'a young pup' who will be 'no bother'). At the end of the film, Dalglish apologises to Hope for his conduct (presumably referring to both the sex and the violence), explaining that he would have behaved differently under 'different' – in other words more civilised – circumstances. Dillon, of course, exhibits no such self-restraint, and Winterbottom's viewing audience is made to feel a certain amount of compassion for the fierce, deposed patriarch who is his own worst enemy.

But *The Claim* reduces this classic conflict between agression and restraint to a predictable truism, especially in comparison with Hardy's subtler treatment of it. Key to Hardy's analysis of this issue is the larger-than-life, irascible, impulsive character of Henchard, whose defiant, irrational masculinity is (at least partly) 'domesticated' over the course of the narrative.[40] The extent to which this occurs, however, is not as remarkable as what George Levine describes as the 'narrative intensity' of his presentation,[41] the extent to which he dominates Hardy's text. In narratological terms, the dimensions of Henchard's characterisation exceed its functions, and it is the former that compel the reader's attention.[42] Henchard's struggle is imbued with tragic dignity, partly by virtue of this charismatic quality (particularly in contrast with Farfrae's much blander presentation), and partly through the narrative's well-documented parallels with Greek and Shakespearian tragedy. Winterbottom's film achieves a similar epic effect through the sheer grandeur of its setting, but it lacks the genuine ambivalence Hardy's text displays towards the inevitable resolution of the conflict between masculinity and domesticity. Ultimately, the requirements of the western genre in the 1990s cause Winterbottom's rendition of this conflict to fall flat. Having shifted its heroic stereotype over the course of the twentieth century from flamboyance to impassivity, from John Wayne to Clint Eastwood, the 1990s western leaves little room for the portrayal of a hero who would have the same appeal for its viewers as Henchard has for a literary audience. Peter Mullan is not fierce enough, not magnificently defiant enough, to engage the viewer's sympathy in the way that it must be engaged if the film is to pack the same punch as Hardy's novel.[43] Nor is Winterbottom's audience made to feel enough ambivalence towards Wes Bentley as Dalglish, who by the end of the film has unproblematically become its hero in a traditional transfer of patriarchal power.

To give Winterbottom credit, Dillon's defeat occurs in grand style. Civilisation finally encroaches, even on the masculine space of the frontier, and it is significant that Dillon's last act of defiance and despair is to burn his house, the symbol of his attempt to live conventionally in a middle-class domestic milieu. As in Hardy's novel, the wronged daughter in *The Claim* rejects the repentant patriarch, who subsequently dies of exposure – not exposure to the eyes of a judgmental society, as in

Henchard's case, but more literally of exposure to the elements. After he sets fire to his house, Dillon wanders away and literally becomes part of the landscape, a black blot resembling a bundle of rags or pile of stones as the camera pulls away. As Mitchell notes, western narrative 'work[s] out the limits of masculinity by defining those who align themselves with the landscape . . . against those . . . who . . . submit to it'.[44] It is significant, too, that after he dies we are shown several views of Dillon lying in the snow; Mitchell contends that 'Westerns can be reduced to oppositions between those who stand and those who fall down . . . The prone are always revealed in the end to be non-men.'[45] As Winterbottom's camera insistently reminds us, Dillon comes to occupy precisely such a position in the landscape, with Dalglish as upright victor removing his hat in a somewhat token gesture of respect as he approaches the body of the fallen patriarch. 'They were like kings', says Dalglish of the pioneers, and by this point, the fallen king theme comes as no surprise, since a man in a tavern scene earlier in the film has already given us a heartfelt recitation of Keats's 'Ozymandias'. The gold miner who trades his claim for Dillon's wife and daughter in the first place also warns Dillon (and the viewer), 'There's no pleasure in it – a man loses heart', as the camera shows us a close-up of the gold dust and nuggets he pours onto the table.

Here, then, is the complication for Hardy's hero, for Winterbottom's hero, and for nineteenth-century manhood in general: the attainment of power and wealth in exclusively masculine terms yields an empty victory. While Hardy's text effectively complicates the bourgeois, domestic alternative, however, Winterbottom's does not. In the film text, domesticity conquers at the end in a standard valorisation of the heterosexual love story. The final long shot pulls back from Dalglish and Hope walking down the street of the burned town, the railroad having bypassed Kingdom Come and doomed it to extinction. The representative of the railroad also represents all it brings in terms of a more orderly, less violent way of life, and the aging patriarch has yielded to the forces of progress. Even the sub-plot based on a love story between one of the whores and a member of the railway crew ends in a wedding celebration, the traditional symbol of successful domestic closure. Despite the hardship of the frontier environment, the overall impression is one of progress and unambiguous triumph, a very different effect from that of Hardy's more muted ending. Elizabeth-Jane's cautious optimism, exemplary of what George Levine calls the tenuous but essential 'compromises' of realism,[46] is overshadowed by the bitter details of Henchard's demise – a fitting conclusion to a text in which middle-class domesticity is not portrayed as particularly attractive, especially for men, even though it is the only viable option.

Overall, *The Claim* constitutes an interesting and intelligent adaptation of its source text for the late twentieth century. Although it mutes the tragedy of Dillon's downfall, offers no counterpart to Henchard's intense homosocial affection for Farfrae, and ends with the traditional closure of marriage, Winterbottom's 'analogy' presents the viewer with some interesting elements of its own in terms of gender issues. For instance, even though the female characters are conventionally divided into whores and 'good' women, a nicely feminist twist is introduced when Lucia, the madam of the brothel whom Dillon has made into 'the richest woman north of Sacramento', becomes the ruler of the new town of Lisboa (named after her father's birthplace) at the end of the film. While men in this present-day western are revealed to need domesticity as 'both the motivation for and the resolution of changing masculine heroisms',[47] women are shown to have other options. And as an exploration of masculinity, Winterbottom's adaptation echoes Hardy's text in its resistance to bourgeois constraints, even if it fails to portray this resistance with Hardy's degree of complexity.

Conclusion

For contemporary viewers, both *Jude* and *The Claim* speak to the difficulty of conforming to cultural constructions of masculinity, in both the nineteenth and twentieth centuries. The other film-length adaptations of Hardy made in the 1990s, Gold's *The Return of the Native* (1994), Agland's *The Woodlanders* (1997), and St Paul's *The Scarlet Tunic* (1998), also address this issue, which frequently translates visually, as in classical westerns, into heroes who literally collapse. These prone 'non-men' are ubiquitous in cinematic adaptations of Hardy: we think not only of Dillon in the snow, but of Jude on the many beds that stand in for his deathbed in *Jude*; of Clym asleep on the floor (see Illustration 8) and the drowned Wildeve in *The Return of the Native*; of Giles stretched out first on the sodden leaves (see Illustration 9) and then on the floor of his hut in *The Woodlanders*; and of the executed soldiers in the penultimate scenes of *The Scarlet Tunic*. These protagonists need help, but it is not clear what form this would take or who would provide it. As Hardy's narrator famously remarks in *Jude*, 'nobody did come, because no one does' (I, v, 27), apart from the female figures who sometimes bend over these fallen forms in grief and alarm (as Hope bends over Dillon, Thomasin over Wildeve, Grace over Giles, Frances over Matthaus). These women appear to occupy a narrative position similar to that of the stock female figure in many Victorian texts, the loving woman who heals the hero's temporary weakness so that he can resume his 'normal' position of strength in the

Illustration 8. Clym (Ray Stevenson) asleep on the floor in *The Return of the Native*, Hallmark: Hall of Fame, 1994.

Illustration 9. Giles (Rufus Sewell) huddled on the ground in *The Woodlanders*, Pathé (UK), 1997.

gender hierarchy. But such ministrations are futile in the face of the cultural difficulties faced by Hardy's film heroes. Their prone position, their loss of erectness, is not temporary but (at least symbolically) permanent, a symptom of their crushing defeat by a gender system as well as a class system in which they can find no place for themselves.

Embedded in Hardy's texts as subversive reproaches to such restrictive systems, these masculine failures perform a similar function on the cinema screen, where the camera frequently dwells on their prostrate bodies. Our response to these fallen heroes is comprised of pity as well as a certain discomfort, an embarrassment at their inability to get up and assert themselves: as lovers and husbands, as autonomous subjects, as capable survivors of modernity – in short, as men. Such mute icons of masculine failure fail to yield the kind of reassurance the viewer of classic adaptations has come to expect in relation to gender issues. Instead, they afford a less immediately pleasurable form of solace, a confirmation of the postmodern sense of the impossibility of 'standing up' to the conflicting demands of virility and restraint that define men's place in a binary gender system, and the further sense of gender itself as a suspect determinant of identity. Like late-twentieth-century men, Hardy's heroes frequently fail in their attempts to negotiate such cultural configurations, both in his novels and in their cinematic reincarnations.

NOTES

1. Albert J. Guerard, *Thomas Hardy* (New York: New Directions, 1964), pp.114–19. First published in 1949.
2. Peter Finch as Boldwood, Terence Stamp as Sergeant Troy, and Alan Bates as Gabriel Oak in Schlesinger's *Far From the Madding Crowd* (and later as Michael Henchard in the 1978 mini-series of *The Mayor of Casterbridge*) are notable exceptions.
3. Wagner's three types of adaptation are discussed in Geoffrey Wagner, *The Novel and the Cinema* (Rutherford, N.J.: Fairleigh Dickinson University Press, 1975), pp.222–31.
4. *Ibid.*, p.146.
5. Tim Dolin, 'Jude Fawley and the New Man', in Penny Boumelha (ed.), *'Jude the Obscure: Contemporary Critical Essays*, New Casebooks (Basingstoke: Macmillan, 2000), p.218.
6. Janet Bergstrom, 'Alternation, Segmentation, Hypnosis: Interview with Raymond Bellour', *Camera Obscura* 3–4 (1979) 89.
7. Dianne F. Sadoff and John Kucich, 'Introduction: Histories of the Present', in Sadoff and Kucich (eds.), *Victorian Afterlife: Postmodern Culture Rewrites the Nineteenth Century* (Minneapolis: University of Minnesota Press, 2000), p.xi.
8. See Pierre Bourdieu, *Distinction: A Social Critique of the Judgement of Taste*, trans. Richard Nice (Cambridge, Mass.: Harvard University Press, 1984).

9. Anne Friedberg, *Window Shopping: Cinema and the Postmodern* (Berkeley: University of California Press, 1993), p.188.

10. Esther Sonnet, 'From *Emma* to *Clueless*: Taste, Pleasure and the Scene of History', in Deborah Cartmell and Imelda Whelehan (eds.), *Adaptations: From Text to Screen, Screen to Text* (London: Routledge, 1999), p.59.

11. Thomas Hardy, *Jude the Obscure*, ed. Patricia Ingham (Oxford: Oxford University Press, 1985). All subsequent page references are to this edition.

12. Patricia Ingham, *Thomas Hardy* (New York: Harvester Wheatsheaf, 1989), p.38.

13. René Girard outlines his well-known theory of mimetic desire, in which the object of desire is invested with erotic interest as a result of being desired by a rival, in *Deceit, Desire and the Novel* (Baltimore: Johns Hopkins, 1966).

14. Thomas Hardy, 'Candour in English Fiction', *New Review* 2 (1890) 17.

15. Thomas Hardy, 'Our Exploits at West Poley: A Story for Boys', in Pamela Dalziel (ed.), *An Indiscretion in the Life of an Heiress and Other Stories* (Oxford: Oxford University Press, 1994). All subsequent references to the text are to this edition.

16. This advice is offset, of course, by the excitement of the 'exploits' of the story, which include finding the headwaters of a river and acquiring the godlike power of changing its course and thus affecting the fortunes of the citizens of two communities – clearly a fantasy of origins and ultimate power (and possibly a figure for writing fiction, an activity which similarly sets out to find the source, and alter the course, of human behaviour).

17. Michael Bracewell, *The Nineties: When Surface Was Depth* (Hammersmith: Flamingo, 2002), p.70.

18. Susan Jeffords, 'The Big Switch: Hollywood Masculinity in the Nineties', in Jim Collins, Hilary Radner, and Ava Preacher Collins (eds.), *Film Theory Goes to the Movies* (New York: Routledge, 1993), p.197.

19. Peter Widdowson, 'Thomas Hardy at the End of Two Centuries: From Page to Screen', in Tim Dolin and Peter Widdowson (eds.), *Thomas Hardy and Contemporary Literary Studies* (London: Palgrave Macmillan, 2004), p.198.

20. See, for example, Kenneth MacKinnon, *Uneasy Pleasures: The Male as Erotic Object* (London: Cygnus Arts, 1997).

21. *Ibid.*, p.62.

22. Conversely, Paul Niemeyer, who agrees that this scene 'fits in with the film's infantilising of Jude', interprets it as straightforwardly 'warm and loving'. Niemeyer, *Seeing Hardy: Film and Television Adaptations of the Fiction of Thomas Hardy* (Jefferson, N.C. McFarland, 2003), p.180.

23. Christine Brooke-Rose, 'Ill Wit and Sick Tragedy: *Jude the Obscure*', in Boumelha (ed.), *'Jude the Obscure'*, p.132.

24. Dolin, 'Jude Fawley', pp.214, 223.

25. Peter Widdowson also notes that 'allowing for the possibility that if Jude "keeps trying" and Phillotson ups and dies one day, there may be the happy ending to the love-story'. See 'Thomas Hardy at the End of Two Centuries', p.193.

26. This, as well as the sickroom scenes in *The Claim*, may in fact be conscious allusions. In a BBC interview with Nev Pierce, Winterbottom

identified *Cries and Whispers* as one of his favourite three movies; see
http://www.bbc.co.uk/films/shootingpeople/michael_winterbottom.shtml.

27. Judith Kegan Gardiner, Introduction, in Judith Kegan Gardiner (ed.), *Masculinity Studies and Feminist Theory: New Directions* (New York: Columbia University Press, 2002), pp.16–17.

28. Jude quotes Ecclesiastes 6:12: 'For who knoweth what is good for man in this life, all the days of his vain life which he spendeth as a shadow? for who can tell a man what shall be after him under the sun?'

29. Peter Widdowson, for example, opines that her 'pert, flirty, self-confident, healthy-young-woman-of-the-1990s mannerisms and expressions seem entirely inappropriate for the . . . "slight, pale . . . bundle of nerves"' Sue represents in the novel. See Widdowson, *On Thomas Hardy: Late Essays and Earlier* (Basingstoke: Macmillan, 1998), p.193.

30. 'Biography for Kate Winslet', *The Internet Movie Database*, 16 Jan. 2005, http://www.imdb.com/name/nm0000701/bio.

31. Frances E. Mascia-Lees and Patricia Sharpe, *Taking a Stand in a Postfeminist World: Toward an Engaged Cultural Criticism* (Albany: State University of New York Press, 2000), pp.93, 99.

32. See *Hardy Review* 4 (2001) 95.

33. In the Thomas Hardy Association's online *Forum* discussion group in May 2001, for example, Goldie Morgentaler called it 'an excellent film, but . . . definitely *not* an adaptation of the novel', an opinion with which at least one other contributor concurred. *Ibid.*, 95.

34. Wagner, *Novel*, p.231.

35. *Hardy Review* 4 (2001) 95.

36. Lee Clark Mitchell, *Westerns: Making the Man in Fiction and Film* (Chicago: University of Chicago Press, 1996); Jane Tompkins, *West of Everything* (New York: Oxford University Press, 1992), p.37.

37. Hardy, 'Candour in English Fiction', 15.

38. See Mitchell, *Westerns*, pp.26–7.

39. *Ibid.*, p.237.

40. The clearest explication of Henchard's domestication is found in Elaine Showalter's well-known article 'The Unmanning of the Mayor of Casterbridge', in Dale Kramer (ed.), *Critical Approaches to the Fiction of Thomas Hardy* (London: Macmillan, 1979), pp.99–115.

41. George Levine, 'Reversing the Real', in Phillip Mallett (ed.), *The Mayor of Casterbridge: An Authoritative Text, Backgrounds and Contexts, Criticism*, 2nd edn (New York: W. W. Norton, 2001), p.413.

42. James Phelan discusses the relationship between a character's dimensions (attributes he or she 'may be said to possess when that character is considered in isolation from the work in which he or she appears') and his or her functions ('particular application[s] of that attribute made by the text through its developing structure'). James Phelan, *Reading People, Reading Plots: Character, Progression, and the Interpretation of Narrative* (Chicago: University of Chicago Press, 1989), p.9.

43. Conversely, Peter Widdowson cogently points out the pitfalls of casting Henchard's character as the main focus of attention, arguing that this

may cause the oppression of women to become 'no more than a reflex of Henchard's character – autocratic, self-willed, self-destructive – rather than an endemic feature of patriarchal society'. See Widdowson, *Hardy in History* (London: Routledge, 1989), p.101.
44. Mitchell, *Westerns*, p.173.
45. *Ibid.*, p.168.
46. Levine, 'Reversing the Real', pp.413–14.
47. Jeffords, 'The Big Switch', p.200.

7   *Far From the Madding Crowd* in the cinema: the problem of textual fidelity

Keith Wilson

Far From the Madding Crowd has an initiatory, if not entirely auspicious, place in the history of adaptations of Hardy's work for performance. It was the first of his novels that he himself attempted, as early as 1879, to shape for the stage. As is well documented,[1] this led in the following year to a collaboration with the critic J. Comyns Carr, and subsequent controversy when the managers of the St James's Theatre, having rejected the Hardy/Comyns Carr dramatisation, staged Arthur Wing Pinero's new play *The Squire*, aspects of whose plot seemed suspiciously close to elements of the Hardy/Comyns Carr work. Prodded into action by an indignant Comyns Carr, Hardy was sufficiently irritated to air his feelings uncustomarily publicly in letters to the press, ensuring engaged audience attention to the finer plot details of both plays when his and Carr's *Far From the Madding Crowd* did finally make it to the stage in 1882.

This early Hardyan dramatic history – indeed, pre-history in relation to the subject of Hardy in the cinema – offers instructive preliminary evidence of the inevitable problems of adapting fiction (created by an individual author for linguistic absorption and imaginative recreation by an individual reader) for media whose terms privilege the collaborative, the performative, and the visual. Virtually every study of the practice and theory of film adaptation reflects at an early stage of its own establishment of conceptual terms what Erica Sheen calls the 'ideological investments [revealed] . . . in the central critical category of adaptation studies: the notion of "fidelity", or "faithfulness to the text"'.[2] Hardy himself (perhaps not altogether surprisingly for a man who once famously responded to requests from music halls to stage his one-act play *The Three Wayfarers* by declaring his willingness 'to let anybody play it for a guinea a night')[3] had quite a pragmatic view of the authorial compromises that might be required to translate a fiction into a viable play. Thus whatever the departures from plot orthodoxy sanctioned for the 1967 film of *Far From the Madding Crowd* by John Schlesinger, its director, and Frederic Raphael, author of the screenplay, their devotion to plot fidelity looks positively slavish by comparison with what Hardy himself sanctioned for his own stage adaptation, which dispensed entirely with Boldwood, invented for Fanny Robin (who drowns herself) a gipsy brother named Will to assume the role of Troy's murderer vacated by the absent Boldwood, and essentially reduced the novel to rustic melodrama.[4]

The majority of adaptations made in Hardy's lifetime attempted more scrupulous fidelity to the originating text, and as a consequence were plagued by a recurrent problem that Hardy himself identified in 1907, on the occasion of Harry Pouncy's presentation in Dorchester of three scenes from *Far From the Madding Crowd* – admittedly a staging experiment that by its very truncated nature was not likely to offer a particularly sure route either to mimetic comprehensiveness or audience comprehension. Hardy wrote to Pouncy after the performance to suggest the audience's need for 'an explanation of the dramatic scenes by a lecturer':

Long experience has shown that knowledge of a particular book, however common, by an audience, can never be assumed . . . Why I think something of the sort desirable is that the people around me – & they were the most intelligent in the room – were somewhat puzzled as to the situation in each case, & did not realize that each man was a different lover.[5]

Even in fuller adaptations of complete novels, this potential discrepancy in response between those audience members who knew the book and those who didn't was often problematic. In the only other stage adaptation of *Far From the Madding Crowd* with which Hardy was peripherally involved, the adaptation made in 1909 by A. H. Evans for performance by the Hardy Players, Evans was so anxious to avoid sacrificing scenes that would be familiar to, and considered indispensable by, the envisaged majority of his audience who knew the novel that he risked rendering the play opaque for those who had not read it, creating a series of cameo moments that succeeded each other with baffling rapidity.[6] Even more sophisticated adapters than A. H. Evans encountered the same problem. The last significant attempt at staging a dramatic adaptation of one of his novels in Hardy's lifetime was a 1926 production of John Drinkwater's version of *The Mayor of Casterbridge*. Noting the continuity problems created by the play's episodic structure, again in part occasioned by the desire to incorporate scenes thought likely to be anticipated by those audience members who had read the book, the reviewer for *The Times* concluded, 'Now and then there was a quick movement; now and then a dramatic thrill. But it was odd how constantly this play kept reminding us of a much grander, profounder story of the same kind that we had read somewhere.'[7]

This is not the place to engage the perennial, if finally somewhat profitless, question of whether a major literary work inevitably generates a play or film of less grandeur and profundity. In relation to film, of course, the answer to the question once seemed self-evident, and dictated by the limits of technology. The earliest film version of *Far From the Madding Crowd*, made by the Turner Film Company in 1915 (with Florence Turner playing Bathsheba), necessarily dispensed with dialogue. As a textual complement to an almost entirely visual experience, those who were present at 11.30 a.m. on Tuesday 16 November 1915 for the film's first showing at the West End Cinema in Coventry Street were presented with a souvenir programme illustrated with stills and containing a helpful synopsis of the story prepared by Hardy himself.[8] This booklet refers to the film as 'a picture play', suggesting the generic rootedness of the new medium in stage drama, an association underlined by the cast list in which two of the actors are described as being 'From the Royalty Theatre'. While no copies of this film are known to have survived, we do have one speculative route to the possible degree of its attempted fidelity to the original novel.

In November 1913, Hardy had agreed to the selling of the right to film *Far From the Madding Crowd* to Sir Hubert von Herkomer, better known in Hardy circles for his role as illustrator to the serial version of *Tess of the D'Urbervilles*.[9] Herkomer died before a film had been made, and rights were transferred to the Turner Film Company.[10] At some point a scenario was prepared, which survives (Dorset County Museum) in the form of a typescript annotated by Hardy as 'mainly Sir H. Herkomer's idea'. Whether this is a script actually prepared by Herkomer (in which case Hardy's annotation may be indicating assistance from other unspecified parties, perhaps Herkomer's son Siegfried, perhaps Hardy himself) or whether it is a script prepared by the Turner producer Larry Trimble, and based on preliminary work by Herkomer, cannot now be known; if it is the latter, it is striking that Trimble is identified as both adapter and producer in the souvenir booklet, with no indication of any indebtedness to Herkomer. Whoever prepared the scenario, and whatever its relationship to the eventual film, it attempts to include, or at least mention in explanatory sub-titles, all the novel's most memorable scenes, including many that the Schlesinger/Raphael film omits. Gabriel watching over the hedge as Bathsheba admires herself in a looking-glass, Gabriel spying on Bathsheba and her aunt in the cow shed, Gabriel's recovery of Bathsheba's lost hat, Bathsheba's rescuing of Gabriel from suffocation, the first Warren's Malthouse scene, Fanny's waiting for Troy outside his barracks, Boldwood's consultation of Gabriel about Bathsheba's handwriting, the sheep-shearing, Troy's attempt to give the watch inherited from his father to Bathsheba, Bathsheba and Troy's meeting on the road with Fanny Robin – all these, and a number of other textually prominent moments that are either omitted or radically transformed in the

1967 film, are scrupulously included in this Herkomer-inspired scenario, with the recurrent elaboration of brief descriptions in the short-hand script annotation 'Business as book'. Hardy himself has added in ms. two scenes, one of the Bathsheba/Troy marriage ceremony, the other of Fanny Robin walking towards the workhouse. Untroubled by the time-consuming demands of dialogue, this detailed scenario, comprising in all thirty-three scenes if one includes the two additions, was for a 'picture play' in the most literal of senses: for all the relative novelty of moving images, it would have generated stylised, tableau-like visual representations of textual moments immediately recognisable to those who knew the novel. Just as surely as most adapters of Hardy's novels for the stage had seen fidelity to the book, sometimes to the detriment of the play, as a primary responsibility, so this script clearly assumes that the film had to include virtually every event that a reader familiar with the text was likely to remember, and hence register the absence of.

If the film itself did indeed attempt to retain this degree of fidelity to textual event, aided by the scenic verisimilitude that came from its having been shot in Dorset, it is not surprising that the *Times* reviewer should have found its evocation of Wessex very compelling: 'One feels that the country in which the action is laid is really the Wessex of the novel and that the farm, the cattle, the sheep are the genuine ones over which Gabrial Oak watched with such care.'[11] But again, as in the Evans stage presentation, fidelity to text does not seem to have proved its own reward, and when in October 1920 Hardy was considering whether to renew the film rights, he observed that the Turner production (or perhaps, as Widdowson suggests in chapter four, the company) 'seems to have been a failure'.[12]

These early attempts at adaptation for both stage and cinema provide a helpful context against which to consider the fidelity question as it relates to Schlesinger's *Far From the Madding Crowd*, especially in light of the conventional assumption that the perceived weaknesses of this film were a function of too submissive a deference to the text (in many cases a claim made, I suspect, by commentators whose own familiarity with the text scarcely equipped them to make this confident judgment). Thus Penelope Mortimer, at the time one of Britain's most influential film reviewers, concluded that Schlesinger's 'devoted, laborious and almost unswerving loyalty to Hardy produces nothing more than a beautifully illustrated edition of the book and that, while harmless, seems curiously unnecessary'.[13] Rita Constabile claims that 'Frederick Raphael's screenplay lifts whole scenes from the novel' (conveniently ignoring the even greater number of scenes it leaves out and the sprinkling of scenes it invents) 'often with dialogue repeated verbatim'[14] (while the occasional phrase is appropriated, there are virtually no scenes with completely verbatim dialogue).

Thus the film gives the impression of textual accuracy to those who don't know the book particularly well, regardless of the quite radical departure at many points from Hardy's novel.

What fidelity in this sense really translates into, I suggest, is moderately careful attention to the main lines of the plot, period atmospheric plausibility (enhanced by exquisitely photographed and leisurely paced rural scenes, with accompanying folk music, to evoke the seasonal rhythms of pastoral life), and landscape authenticity. However much Julie Christie and Terence Stamp may look like the youthful cult celebrities of the 1960s that they were,[15] Schlesinger's Wessex itself looks like the real thing because, unlike the landscape of Polanski's *Tess*, it is. While the imaginatively authentic setting could and did generate its own literal-minded version of reader dissatisfaction in some of those who knew Dorset and Wiltshire sufficiently well to undermine their capacity for willing suspension of disbelief in relation to this screen Wessex (how *did* those rural foot-sloggers manage to move so effortlessly between Devizes, Shaftesbury, and Maiden Castle?), the film was seen to have got its setting almost breathtakingly right, with Nicholas Roeg's magnificent – on occasion aerial – panning shots giving generous embodiment to the supposedly cinematic qualities of Hardy's perspectival imagination.[16] Such visual evocativeness and opulence must have been thought to go a long way towards bridging the perennially troublesome expectation divide between those audience members who know the text and those who don't, helping to disguise some of the motivational and structural elisions that weaken the film, not just as a version of Hardy's novel but on its own cinematic terms.

In the space available, I can explore only a few of these, and will do so primarily in relation to elements that affect the characterisation of Sergeant Troy, whose emotional motivations in the film seem to me opaque almost to the point of complete impenetrability.[17] For all Hardy's familiar predilection (manifest in characters like Aeneas Manston in *Desperate Remedies* or Alec D'Urberville) for utilising the character typology of melodrama in creating destructive womanisers, he gives a striking degree of psychological complexity to the character of Frank Troy, a complexity which is entirely lost in the film. While even in the novel there is a distracting contradiction between Troy's treatment of Fanny Robin in life and the emotional excess of his rejection of Bathsheba over Fanny's coffin ('This woman is more to me, dead as she is, than ever you were, or are, or can be'),[18] the book does construct subtle situational threads and imagistic clusters that cumulatively provide a convincing explanatory context for Troy's temperamental extremes.

I would like to tease out some of these interwoven motifs as they are established in the book. Boldwood, as well as being the patron of

Fanny Robin whom he had schooled and found employment for with Bathsheba's uncle, is also the source of the details of Troy family history that help flesh out Troy's character. As this family history was originally conceived, Troy's physician father had a taste for country living that led to professional ruin, his debt-ridden departure from the area having consigned his erstwhile bright and personable son to a dreary life as a Casterbridge copying clerk, from which he escapes by the 'wild freak of enlisting' (FMC, xv, 100). As Hardy further refined over successive revisions the details of Troy's past, he acquired the romance of a French governess mother, and ultimately, at the cost of illegitimacy, an aristocratic father.[19] Thus Troy, who in the film is little more than a uniformed popinjay with a flirtatious gift of the gab, in the novel has a past and an equivocal paternity to help account for his emotionally unstable, feckless, and sexually predatory present.

The fact that Bathsheba too had a father, similarly inclined to serial bankruptcy, who 'was one of the ficklest husbands alive' (FMC, viii, 55), is surely of suggestive psychological interest in relation to her infatuation with Troy, but this information too is excised (along with the malthouse scene that provides it) from the film. Troy's family past is made further relevant to his manipulation of Bathsheba in his attempt to persuade her to accept his father's watch, which itself undergoes an evolution into greater grandeur through Hardy's successive revisions, acquiring ultimately an engraving of the crest of the Earls of Severn with their motto '*Cedit amor rebus* – "Love yields to circumstance"' (FMC, xxv, 375), a sentiment surely very relevant to the disabling network of sexual crossed purposes in which the major characters are snared. This is the same watch that contains the lock of Fanny's hair that will be a prime motivation, along with the suspicions aroused by Bathsheba's witnessing of the surreptitious conversation between Troy and a bedraggled woman asking about Casterbridge Workhouse, for Bathsheba's disastrous opening of Fanny's coffin. During this roadside exchange (FMC, xxxviii, 228), Troy provides a crucial indication of why Fanny's death should have such an effect on him: as previously mentioned to Boldwood (FMC, xxxiii, 205), he had been searching unsuccessfully for her before marrying Bathsheba, and had assumed that she had deliberately gone away from him or died. Thus his constitutional will to seduce notwithstanding, there is very strong textual evidence that Troy, in as far as he is capable of anything resembling genuine emotion, does indeed love Fanny to a degree that he has never loved Bathsheba, and that Bathsheba may indeed have grounds for worrying that he finds Fanny Robin's golden hair 'more beautiful than my miserable black mane' (FMC, xl, 238).

This much fuller context helps provide some indication of why one of the film's most commented upon departures from the novel, the change in the colour of Bathsheba's hair, *is* actually a matter of some significance, for reasons that have nothing to do with whether Schlesinger wanted to capitalise opportunistically again on Julie Christie's sixties golden-girl image after conspicuous success with it in his previous movie, *Darling*. For what does the film provide in substitute for Hardy's carefully constructed motivational and situational network? No significant past for either Troy or Bathsheba and therefore nothing to suggest the possibility of shared familial vulnerabilities; no connection of Boldwood with Fanny (a connection in the book that leads directly to Bathsheba's first awareness of Boldwood, when he goes to her house not to offer assistance to the new young farmer, as in the film, but to enquire for news of her vanished servant); no indication that Boldwood or anyone else knows anything much of Troy's past; no Bathsheba-witnessed conversation about Casterbridge Union between Troy and a mysterious young woman on the evening before Fanny dies there; no watch; no lock of hair; no sexual insecurity in Bathsheba because of Fanny *until* Fanny is lying unthreateningly in her coffin; and no indication at all between Troy's desertion of Fanny on their ill-starred wedding morning and her desperate appeal to him on the day before her death that he has given her a second's thought. In short, actions unfold in an exquisitely photographed motivational vacuum.

One substitution for these excisions worthy of particular note is the clock-cum-music box with its revolving soldier-bugler, Troy's wedding present to Bathsheba, presumably adopted for the film as a more playfully mobile avatar of the missing watch. Nice touch though this is, with its coy self-reference on Troy's part and its ominous warning of the relentless passage of time, a reflexive self-consciousness that can be utilised in the film's closing moments to offer ironic accompaniment to Gabriel and Bathsheba's felicity as they settle down to married life together, it makes no contribution, unlike the watch and its golden secret, to an understanding of what makes these characters act as they do. It is, therefore, almost appropriate that the relative dispensability of this terminal image should have been brutally signalled in its cutting from American prints of the film to provide a more upbeat ending and to help reduce the running time of a movie that American audiences found tediously slow-paced.[20]

These criticisms of what is still, nearly forty years on, one of the best adaptations of Hardy's work to the screen are not founded in a merely conventional and literal-minded complaint that the film is not faithful in substantive detail to the book, nor that the adapter is relying on an audience's antecedent knowledge of the text to fill in the motivational gaps. They rest on the view that, in its pursuit of a certain surface kind of, primarily visual, atmospheric fidelity, this film, successful in many ways though it is, sacrifices the book's imaginative logic without adequately substituting an alternative cinematic one of its own. And what this uncertain hesitation between the presentational imperatives of two associated, but finally very different, imaginative media inevitably leads to is a motivational blurring or continuity illogic even in some of those episodes where the film does retain key elements of the originating plot. I would like to consider three such episodes that the film *does* retain, but in modified form, and whose decontextualisation manifests this slippage in the story's translation from text to screen.

The first relates to the vigorous spring-cleaning at Bathsheba's new home that, in the film though not in the book, leads to her discovery of the valentine card that she sends to Boldwood, with such unfortunate results. As we have already seen, the excision of Boldwood's protective concern for Fanny Robin and reputation for kindness from the film makes his offence-causing appearance on horseback at Bathsheba's front door in the middle of the domestic turmoil appear contrived: why would this supposedly cold and self-contained man, so hopeless in his dealings with women that, as one of Bathsheba's servants observes in the film, ''tis said he has no passionate parts', come in person to offer his assistance to a woman he does not know? But even more strained is the presence of the valentine itself. Why amidst the dust, dirt, and detritus through which Bathsheba and her employees are hacking their way, in the former household of her uncle, an aging male so unromantic and careless of circumstance that he leaves dreadful macassar-oil stains on his furniture, does a pristine valentine suddenly pop up as if newly lifted from the card racks? In the original, Bathsheba has bought it the day before as a gift for Teddy Coggan, and is moved to send it to Boldwood not through irritation at his equestrian impertinence but out of pique at his failure to pay any attention to his beautiful new neighbour in church that morning. But injured vanity as a motivation for Bathsheba's action has disappeared from the film, rendering her sending of the unconvincingly located valentine a punishment of Boldwood for social presumption rather than sexual inattentiveness.

Another cross-media continuity problem relates to what is possibly the film's most memorable scene, Troy's dazzling of Bathsheba with his sword exercises (see Illustration 10), an episode transferred from an enclosed 'hollow amid the ferns' (FMC, xxvii, 159) to a more dramatic, militarily resonant, and immediately recognisable setting, Dorchester's most famous historical site, the ancient hill-fort of Maiden Castle. This is one of the most universally praised episodes in the film. Niemeyer has commented on the cinematic enlargement of the scene, 'with Troy running up and down the slopes and waving and thrusting his sword with a look of ecstatic fury on his face', a display that ends with his climactic thrust of

Illustration 10. Sergeant Troy (Terence Stamp) displays his swords-
manship in *Far From the Madding Crowd*, MGM, 1967.

the sword into the ground in front of Bathsheba.[21] As a visual evocation
of Troy's dangerously threatening masculinity and Bathsheba's aroused
psycho-sexual fascination with him, it is a dazzling set piece. But what
is that doomed caterpillar suddenly doing on Bathsheba's bosom now
that the sword-play is taking place in these open expanses? In the original

episode, where Bathsheba advances towards the trysting place by suggestively pushing her way through 'tall thickets of brake fern . . . their soft feathery arms caressing her up to her shoulders' (FMC, xxvii, 159), no undue athleticism is required of the caterpillar to get it into position to be spiked by Troy's glittering phallic sword.

And perhaps the most naggingly obtrusive of all these surviving signs of adaptive strain: in the film, what *are* Troy's motivations for consigning himself to the waves? He has thus far displayed virtually no capacity for emotional or speculative subtlety, with the result, as we have seen, that his recent outburst over Fanny's coffin has seemed gratuitous and excessive. As he descends to that beautiful sweep of coastline to the plaintive strains of 'The Bold Grenadier', he looks mildly disconsolate but far from disablingly careworn, idly slashing at the grass with a switch and galloping down the cliff pathway in a solitary civilian echo of his earlier martial descent down the flanks of Maiden Castle towards the bedazzled Bathsheba. In the book, his motivations are clear: 'A composite feeling, made up of disgust with the, to him, humdrum tedium of a farmer's life, gloomy images of her who lay in the churchyard, remorse, and a general aversion to his wife's society impelled him to seek a home in any place on earth save Weatherbury' (FMC, xlvi, 281). After a long and exhausting walk, his 'nature freshened within him' (FMC, xlvi, 282) and he decides to rest and bathe, only to be carried out to sea by a forgotten current. By contrast, the film gives little indication of the reason for his desertion of Bathsheba, who is after all still his meal-ticket as well as his wife, beyond that carelessly suggested by the unearned emotional excess of his outburst over Fanny's coffin. He *could* be attempting suicide, as some commentators have assumed, presumably assisted in their assumption by his recent labouring over Fanny's grave and the melancholic pace of the song. But there is not the slightest genuine indication that he is, or emotionally plausible suggestion as to why he might be.[22] Nor, of course, is there any immediate indication of a rescue.[23] The episode becomes little more than a laborious, but again beautifully photographed, plot/continuity contrivance of uncertain significance.

Schlesinger's *Far From the Madding Crowd* was the first major film adaptation of a Hardy novel and, as suggested earlier, is arguably still the best. In identifying some of the adaptive problems it faced and could not entirely satisfactorily solve, one is perhaps indicating finally unresolvable tensions between film and book text that are an inevitable and long-recognised function of the role played in adaptation by that most demanding, heterogeneous, and hence unpredictable of collaborators: an audience. When Hardy laboriously explained to Harry Pouncy what was needed to make his scenes from *Far From the Madding Crowd* more

audience-friendly for those who hadn't read the book, without sacrificing the goodwill of those who had, he was adumbrating a problem that
no film-maker who wishes to survive the fidelity test and avoid the pitfalls presented by that 'central category of adaptation studies' can either
ignore or entirely solve. The Schlesinger/Raphael collaboration, unlike
the Hardy/Comyns Carr one, perhaps came as close to a solution as can
realistically be expected.

NOTES

1. For full discussions of both the play and the controversy, see James F. Stottlar,
   'Hardy vs. Pinero: Two Stage Versions of *Far From the Madding Crowd*',
   Theatre Survey 18 (November 1977) 23–43; Pamela Dalziel, 'Whose *Mistress*?
   Thomas Hardy's Theatrical Collaboration', *Studies in Bibliography* 48 (1995)
   248–59; Keith Wilson, *Thomas Hardy on Stage* (London: Macmillan, 1995),
   pp.25–9; and Suleiman M. Ahmad, '*Far from the Madding Crowd* in the British
   Provincial Theatre', *Thomas Hardy Journal* 16 (2000) 70–83.
2. Erica Sheen, Introduction, in Robert Giddings and Erica Sheen (eds.), *The
   Classic Novel: From Page to Screen* (Manchester: Manchester University Press,
   2000), p.2.
3. Thomas Hardy to J. M. Barrie, 1 December 1911, in Richard Little Purdy
   and Michael Millgate (eds.), *The Collected Letters of Thomas Hardy*, 7 vols.
   (Oxford: Clarendon Press, 1978–88), vol. IV, p.194.
4. The only surviving copy of the Hardy/Comyns Carr adaptation is the one
   submitted to the Lord Chamberlain's office before the Liverpool production
   (British Library Additional Manuscripts 53267, item 29).
5. Thomas Hardy to Harry Pouncy, [21 October 1907], in Purdy and Millgate
   (eds.), *Collected Letters*, vol. III, p.280. This is precisely the solution that
   Granville Barker adopted when he staged an adaptation of *The Dynasts* at the
   Kingsway Theatre in 1914, foregrounding a Reader who in direct address to
   the audience set the successive scenes.
6. The first scene began with Gabriel's lamb-bearing visit to the cottage of
   Bathsheba's aunt (during which the audience was informed of Bathsheba's
   antecedent rescuing of him from suffocation). No sooner had Bathsheba
   departed, having refused his offer of marriage, than Cainey Ball rushed in
   to tell everyone that Gabriel's sheep had just disappeared over the edge of
   the chalk-pit. Gabriel was still coming to terms with this when Jan Coggan
   arrived to tell everyone that Bathsheba had inherited Weatherbury Farm. By
   the beginning of the second scene, Gabriel was already employed at the farm
   (the rickyard fire having occurred in the break between scenes) and a formerly
   unidentified woman named Fanny – who never actually appeared on stage –
   had seemingly disappeared (see typescript in the Dorset County Museum).
7. *The Times*, 9 September 1926, p.10.
8. Hardy had been asked to prepare this in a letter, dated 2 November 1915,
   from F. H. Waters of Hepworth Publicity. The synopsis, pencilled out by
   Hardy on the back of Waters's letter, is printed in full in Michael Millgate
   (ed.), *Thomas Hardy's Public Voice: The Essays, Speeches, and Miscellaneous*

Prose (Oxford: Clarendon Press, 2001), pp.363–5. A copy of the souvenir booklet can be found in the Dorset County Museum.

9. See Thomas Hardy to Sir Frederick Macmillan, 21 November 1913 and 26 November 1913, in Purdy and Millgate (eds.), *Collected Letters*, vol. IV, pp.322, 324. An undated contract between Hardy and Herkomer, signed by Hardy but later cancelled, as well as a revised agreement (dated 2 December 1913) signed by Herkomer but not Hardy, survive in the British Library.

10. See Thomas Hardy to Sir Frederick Macmillan, 1 June 1915 and 9 June 1915, in Purdy and Millgate (eds.), *Collected Letters*, vol. V, pp.106, 111.

11. 'A Wessex Film', *The Times*, 17 November 1915, p.5.

12. Thomas Hardy to Sir Frederick Macmillan, 9 October 1920, in Purdy and Millgate (eds.), *Collected Letters*, vol. VI, p.42.

13. 'When Loyalty Isn't Quite Enough', *Observer*, 22 October 1967, p.28.

14. Rita Constabile, 'Hardy in Soft Focus', in Michael Klein and Gillian Parker (eds.), *The English Novel and the Movies* (New York: Frederick Ungar, 1981), p.155.

15. This was recurrently noted in reviews at the time, and wittily encapsulated from the distancing perspective of the late 1980s in Peter Widdowson's identification of 'the instantly recognizable 1960s film face of Christie with her Mick Jagger mouth' and 'Stamp with his arrogant George Best features' (' "Tragedies of Modern Life"? "Thomas Hardy" on Radio, TV, and Film', in Widdowson, *Hardy in History: A Study in Literary Sociology* (London: Routledge, 1989), p.109).

16. For other discussions of Hardy's supposed 'cinematic' techniques, see the references in chapter one, notes 3–6.

17. For a more positive view of both the film characterisation of Troy and other elements of the film, see Fran E. Chalfont, 'From Strength to Strength: John Schlesinger's Film of *Far From the Madding Crowd*', in Norman Page (ed.), *Thomas Hardy Annual No. 5* (London: Macmillan, 1987), pp.63–74.

18. Thomas Hardy, *Far From the Madding Crowd*, ed. Rosemarie Morgan (London: Penguin, 2000), p.263. All subsequent references to the novel are to this edition, and are cited parenthetically.

19. For details of these modifications, see *ibid.*, pp.367–8.

20. For a discussion of the film's relative failure in America, see Gene D. Phillips, *John Schlesinger* (Boston: Twayne, 1981), pp.80–92.

21. Paul J. Niemeyer, *Seeing Hardy: Film and Television Adaptations of the Fiction of Thomas Hardy* (Jefferson, N. C.: McFarland, 2003), p.87.

22. See, for example, Phillips, *John Schlesinger*, p.85, and Niemeyer, *Seeing Hardy*, p.89.

23. For Peter Widdowson, this invitation to assume that Troy has drowned himself represents a 'compression and sharpening of the story line' (Widdowson, *Hardy in History*, p.108), but he leaves unexplained why such plot concentration should be the logical result of a gratuitous misdirection unrooted in Troy's antecedent characterisation.

8 Staging the *Native*: aspects of screening *The Return of the Native*

Rosemarie Morgan

The spectatorial mode of the motion-picture story necessarily engages audiences in direct sensory experience: hearing and seeing as well as exercising the imagination. Yet more complicitly, the listener-spectator is conjoined to speaker-performer in the same spatio-temporal experience. The exposition of highly personal events offered up to public scrutiny, feelings and situations frequently interiorised and even protected by privacy laws in the real world, and often regarded as too intimate to be rendered visible to the spectatorial eye, can provoke schisms in cultural orthodoxy. This is fuelled by the nature of the filmic image which opens up a 'potentially limitless range of readerly interpretations [and] produces a fluid relationship between eye and object'.[1] (This 'relationship', when it arises in the literary text, tends nowadays to be stigmatised by the moralistic critic as 'voyeurism'). Any affront to cultural orthodoxy leads to censorship or, in anticipation of this, what Hardy experienced as bowdlerisation of his work – in film-making terms, 'taking liberties with the adaptation'.

'Taking liberties' in turn provokes controversy. Confronted by altered story-forms and deviance in transpositions the accusation is frequently 'inauthenticity'. Yet such transpositions go back as far as Chaucer and deep into time. In most instances it is the quality of the innovative transposition or adaptation which distinguishes the appropriated story as an art-work in its own right – distinct from its previous manifestation and autonomous in its vision. Likewise the prevailing ideologies of the society, as imposed, in ancient times, by Boccaccio and Chaucer upon the balladic oral story, are nowadays imposed upon screen stories. However loose or literal the film, whatever the degree of 'fidelity' to its source, the cinematic version must needs modify the content of the original. It is for this reason that such modifications, since they have meaning, must be told. They, primarily, are the signifiers of the tale.

It is with these specific considerations in mind that this brief study of Jack Gold's 1994 screen version of *The Return of the Native* (published in 1878) will concern itself. In what manner and with which modes of transposition from text to screen does this tale get told? What, if any, prevailing ideologies are nowadays infused into staging Thomas Hardy's *The Return of the Native*?[2]

The last question is the easier to answer: Hardy's story is now pure romance. I use the term conventionally, in classic parlance, *amor vincit omnia*. The 'love that conquers all' in the screen story is not only that of Thomasin and Diggory Venn, which was in fact merely an alternative 'happy ending' grudgingly inserted by Hardy paying lip-service to market requirements, but also that of Clym and Eustacia. The closing scene features Clym (Ray Stevenson) preaching on Rainbarrow *not* on 'morally unimpeachable subjects' (RN, VI, iv, 396) but, in the grandiloquent words of, say, *True Romance* magazine, on the undying nature of love and the 'beauty of truth which never dies' (not in Hardy). As Clym speaks his face is illuminated to a radiant glow and the camera closes in on a vision of Eustacia (Catherine Zeta Jones) gazing lovingly upon him from a nearby hillside. The scene concludes with an omniscient, aerial view encircling and gradually distancing the picturesque scene. This celestial moment is accompanied by a sound track of soaring violins.

At this point it is worth noting that in his 'General Preface' to the Wessex Edition of 1912 Hardy classifies his prose fiction in three ways: 'Novels of Character and Environment', 'Romances and Fantasies', and 'Novels of Ingenuity'. He places *The Return of the Native* in the first category, not the second of 'Romances'. At the risk of over-simplification, Hardy's novel features an 'Environment' of some severity, rigour, and turbulence: endurance and mutability triumph overall. The Egdon microcosm also epitomises a balance of conflicting forces of upheaval and stability, dissonance and harmony, attraction and revulsion. As to 'Character': a series of misfortunes arises from the characters' 'conflicting forces' – their unfulfilled aims, misbegotten ambitions, frustrated desires, oppressive class and sexual double-standards. Tragedy is the outcome.

The film, conversely, features an idyllic, idealised pastoral environment. The degree to which ancient Egdon has been transposed to a modern notion of a Golden Age setting (filmed on Exmoor), places it, at times, out of all recognition: undulating grassy meadowlands replace rough heather and gorse moorland, a glistening river meanders where Hardy has a timeworn Roman road, incandescent waterfalls cascade in place of man-made weirs (a form of dam), and sheep graze on verdant hillsides. And where the film portrays the age-old rural practice of reddling the under-shanks of rams Hardy presents no such thing (reddling marks the ram which in turn stains the impregnated ewe thus colour-coding for lambing-down). There are no sheep on Hardy's Egdon. Geologically speaking, reddle-clay, or hydrated ferric oxide (which gives the clay its colour), is absent on heathland terrain. Hardy's Venn is a reddle *trader*; he has nothing to do with tending flocks of sheep – indeed the nearest trading station for reddle is over fifty miles from Egdon on the Wessex map.

It is important to differentiate between pastoral idylls, where grazing sheep traditionally represent peace and tranquillity in Golden Age ideology (not to mention biblical connotations of paternalism, sanctity, and salvation), and the 'sombre' quality of the 'Egdon waste' (RN, I, i, 9–10), where no sheep-grazing pastures exist: the only herbivores are heathcroppers (wild ponies) grazing on heather and furze. Ideologically speaking, the romantic 'sheep-may-safely-graze' psalmic image of a rural England environment is not at all what Hardy aims at, microcosmically speaking. Indeed, Hardy's reddleman remains an outsider, literally and figuratively; this is pivotal to the moral universe of his story. For example, moral values, moralising attitudes (as exemplified by Venn), impinge on the Egdon world from an external, puritanical, middle-class culture beyond it. Susan Nunsuch's witchery and the primitivism of local superstitions are but ancient shades of Venn's 'imported' social mores prescribing a blame-shame culture and the victimisation of nonconforming women. Prevalent as superstitious practices may be (Hardy tells us) in rural culture, they serve to fill an emotional or psychological need to explain and externalise fears of difference and of the unknown. Social mores, by contrast, shape human lives. Class division, for example, shapes Mrs Yeobright's attitude to Eustacia and also plays a part in the alienation of her son. This is not to say that Mrs Yeobright is the instigator of human tragedy, rather that her class values and social attitudes, internalised from the world beyond the novel, are a factor. And the repercussions are profound. Nunsuch, on the other hand, provides the means for externalising the social prejudice against Eustacia but plays an insignificant part in putting individual lives in peril.

The film, then, transposes an idyllic, idealised pastoral world on to Hardy's Edgon and in so doing resituates the reddleman from outsider and intruder and, at crucial points in the novel, a demonic figure, to a more benign character central to the community. Where in Hardy, Venn is regarded as an alien figure, the screen story transposes him to a neighbourly denizen, a go-between whose malign role and meddling (note the internal echo with reddling) is nowhere apparent. In fact, the movie shows the reverse: Mrs Yeobright thanks him graciously for regaling local gossip; there is no gambling scene to expose the dire consequences of his meddling, and his harassment of Eustacia, such as deliberately catching her ill-prepared (undressed) for visitors or humiliating her with offers of becoming a lady's maid in Budmouth, is nowhere in evidence.

Clearly a film has to be selective and Venn's role in the original story is complex. Alexandre Astruc observes that 'one of the traditional problems of film has been its difficulty in expressing thought and ideas'.[3] Venn is primarily a symbolic, allegorical figure. He trades on stamping indelible markers on sexually active creatures ultimately to stain the pregnant female; likewise he preys on the sexually active woman, Eustacia, tormented as she is with sexual hunger. Is he the latter-day equivalent of the sexual predator?

In his early novels, as I have argued elsewhere,[4] Hardy offers his readers an array of Grundyan censors; these implied censors diminish with time as his growing reputation empowers him to speak with a greater degree of candour. In the early novels, however, it is possible to detect a Grundyan watchdog who proffers a judgmental 'voice' intertextually, mainly directed at Hardy's sexually hungry girls. This "voice" occasionally infiltrates the consciousness of select characters who in turn utter those moralistic observations of which the *Cornhill* editor, Leslie Stephen, wished there were more. The implied censor, omnipresent in most contemporary Victorian narrative proscriptions on women, redeemed many an authorial indiscretion (in editorial eyes) when applied judiciously to Hardy's 'sexy' ('wayward') women. Stephen would have rejoiced if Hardy had also applied the 'Grundyan' device to mediate the sacrilegious talk of his rustics.

In Hardy, Venn personifies the moral-watchdog in extremis: he even conceals himself with turves (aligned overtly with the devil) so he can crawl unnoticed to spy on the unsuspecting lovers, Eustacia and Wildeve. But his figurative role, 'expressing thought and ideas', remains more opaque and is frequently overlooked or even elided by critics, especially those applauding the reddleman's punitive attitude to Eustacia. The most transparent of signifiers, in Hardy, is that Venn bears a demonic guise. This is critically important to the epistemology of the novel where it brings the reddleman closely into line with Gide's devil, who operates in guises of plausibility.

Needless to say, this is not the stuff of romantic films. A modern audience must have heroes. Accordingly, heroism (not demonism) is transposed onto Venn's role, most obviously in the drowning scene. Here he becomes the focus of the action, leaping into the water intent upon rescuing Eustacia (camera close-up). He will be her sole rescuer! Conversely, in Hardy she is pulled from the water by several men and not until some time has elapsed after the other bodies have been recovered.

Hardy, as is commonly known, was irritated by romantic plots with happy endings. He held that the conventional Victorian denouement, getting-married-and-living-happily-ever-after, imposed a perniciously false coloration on life – within the novel and beyond in the ideology of the culture. Indeed, had he had his way with his editors he would have abandoned this convention altogether, even as early as *Far From the Madding Crowd*.[5] Understandably, however, given the disapproval he encountered from editors when submitting *The Return of the Native* for serial publication,[6] he capitulated to a degree of judicious decorum: he would provide a marriage for Thomasin but Eustacia would flee her ties and remain unclaimed at the last.[7] Hardy apparently saw Thomasin, the conventionally '*good*' heroine, as dispensable, in terms of sacrificing her to market needs, or at any rate, more amenable to those prevailing ideologies which dictated what was 'good' for women and what 'good' women did. The fact that he italicised the word '*good*' in a letter of February 1878 to his illustrator, Arthur Hopkins, bespeaks his wry humour at the stereotypical Victorian polarisation of women.[8] Although in terms of her status as heroine '*good*' little Thomasin might have achieved a higher stature as lonely widow ('good' women like 'good' men should suffer, after all), and although states of isolation and emotional hunger are more consistent with the great 'waste' that is Egdon's postlapsarian wilderness of lost and roaming souls, the 'good' deed was pragmatic. Hardy had a living to make.

Nor was it the first judicious adjustment Hardy made to this 'Novel of Character and Environment'. Eustacia had already undergone significant modifications. Like Bathsheba before her, Eustacia had emerged from Hardy's pen, in the first flush of writing, a spirited 'bad girl' of some considerable power, prone to fits of temperament and witching-hour passions. With Bathsheba, *Cornhill* editor Leslie Stephen had enforced specific revisions – among them, anger modification. Anger was out (nice women didn't) and vexation was in. Eustacia's case is more extreme, however: she is considerably more nonconforming than her predecessor. Aware of this and apparently having learned prudence from Stephen, Hardy made the revisions himself.[9]

If John Paterson, author of *The Making of 'The Return of the Native'*, aptly represents patriarchal views of women, Hardy was well advised in his cuts. Paterson works on the assumption that Eustacia, more expressive, galvanic and excitable in the Ur-text, is not just 'bad' but seriously evil: her 'hot words of passion' are 'demonic' and her anger manifests 'satanic pride' (Paterson's words).[10] Would male anger be thus interpreted? Of course not. Here is a typical example: where the lonely girl 'laughs at herself . . . sighs between her laughs, and [gives] sudden listenings between her sighs', Paterson labels this 'diabolism'.[11] This is quite extraordinary! It reeks of Victorian asylum mentality where women were incarcerated for emotional outbursts and uncontrolled passions.

I use the word 'extraordinary' advisedly. For a close reading of *The Return of the Native* shows that this orphaned 'young girl' (RN, I, vi, 61) only *just about* manages to cope with her emotional conflict, mainly by taking long walks (I, vii, 73). Clinical depression and bi-polarism were not certified diagnoses in Hardy's day. He speaks instead of 'hypochondriasis' (I, vi, 65).[12] However, he clearly understands her dilemma (walking is still recommended today for depression), and makes it plain enough to the reader, detailing her mood swings, her 'desponding reverie' (I, vi, 59), her 'languid calmness, artificially maintained' (I, vi, 63), the 'eating loneliness' of her days (I, vii, 71), her sense that 'nothing is worthwhile', and her deep 'depression of spirits' (I, vii, 73). These psychological stresses, manifest in fits of excitement commingled with gloom, ultimately overwhelm her completely when struggling with the unbearable upheaval of her marriage: in the 'chaos of her mind', she breaks down at the last, reduced, in a 'rocking movement' of her body, to a state of emotional collapse – 'the wings of her soul were broken' (V, vii, 345–6).[13]

Certainly Hardy attributes to Eustacia a local reputation, on Egdon, of witchcraft, and if for the heathfolk there is a synonymity between witch and demon then this may transfer to Venn's harassment and persistent stalking of her but it does not excuse his Peeping-Tom habits.[14] Such an assimilation of local superstition tends to evince his prejudice and ignorance. Notwithstanding her psychological disorders her powers of enchantment will incite the superstitious rural community and the educated re-immigrant alike to demonise her. Hardy would have been aware of the injustice – that men (including Venn) will both lust after her and fear her spellbinding power over them while women will blame her for men's desires.

It is with prudent foresight, then, that Hardy revised the Ur-text and modified the witchery aspect. Indeed if an educated critic of the 1960s can fall prey to sexist attitudes, attributing demonism to the enchantress (who fills men's hearts with cravings), while simultaneously adopting the attitudes of simple-minded heathfolk for whom anything unfamiliar is to be feared and maligned, for whom the inexplicable remains, perforce, supernatural, then what hope would there be of gaining the common reader's understanding of this beautiful but troubled young woman?[15]

Predictably, given the millennium years' preoccupation with phenomenalism, indeterminism, and psychic phenomena, the screen story does not treat witchcraft as a hostile force. Rather, the main characters simply humour the notion Paterson finds so disturbingly satanic. Only one incident, intended as an act of exorcism, features seriously enough to lend a moment of high drama to the story. This is Nunsuch's vicious stocking-needle stabbing of Eustacia in church.[16] The film maximises the explosive effect of this scene. First, it is re-situated from a regular Sunday service (as in Hardy) to the Thomasin/Wildeve wedding ceremony. Hence a double drama now occurs: there is Nunsuch's act of violence itself and, in addition, the classic dramatic gimmick of a marriage ceremony interrupted by a rival figure (although in Hardy Eustacia repudiates conventional wifedom; this is part of her heterodoxy in Victorian eyes). Second, the incident is given visual emphasis by the use of repeated zoom shots in rapid succession and, in fluid continuity, focusing upon the fanatical malevolence of Nunsuch's unpleasant face then cross-cutting to the unsuspecting beauty whose flawless loveliness intensifies the sense of profane impalement. This adaptation of the stabbing scene preserves, of course, the film story of pure romance: yet again the benighted 'beauty' is being mercilessly persecuted.

The stocking-needle episode aside, the witchcraft motif remains inconsequential in the film story: Nunsuch does not lay a curse on Eustacia (as in Hardy, 'The Lord's Prayer repeated backwards'), nor does she fashion a waxen image into which she thrusts 'with apparently excruciating energy . . . as many as fifty [pins] . . . Some into the head of the wax model, some into the shoulders, some into the trunk, some upwards through the soles of the feet' (RN, V, viii, 348). Instead, she somewhat laconically takes a ribbon worn by Eustacia and tosses it into the fire. Wildeve is equally nonchalant. In one of his night visits to Eustacia he tries to snatch a kiss or two and teases, 'Maybe you are a witch. You can keep *me* in pain until morning.' Eustacia simply looks bored while the camera indulges in repeated close-ups of her beautiful face in the moonlight. Alternatively, in trying to draw his granddaughter indoors late at night as she queries (wistfully) 'Do *you* think I'm a witch?' Captain Drew (Vye) simply jests, 'Well if you *are*, there isn't a prettier one!' (none of the above is in Hardy).

This lighthearted approach to witchcraft is anomalous given the tendency of the film towards romance. Witchcraft lends itself readily to scenes of moonshine, mystery, and entrancement and, if treated a little more imaginatively, might have added dramatic colour to what is a somewhat insipid production. True, Hardy's depiction of Nunsuch's spells and incantations is sinister and cruel. But a touch of the irrational and uncanny can certainly intensify a romance. Recent films as different as *The Purple Rose of Cairo* and *Eyes Wide Shut* sustain romantic plots despite thematic complications of fantasy, psychic violence, surrealism, and other bizarre occurrences.

The dissonance in Hardy's *The Return of the Native* is critical to our understanding not only of Eustacia's characterisation but also of the human relationships evolving, Egdon-wise, in turmoil, fortitude, darkness, and light – ever subject to the vagaries of time, upheaval, and change, perpetually in flux. But not so in the film version: there is not a whisper of dissonance. The romance genre reflects a far more sedate (even sedated?) culture in terms of audience expectations: no doubt romance offers an analgesic, a mollification of harsh reality. Or a panacea.

Whatever Jack Gold was looking for in Hardy's novel, it was not psycho-logical drama, emotional conflicts, contradictory states of mind, or the moral blinding of personal desire. What results is rather a story of well-meaning folk constantly and fatefully missing each other's tracks (which is, of course, one aspect of Hardy's complex tale). And all rests upon (romantic) determinism. The principals are all portrayed as if slightly drugged: swallow the 'fate' pill and everything is taken care of, all in the name of love's sweet illusion.

To take a brief example, Clym, arriving back at Egdon from Paris, catches a glimpse through the fog of a dream-like figure, a shrouded woman wistfully tending a white pony. The mist swirls and she is gone. He then spends the entire evening at Bloom's End preoccupied with the chimera, gazing out on the night heath while his mother exasperatedly tries, without success, to regain his attention. The pointers are obvi-ous. But the manner in which they are made obvious indicates that the screen story intends predestination to signify causality. As if abiding by a horoscope reading, Clym takes this incident as fateful. No explanation is necessary; a glimpse of the dream-woman is a premonition and that is that.

This makes for a disappointingly predictable film. Where is the tonic-ity, the winding-up, the potency of a story which should, at times, be *un*predictable? Equally problematical, Clym now lacks credibility as an enlightened mind fresh from the Paris of the late 1840s where social-ist philosophies were already shaping modern thought. For all his high-minded aims he's just another superstitious Egdon eremite. Perhaps this should not create problems of plausibility given the romantic (illusion of love) focus of the film, but it does: Clym's vocation to 'enlighten' the locals includes battling the irrational and superstitious, yet this passive, spellbound man is himself wholly susceptible to the power of spells.

Dissonance, ambivalence, indeterminism, and a studied watch-fulness[17] characterise the narrator(s) of Hardy's *The Return of the Native* – the passive acceptance of the film narrative is nowhere in evidence. Nor is there any point in the screen story where this is ruffled. Even as the (supposedly) suicidal Eustacia seeks out her grandfather's brace of pis-tols above his bed there is a singular lack of urgency about the scene: the camera work is poised, middle-distance (no disturbing low angles, no hand-held-camera instability); the lighting is soft, not high-contrast or

Illustration 11. Eustacia (Catherine Zeta Jones) ponders suicide in *The Return of the Native*, Hallmark: Hall of Fame, 1994.

harshly unsettling (no sense of anguish); and there is no build-up of tension whatsoever (Hardy, conversely, cross-cuts the scene). Moreover, the entire event is transposed to a public arena – to the relaxed comfort of the downstairs living room where Eustacia's grandfather notices her glance and removes the guns for cleaning. Hardy, on the other hand, chooses the emptied spaces of the second-floor bedrooms and it is the infatuated Charley who – deeply concerned by her strangeness of manner – follows her upstairs, notices her entry to her grandfather's room, tracks her movements closely as she leaves and, before she returns, secretively removes the weapons:

She turned and went up the second time – softly and stealthily now – and entered her grandfather's room, her eyes at once seeking the head of the bed. The pistols were gone. The instant quashing of her purpose by their absence affected her brain as a sudden vacuum affects the body: she nearly fainted. Who had done this? (RN, V, v, 328).

The film adaptation inevitably undermines Eustacia's status as tragic heroine. The idea seems to be to sustain romantic elements at all costs and to provide audiences with well-processed fare for instant consumption and easy digestion. Not surprisingly the denouement, the death scene itself, is wholly palatable and undisturbing. Eustacia stands on the bridge staring down at the rushing torrent of the waterfall where she will imminently drown (see Illustration 11): there is no sense of lurching dread, no dark foreboding, no tonal strain or ferment. On the contrary, the visual emphasis (as in the earlier 'pistols' scene) rests upon Eustacia's (Catherine Zeta Jones's) physical beauty thus eliding, entirely, the tragic significance of a suicidal mind breaking under pressure.

The emotional undercurrents of a scene do not necessarily rest with the skills of the actor. Cinematographic expertise also comes into play. There is, for example, a psychological difference between employing a stationary camera (stable) or eye-level shot (seldom disorienting or disturbing) and a moving camera with angle shots, which imparts a sense of agitation; indeed, the hand-held moving camera intensifies undercurrents of emotional instability and if held at close range can instantly convey jumpy, ragged states of mind. The camera work in the two key scenes aforementioned is smooth, seamless, and poised, conveying no sense of disorientation, anxiety, or crisis.

Imminent danger, momentarily suggested in the 'bridge' scene as the camera cuts to the swirling waters beneath, is severely undermined by cross-cuts to the beautiful face, by the sound track's reiteration of the angelic chorus (which plays constantly throughout), and by repeated focus on the group of observers (Thomasin, Clym, et al.) from which no motion of felt urgency emanates to accelerate the dramatic pace. The main indication of crisis is put in Thomasin's hands whose tinny little Sunday School voice yelling out 'She's in the water' carries no force or conviction. Additionally, the inertia and physical distance of the loosely framed group of observers allows for too much slack at the point when the implosive action of Eustacia's vanishing body occurs (why are they all just standing there?). When she reappears in the waters beneath, the (would-be) mortal impact of her fall is altogether lost. A tightly framed shot with the figures about to break from it would have added a sense of tension, as would narrowing the spatial gap from the scene of disaster.

Most problematic, however – and this *does* cause the viewer some anxiety (if for the wrong reason) – is the fact that the 'white water' beneath the bridge flows over visibly treacherous rocks and it was at this point that, with an unsuccessful effort at suspension of disbelief, I was deeply concerned that if Eustacia should fall, as fall she must, she wouldn't drown at all but would knock herself out.[18]

Returning to 'beauty shots', Paul Niemeyer makes a similar point. Concerning Mrs Yeobright's fatal trip across the heath on a scorching summer's day[19] only to be confronted at her son's house by a face at the window and no one at the door to let her in, Niemeyer asks the question, 'Why does Eustacia stay at the window so long that the camera is again allowed to devour her beautiful features?'[20] This is indeed a gratuitous cinematic gesture as well as a highly unconvincing scene. Eustacia's intention, after all, is to remain concealed. The over-exposure of the scenic action and the sagging spatial frameworking here is not only clumsy cinematography but an insult to the viewer who is deemed, presumably, to be too dim-witted to grasp the implications of the face at the window: a sudden, brief glimpse would be enough.

Space, after all, is a medium of communication. As Giannetti argues,

One of the most elementary, yet crucial, decisions the film director makes is what shot to employ vis-à-vis the materials photographed . . . How close should the camera get to the subject – which is another way of saying how close should *we* get to the subject, since the viewer's eye tends to identify with the camera lens . . . The film frame is also a kind of territory, though a temporary one, existing only for the duration of the shot . . . The less we see, the more mysterious and inaccessible he [the subject] will seem.[21]

In sum, the film genre of *The Return of the Native* best fits the category of historical romance,[22] an unabashed prettification of the past. The emphasis, in costume, scenic backcloth, musical score, and cinematography, rests upon the picturesque and the lyrical, the ideological emphasis relies upon the rural legend of the 'cool sequester'd vale of life'.[23] The Egdon paradigm as represented by Hardy, of rough and rushing weirs, arid heathlands, turbulent weather, and lynchet-fretted barrows, is modified in the film to suit a modern audience's idea of 'old England'. Rugged Egdon, its characterisation as a unique entity, becomes an idealised rural landscape with incandescent waterfalls (there is none such in Hardy), flanked by hills that are 'alive with the sound of music' (indeed the aerial shots are strongly reminiscent of the opening scenes of *The Sound of Music*).

In general, for staging *The Return of the Native*'s natural world, the *mise-en-scène* relies upon camera angles ranging from high to deep-focus: this aptly conveys a sense of space and an omniscient point of view. The figures in the landscape, however, are not naturalistic: they are, in the main, stagey and theatrical. The sense is that the film characters represent no contemporary human condition (as in Hardy) but an *idea* of what a Hardy novel should be. Take the opening scene with Eustacia striding the wide, spectacular hills (heavenly choir singing) in swirling folds of an opulent blue cloak while intermittently flinging back her head – shrouded in a monk-like cowl (see Illustration 12). This last un-hooding image is effective in evoking her sense of suffocation and constraint but, with an inconsistency typical of the film throughout, the visual impact, suggestive of *inner* enclosure, is undermined by the framed composition of her free body taking full command of the *outer* world: the vast, open, unfettered terrain. The camera meanwhile cross-cuts to visual elements corresponding to the idea of a Hardyan-Egdon scene: furze-cutters emerge

Illustration 12. Eustacia (Catherine Zeta Jones) in *The Return of the Native*, Hallmark: Hall of Fame, 1994.

in the foreground, heathcroppers are briefly framed, while a long-lens shot juxtaposes the seemingly oblivious heroine striding the hills which, at this point, is not, geologically speaking, a heath at all. The sequence concludes with Eustacia's mounting the summit of the hillside where she breathes something inaudible about 'dying for love' whereupon, with a touch of the epic, the camera circles dizzily in an aerial shot – intended, perhaps, to convey a sense of overweening destiny.[24]

Returning to the lone beauty-cum-witch who no longer features as a persecuted figure cloaked in superstition and fear, it appears that modern ideologies, ironically, reflect something of the decorum Hardy's Victorian editors also tried to impose on his work. 'Decorum' *is still pertinent* to Eustacia's characterisation: Hardy's 'rebellious woman' (RN, I, vii, 73) never raises her voice in anger in the film story; she does not cry out 'vehemently' in the face of Clym's complacency as furze-cutter: 'I would starve rather than do it . . . I will go and live with my grandfather again' (RN, IV, ii, 248), and if her 'wrath and fervour' may 'be somewhat thrown away on [Hardy's] netherward Egdon' (RN, I, vii, 69), there is none whatsoever to be 'thrown away' in the screen tale. Nor does she mutter imprecations to herself or 'soliloquise aloud' (RN, V, vii, 346). On the contrary, her voice throughout is sweetly submissive, measured, and controlled, and her demeanour modest and unassertive in keeping, I suppose, with the current idea of the stereotypical Victorian 'lady'. Even her sensation-starved habit of dragging strands of her hair though the furze as she walks on the heath (possibly a form of algolagnia) is substituted in the film by Clym's brushing it! Indeed, if this is a woman who 'had advanced to the secret recesses of sensuousness' (RN, I, x, 96), this is nowhere evident. Even more oddly, in this day and age of sexual explicitness, her bedroom 'shivers', 'heavy breaths', and 'shudders' (RN, I, vi, 67) remain a feature of Hardy's novel alone.

Does this muting of plot, character, and scene reflect a failure of projection into the historical past where Hardy shows a deep complexity of environment and character? I doubt it – with the vast array of research resources available I suspect that it is quite simply the director's deliberate choice. Happy endings (relatively speaking) appear to be mandatory in adaptations of Hardy's novels. Modern audiences, like the readers of the Victorian novel, favour illusion over reality. The film is thus unfaithful to the novel at the level of what Giannetti calls 'realism', which should involve a rejection of 'clichés, stale conventions, stock situations and characters . . . glib happy endings . . . and other forms of phony optimism'.[25] This could be said of Hardy's story but not of Gold's film.

NOTES

1. Martin Halliwell, *Images of Idiocy: The Idiot Figure in Modern Fiction and Film* (Aldershot: Ashgate, 2004), p.17.
2. My references are to the first edition of *The Return of the Native*, ed. Tony Slade (Harmondsworth: Penguin, 1999). My intention, in using the first edition, is to keep as close as possible to Hardy's first writing – created at that

unique historical moment before public opinion, editors, and critics could in any way impose or influence revisions to the text.

3. Louis D. Giannetti, *Understanding Movies*, 5th edn (Englewood Cliffs, N. J.: Prentice Hall, 1990), p.350.

4. See Rosemarie Morgan, *Women and Sexuality in the Novels of Thomas Hardy* (London: Routledge, 1988), especially chapter three, 'The Heresy of Passion: *A Pair of Blue Eyes*'.

5. See Rosemarie Morgan, *Cancelled Words: Rediscovering Thomas Hardy* (London: Routledge, 1992).

6. Leslie Stephen, editor of the *Cornhill*, took one look at the opening chapters and declared it too dangerous for a family magazine, but eventually *Belgravia* agreed to publish it.

7. In 1912 Hardy added the following footnote:

> The writer may state here that the original conception of the story did not design a marriage between Thomasin and Venn. He was to have retained his isolated and weird character to the last, and to have disappeared mysteriously from the heath, nobody knowing whither – Thomasin remaining a widow. But certain circumstances of serial publication led to a change of intent.
>
> Readers can therefore choose between the endings, and those with an austere artistic code can assume the more consistent conclusion to be the true one. (Thomas Hardy, *The Return of the Native*, ed. Simon Gatrell (Oxford: Oxford University Press, 1990) p.472).

8. Richard Little Purdy and Michael Millgate (eds.), *The Collected Letters of Thomas Hardy*, 7 vols. (Oxford: Clarendon Press, 1978–88), vol. I, p.52. All further references to this edition will appear in brackets in the text.

9. Vigilant of prevailing codes of decorum Hardy wrote to his illustrator, Arthur Hopkins (Feb. 1878), 'I think you have chosen well for the May illustration – certainly the incident after the mumming, with the mummers looking on, will be better than the mumming performance itself. Eustacia in boy's clothes, though pleasant enough to the imagination, would perhaps be unsafe as a picture' (*Letters*, I, 54).

10. John Paterson, *The Making of 'The Return of the Native'* (Berkeley: University of California Press, 1960), pp.18–19.

11. *Ibid.*, p.19.

12. *Hypochondriasis*: 'a generic term for a range of neurotic psychological disorders such as mild depression, low spirits, irritability, and vague and apparently baseless dissatisfaction with one's lot' (Slade (ed.), *Return of the Native*, p.406, note 8).

13. Helen Small, in her 'Chances Are: Henry Buckle, Thomas Hardy, and the Individual at Risk', criticises Eustacia's story with surprising naivety for 'not offering a model for thinking either more directly about how one acquires a vision of community, or about individual moral agency' (79). This is entirely irrelevant given that, in common with her author, Eustacia regards herself as an outsider and essentially hermetic. Equally surprisingly, Small decides that Eustacia's characterisation is 'anachronistic . . . egoism' and 'Romantic individualism', offering no psychoanalytical insights despite the title of the volume in which her article appears, *Literature, Science, Psychoanalysis,*

1830–1970, ed. Helen Small and Trudi Tate (Oxford: Oxford University Press, 2003), pp.64–85.

14. Venn claims protection of Thomasin's interests: this would avail him nought in a modern court of law all too familiar with the stalker's 'protection' excuse.

15. On the young, alluring woman subjected to accusations of witchcraft, see Nancy van Vuuren, *The Subversion of Women* (Philadelphia: Westminster Press, 1974). Certain critics claim Hardy's revisions to Eustacia's characterisation expose autobiographical ambivalence rooted in attempts to conceal his obsession with a young woman in his past. But both Eustacia's characterisation and the Egdon paradigm (the 'Quiet Woman' is quiet because headless) suggest the influence of George Sand, whom Hardy was reading at the time.

16. Hardy's naming of 'Nunsuch' is acute. The Celtic language employs the same word for 'nun' and 'witch'. This goes back to the days of the *Malleus Maleficarum*, as do the similar habiliments of nun and witch.

17. Hardy's 'cinematographic' insights are worth noting: he held that the art of observation lies in seeing great things in little things, the whole in the part. The storyteller requires, then, not only an intuitive power but a synecdochic vision which perceives and seeks to represent the whole picture in a microcosmic fragment, as in capturing the whole tune in a few bars. He also sought, he said, to make visible that which is normally unseen. This implies a proleptic understanding of visual technology. Likewise he viewed the world microscopically, telescopically, even kaleidoscopically: I would call this attribute 'spectroscopic' – it is the gift of the film director.

18. Where Hardy leaves Eustacia's suicide ambiguous – confusing light-signals could have misled her, especially given her disturbed mental state – the film story does not. As far as the mores of the prevailing society are concerned, many Victorian readers would have condemned suicide as an offence against Church, God, and State. Likewise Hardy's (censoring) editors. With due respect to the newscasting censorship of the Nine-Eleven suicides at the Twin Towers site (unlike Europeans, Americans were not permitted to view the full, uncensored footage), the millennium audience (and film director) is less likely to censor suicide.

19. This is possibly one of the most implausible scenes in the film. It is set in winter, the trees are bare: Mrs Yeobright does not therefore suffer a heatstroke. No adders are featured (which anyway hibernate); hence, when she rests on the heath there is no reason for Johnny Nonsuch's alarm nor for her death.

20. Paul J. Niemeyer, *Seeing Hardy: Film and Television Adaptations of the Fiction of Thomas Hardy* (Jefferson, N. C.: McFarland, 2003), p.224.

21. Giannetti, *Understanding Movies*, pp.56–9.

22. The film also has attributes of the Classical genre: 'a slightly stylized presentation that has at least a surface plausibility' in which 'the images are determined by their relevance to the story and characters, rather than a desire for authenticity . . . classical cinema is story oriented . . . A high premium is placed on the entertainment values of the story, which is often shaped to conform to the conventions of a popular genre' (*ibid.*, p.5).

23. Thomas Gray's line is from 'Elegy Written in a Country Churchyard' – the first line, 'Far from the madding crowd's ignoble strife' forms Hardy's title to his fourth published novel. Hardy's title is of course ironic: 'ignoble strife' provides the underlying motif to the entire novel.
24. However, the melodramatic bonfire scene on the Barrow is highly effective. Note: the ancient Hallowtide celebrations and lighting of fires have been superseded by Guy Fawkes Night festivities (which have borrowed much from pagan rituals): these celebrate the 'Gunpowder Plot' of 5 November 1605, when an uprising of English Catholics conspired, unsuccessfully, to blow up the Houses of Parliament.
25. Giannetti, *Understanding Movies*, p.312.

9 Screening the flashback: three ways of opening *The Mayor of Casterbridge*

Philip Allingham

As both *The Claim*, Michael Winterbottom's 2001 film adaptation of Hardy's *The Mayor of Casterbridge*, and the 2003 screening on the Arts and Entertainment Network of a more conventional adaptation well illustrate, the 1886 novel about a 'Man of Character' continues to engage the minds of the present generation. The very first adaptation of this novel, as Peter Widdowson mentions in chapter four, was Sidney Morgan's 65-minute silent film of 1921, made with the author's cooperation in Steyning, Sussex, and 'on location' in and around Dorchester.[1] Although British film-maker Thorold Dickinson planned to produce a cinematic treatment of the novel for 1950's 'Festival of Britain', the project fell through, possibly because Hardy's tragedy was inconsistent with Britain's need for celebration, and possibly because he could not fully integrate the mayor's housekeeper, Mrs Trimlett, his comic replacement for Susan Henchard, whom he cut because he failed to see her function in the plot as a palpable claim on Henchard's loyalties and a symbol of how the past affects the present.[2]

The first 'talkie' based on *The Mayor of Casterbridge* is surprisingly recent: the seven-part BBC television serial of 1978, directed by David Giles, which was popular as a high-brow soap-opera on both sides of the Atlantic. In the United States it was an offering of *Masterpiece Theatre*, hosted by that affable Anglo-American broadcaster-journalist Alistair Cooke. Perhaps as a result of ITV's decision finally to screen their three-hour television adaptation, directed by David Thacker, on 3 September 2003 (it had been completed in 2001), the BBC released its 1978 serial in a three-DVD boxed set in 2003.[3] All three versions of *The Mayor of Casterbridge* are therefore currently available for viewing; they also raise interesting questions about the processes of adaptation.

When a screenwriter attempts a cinematic adaptation of *The Mayor of Casterbridge*, he or she is immediately faced with integrating and providing continuity for the story's earlier events. In producing a series of twenty tableaux for its 1886 serialisation, illustrator Robert Barnes easily assimilates the story's opening flashback into his pictorial commentaries on the characters, the settings, and the moments of crisis in each weekly instalment. Barnes does not show the actual wife-sale, possibly because it smacked too much of the sensational. What he does show is the furmity seller, who straddles the twenty years between Susan's original sale and her return in search of Henchard. For cinematic adaptation, however, there seems no avoiding the wife-sale, the aging of the actors who play Susan and Michael Henchard, or the need to show how past events affect the present. The novel's opening sequence in particular has presented problems in narrative and visual continuity with which each screenwriter and each director has had to grapple.

The flashback, of course, is a narrative device that considerably predates the cinematic era, the first instance occurring in Homer's *Odyssey*. Although it has proven especially useful in such films as Orson Welles's *Citizen Kane* and such plays as Arthur Miller's *Death of a Salesman*, providing the audience with the knowledge of antecedent events necessary to the development of theme, character, and plot, a writer employing this device often finds it difficult to signal such a shift in story-time. Continually, readers of *The Mayor of Casterbridge* 'must supply the present scene with meaning by considering the past of the novel'.[4] Screenwriters too have found it difficult to find a cinematic equivalent to turning back the page, to make the past and present co-exist in the minds of viewers. In what follows I will focus on the ways in which the successive screen adaptations of *The Mayor of Casterbridge* handle this particular challenge in their respective opening scenes.

Dennis Potter's BBC television adaptation (1978)

Since screenwriter Dennis Potter decided to adhere to Hardy's text whenever possible, he was compelled directly to confront the problems associated with the opening flashback. Hardy clarifies Henchard's age only at the close of the opening episode when the youth vows to 'avoid all strong liquors for the space of twenty ['twenty-one' in the 1912 edition] years to come, being a year for every year that I have lived'.[5] Potter by contrast makes Henchard grumble at the outset that he was just eighteen when he married. Since Alan Bates was already forty-three, and his co-star Anne Stallybrass thirty-eight, they make an unconvincing young couple.[6] Alan Bates does his best to convince us of his character's youth, appearing both thinner and more agile in the flashback. Past and present are also well distinguished by the sunny day on which the wife-sale occurred, as opposed to a gloomier day in the present, and by the finger-post two miles outside of the village of Weydon-Priors, which appears firmly upright and freshly whitewashed in the past, but is now dilapidated.

The primitive agricultural prints which accompany the opening credits also imply a return to a simpler age in which viewers can accept the fact that such a wife-sale may have occurred. The unnaturally large hand grasping a sheaf of wheat represents both the John Barleycorn figure of the rags-to-riches Mayor and the veteran of stage and screen, Alan Bates, then associated in the minds of many television viewers with Gabriel Oak in Schlesinger's *Far From the Madding Crowd* (1967).[7] Having been seen on television and in some of the most popular British films of the 1960s, by 1978 Bates's face and manner of acting were already familiar to viewers on both sides of the Atlantic. His name in the opening credits of *The Mayor of Casterbridge* must have seemed an assurance that viewers would be treated to a sensitive and convincing portrayal of the volatile Hardy protagonist.

Among the other agricultural plates in the credits, a haywain suggests a Constable-like vision of 'Olde England' as well as the economic forces behind the tale. Finally we come to the frame 'with Anne Stallybrass' – most conspicuously seen as Jane Seymour, the wife of another male tyrant in the 1971 mini-series *The Six Wives of Henry VIII* – and a plate of coins, bills, and hands to suggest the wife-sale. The previous acting credits of the male and female leads created for viewers in 1978 personas of Bates and Stallybrass. Thus, the television audience's pre-viewing experiences may have conditioned their reception from the outset, the illustrations in the credits echoing Hardy's theme of the inescapable influences of the past, of memory, and of guilt. The title 'Part One' dissolves into the mists of the Wessex moors (also metaphorically the mists of memory) as two women dressed in mourning walk determinedly towards us. The older woman carries her bundle close to her, as if it were an infant, preparing us for the image of her earlier self. In the text, they walk with joined hands, in contrast to the physical alienation of Henchard and his wife earlier at this spot, when Henchard walked several paces ahead of his wife. In the film Elizabeth-Jane walks beside her mother but complains, 'We don't even know where he is, whether we're going away from him, or towards him, or what!' Her petulance and the familiar landscape trigger in her mother's mind images of another unruly late-adolescent upon whom adult responsibilities and cares had been thrust, her former husband. 'You were thinking of poor father', remarks the girl, in ignorance of the transaction at Weydon fair two decades earlier, producing her mother's ironic rejoinder, 'Yes, in a way I was.' This invented dialogue, with alternating close-ups of mother and daughter, heightens the irony of the lines taken from the novel with minor alterations:

'It was here I first met with Newson – on such a day as this.'
'First met with father here? Yes, you have told me so before. And now he's drowned and gone from us!' (MC, iii, 20)

In Potter's screenplay, past and present vie for dominance in the mother's consciousness as the women thread their way though the fair, which is still enjoying a thriving trade, despite the fallen condition of Mrs Goodenough. Regardless of Elizabeth-Jane's insisting with bourgeois class-consciousness that speaking to the ragged vendor 'isn't respectable' (MC, iii, 21), Susan enters the furmity vendor's small, circular tent (supplied by Potter, perhaps to keep the daughter from overhearing the ensuing conversation) in hopes of learning about what happened to Henchard after that fateful night. Her daughter is not engaged (as in Hardy's text) at 'some stalls of coloured prints' (MC, iii, 20) but in watching a Punch and Judy show – another nice piece of Potter irony, since her mother's first marriage was characterised by 'nothing but temper' (MC, i, 13). There is then a flashback to the same place twenty years earlier as Henchard seeks consolation in alcohol. Potter then initiates the mock-auction after which the scene abruptly shifts to Henchard's awakening in the abandoned tent; as Mrs Goodenough puts up the last bench, a cock crows, literally denoting daybreak but perhaps suggesting betrayal, as in the New Testament. Cut to a close-up of the mature Susan in the present, in Mrs Goodenough's much smaller tent. At the old woman's reiterated offer of a drop of rum, the scene suddenly shifts to the council dinner as a belligerent Henchard proclaims his teetotalism rather than, as in the novel, to young Henchard's taking his Bible-oath.

The pivotal figure in both scenes is Henchard, still irascible and controlling events, but older and heavier. His fluffy hair like Susan's is now tinged with grey, but in terms of personality he seems the same as he vociferously rebukes a waiter for attempting to pour him a glass of wine. In the darkness outside, a covered wagon bearing Susan and Elizabeth-Jane approaches, prompting viewers to ponder how Potter will effect the reunion that Hardy's text requires. Further situational irony is afforded by Potter's making the vehicle by which the women arrive one of Henchard's, although his name on the spatterboard is partially obscured by a tarpaulin and therefore presumably unseen by either of them. Thus the business and narration of the first four chapters are synthesised in the memories of the abused wife, leaving us to deduce much about her subsequent liaison with Richard Newson from the few remarks dropped by her daughter during their fairground visit. Despite the length and detail of the 1978 production, in other words, the screenwriter relies upon his viewers' familiarity with the original text in order fully to comprehend these early scenes. However, the use of well-known actors (bringing with them the authority of their previous roles) helps to reinforce the pervasive sense crucial to the text of the weight of the past and its inherence in the present.

David Thacker's ITV adaptation (2001, 2003)

David Thacker's production, as we have seen, although filmed in 2001, was not televised in either Britain or the States until late in 2003. Then the film was released on DVD on 23 September by A & E, no longer 'edited for television'. Televised, it seemed precipitate, lacking sufficient transition between scenes. For example, there was a sharp cut from Henchard's face immediately after the wife-sale to the interior of the country church in which he swears off liquor. However, when released a month later on a single DVD, the latest film adaptation seemed quite restored, although not perhaps to the fullness of Dennis Potter's 1978 six-hour mini-series.

The visual format of the latest adaptation's DVD cover offers us a useful 'advanced organiser' for interpreting the disk it contains: the past (front) is juxtaposed against the present (back), with the largest figure being 'young' Michael Henchard (Ciarán Hinds, centre right). His unsmiling visage beside the caption in block capitals 'THE CAPTIVATING STORY OF LOVE, HONOUR, FAMILY, AND BETRAYAL' is superimposed upon the smaller, shadowy figures of 'young' Susan (centre left), smiling down upon an infant in swaddling clothes, and of the youthful Henchards walking towards us (in the film, first through fields and finally on a gravel cart-track to Weydon-Priors), he supporting his rush basket of implements on his back, she carrying the baby. Above all these figures the patriarchal signifier 'MAYOR' in large-font red letters dominates the top register. The back cover repeats the same lettering, but sits above a cluster of three images of equal size (Farfrae, Lucetta, and the grown-up Elizabeth-Jane) and a three-paragraph 'blurb'.

The opening paragraph of this blurb, inevitably charged with public-relations promotion hyperbole, specifically attributes the wife-sale to the young husband's intoxication: 'Destitute and drunken, Michael Henchard is an itinerant farmhand who sells his wife and daughter to a sailor in a moment of alcohol-fuelled desperation.' The actual experience of watching the opening scenes, however, works against this facile interpretation of Henchard's behaviour. The fast-paced opening sequence does not establish the present with a mature Susan accompanying her grown-up daughter to Weydon Fair, as in the 1978 mini-series. What follows, then, is prologue, not flashback, as the tanned, healthy, sturdily dressed couple bear with them the nimbus of 'stale familiarity' that afflicts their shabbily garbed textual counterparts; as in the text, not a word is exchanged between them as the husband reads a ballad sheet and the wife is absorbed by her infant. There is no intervening mid-road discussion with a turnip-hoer about the impossibility of renting a cottage, a scene that Hardy uses to establish the poverty and unemployment that grip the cornlands – in fact, the pair exchange words with nobody until they are inside the tent bearing the small sign, 'Good furmity sold here.' No air of decrepitude blights the holiday atmosphere suggested by the spotlessly white tents of various dimensions and the frolicking children. In place of Hardy's list of specifics about the mixed nature of the stalls – 'peep-shows, toy-stands, wax-works, inspired monsters, disinterested medical men . . ., thimble-riggers, nick-nack vendors, and readers of Fate' (MC, i, 7) – the screenwriter and director give us a moment-to-moment montage accompanied by a look of wonder on the smiling face of Susan Henchard. In a rapid succession of images, we have a sense of how she perceives the throng: a puppet-maker; a fiddler, playing; a group of empty kegs; horned sheep in a pen; horses and cattle being sold by a respectably dressed male auctioneer who cries, 'Sold for forty shillings!' and offers 'a very promising brood-mare not five years old' (dialogue derived directly from chapter one, but only heard from within the tent in the text); a peep-show; a soldier in red dress uniform; and a scene in which a bare-chested strongman throws a skittle at a dummy in female clothing, perhaps intended to be emblematic of this society's inveterate misogyny.

So rapid is this montage that its peculiar effects may not register consciously with viewers, but it seems to be serving as subtext for how Henchard has blamed his ill-fortune on his having married early and as foreshadowing how he intends to rid himself of Susan. An interesting touch is the presence of banners with figures on them, evident too in the background of Barnes's second illustration for the *Graphic*'s 1886 serialisation, 'The hag opened a little basket behind the fire, and, looking up slily, whispered, "Just a thought o' rum in it?"' (see Illustration 13). These decorative banners that fill the rear register of Barnes's plate are undoubtedly an authentic touch, since such icons represent for the unlettered Hodges of Dorset the goods and services available at the various stalls.

Michael (Ciarán Hinds) and Susan (Juliet Aubrey) can hardly be labelled 'young' as in Hardy's opening chapter (MC, i, 10), so that the husband's gruffness seems more a matter of disposition than a reaction to the hard knocks of recent circumstance or his being incapacitated by the liquor after a long day's tramp. Hardy makes it clear that one

Illustration 13. 'The hag opened a little basket behind the fire', illustration by Robert Barnes for part 2 of the serialised version of *The Mayor
of Casterbridge* in *The Graphic* 33 (9/1/1886), p.41 (National Library of
Scotland).

of Michael Henchard's chief motivations for auctioning off his wife and child is the economic liabilities they constitute. Susan is literally 'no good' (MC, i, 10) to him since she and the child impede his mobility; if, contends the young husband, he were divested of the responsibilities of wife and child, as 'a free man' (MC, i, 9) he would make his fortune in the fodder business. Although Hinds's Henchard consumes several bowlfuls quickly, he expresses little relish and exhibits none of the signs of inebriation which Hardy describes as Henchard quickly descends from serene drunkenness to joviality, argumentativeness, and heated anger. He shares the 'contemplative bitterness' of Hardy's character, but is hardly 'fuddled' (MC, i, 9–10). The camera several times dwells on the anxious, distressed face of Susan in this scene; she is standing behind Henchard and to his left, while the furmity vendor, further back, observes matters from the right. In broad dialect, Henchard proclaims, 'I'm open to an offer for this gem of creation', then swiftly ups the bid to five guineas; momentarily, it seems there will be no sale after all. 'Yes or no, for the last time', he calls. Suddenly, from across the table rather than 'from the doorway' (MC, i, 12) of the tent, Newson simply says, 'Yes.' Occupying the left half of the screen, he is not dressed at all like a sailor, but wears a green-brown jacket, blue stock, and neckcloth.[8] 'You say you do?' queries Henchard, shown full-screen, head and shoulders. 'Saying's one thing, paying's another: where's the money?' As the camera pulls back, Newson rises and reaches into his left jacket pocket, the light from the doorway now framing his figure. Newson lays five large notes (not a single five-pound note, as in the text) and afterwards five coins on the table before the seated Henchard, who views the act with apparent satisfaction rather than with either apprehension or temper. Susan then makes a final, low-keyed plea for her husband to reconsider. 'I take the money, the sailor takes you', Henchard coolly responds, although how he recognises the man as a sailor we cannot tell. 'Very well, the bargain's complete', concludes Henchard as Newson crosses behind the centre-pole of the tent to Susan. This is shot from behind Henchard, from the furmity woman's perspective, perhaps foreshadowing her bearing witness against Henchard later.

That the figure of the old furmity vendor may appear again and prove crucial in the turning of Henchard's fortunes may be signalled by the casting of television and film veteran Jean Marsh in the role. In contrast, the five principals in the cast of the 2001 ITV production provided relatively fresh (or, at least, unfamiliar) faces for the August 2003 television audience.[9] The dialogue from Hardy's text is shortened and sharpened to advance the action speedily to Susan's abrupt departure. She seems quite agreeable to the transaction as she calmly lays her wedding-ring on the table, rather than, as in the text, flinging it across the room. The scene is curiously uncharged: Susan does not 'sob bitterly' and no look of 'stolid concern' mars Henchard's impassive features. Neither he nor we are 'conscious of his alcoholic load' (MC, i, 14). Neither alcoholism nor economic privation and unemployment but rather some long-standing grievance has precipitated the wife-sale in Whitehead's screenplay.

Unlike his counterpart in the 1978 mini-series, Henchard does not pass out in a stupor under one of the benches, then wake up disoriented the next morning only to recall by virtue of the wedding-ring the events of the previous evening. Rather, there is a sharp cut to Henchard's determinedly marching along an escarpment. The morning sun then streams not through the crevices in the canvas of Mrs Goodenough's tent, but through the windows on the left side of a quiet, whitewashed church interior. At once, the double doors fly open simultaneously, and Henchard stands on the sandstone floor, his arms wide, holding them. Adrian Johnston's theme for the film rises as in close-up he takes off his hat. The camera pulls back, revealing a great Bible on a lectern (left) as he shrugs off his rush basket and deposits it in the foyer. His form is emphasised by the circular script on the interior archway and the three-part scroll above the squared entrance. The camera closes in and the music rises as, taking up the Bible and holding it to his chest, Henchard kneels and makes a vow that is a close paraphrase of what Henchard vows in the text. The revised text, as opposed to that of the serial, reads 'the space of twenty years to come' (MC, ii, 18), so that the termination of this oath will coincide approximately with the decline of Henchard's fortunes after Susan's death. He looks down, awestruck, upon the book, and kisses it; then his face fades from the screen as three trees in a line, with flat fields beyond, are superimposed. That man, implies the fadeout, has disappeared. Next, two bonneted women pass from behind the left to the centre tree, and '19 years later'[10] comes up, reinforcing the linear nature of this film's narrative structure.

In mourning, Elizabeth-Jane (left) and Susan (right) in a head-to-waist shot descend into the fairground, signified metonymically by a goat (right), a child (left), and a wagon (rear). That we are back at Weydon-Priors is implied by the continuity devices of the banner (directly above Mrs Goodenough's head), the totem pole, and the female dummy, which visually connect past with present. Elizabeth-Jane's urging her mother not to speak with the one person who connects past and present, the old, disreputable furmity vendor, seems curiously unmotivated because Whitehead has cut 'it isn't respectable!' (MC, iii, 21), perhaps to render his young heroine more attractive (and more credible in her role as what Pamela Dalziel has termed 'sympathetic and perceptive observer'[11]), exonerating her from politically incorrect middle-class snobbishness or class-consciousness.

Susan's interview with the 'tentless' (MC, iii, 21) Mrs Goodenough occurs out in the open (in accordance with the text, and not in a tent, as in the 1978 production), but out of Elizabeth-Jane's hearing, establishing her as a focal character. Neither Susan nor Mrs Goodenough has aged much; although the furmity vendor is decidedly grimier, she wears the same clothing, hat, and linen head-covering. Her pewter bowls and spoons are to be taken as survivors of her former prosperity (and thereby provide visual continuity), although Hardy specifies that, having lost all vestiges of that former time, she serves furmity 'in a couple of chipped yellow basins of commonest clay', as in the 1978 adaptation. Susan smiles good-naturedly and shakes her head almost wistfully rather than 'bitterly' at the vendor's 'old trick' of offering 'a thought o' rum in it' (MC, iii, 21–2).

When Mrs Goodenough's memory seems to fail her as to where Henchard had said he had gone, Susan turns to leave, whereupon the furmity-woman cries, 'Wait!' and holds up and rubs together the fingers of her left hand. The gesture re-emphasises the money-morality which led to Henchard's selling his wife in the first place. Susan's coins seem to stimulate the vendor's memory as she blurts out, 'Casterbridge'. In the next moment, Susan and her daughter are seen in silhouette against the sky. Emulating Hardy's text, the transition from past wife-sale to the moment of reunion is thus completed in a purely linear fashion, obviating the need for the continual fade-outs and fade-ins of the 1978 series. It is a more straightforward approach to the challenge Hardy poses but still succeeds in highlighting the importance of Henchard's past.

Michael Winterbottom's *The Claim* (2001)

To assimilate the flashback into the body of the narrative, screenwriter Frank Cottrell Boyce and director Michael Winterbottom opted for an entirely different approach from that taken by either Potter or Whitehead. *The Claim* does not open on some byroad or trail, but *in medias res* in the raw mining town of Kingdom Come itself, the backdrop of Hardy's Wessex, as Simon Gatrell observes in chapter three, having been replaced by California's majestic Sierra Nevada. One might be reminded momentarily of the genial gold-rush society of Alan Jay Lerner and Frederick Loewe's *Paint Your Wagon* (1969) or the rough-and-tumble town of Robert Altman's *McCabe and Mrs Miller* (1971), but the swift justice of Mayor Daniel Dillon (Peter Mullan) soon dispels such associations in the whipping scene that immediately proceeds his brief initial interview with

Hope Burn (Sarah Polley of *The Road to Avonlea*), the film's Elizabeth-Jane figure. The mountain setting is an insistent presence that constantly reminds the audience that the story occurs on the frontier, far away from the culture and societal restrictions of the eastern United States and Western Europe. Here, the law is whatever the town's richest citizen conceives it to be: 'In keeping with moving the location to a place where "civilization" is still being formed, the storyline and characters have been made into more basic, perhaps even less civilized, versions of what Hardy originally created.'[12] Although the possible public exposure of the wife-sale poses a threat to neither this mayor's reputation nor his business, the arrival of the mayor's ex-wife imposes certain personal constraints upon Dillon, whose ultimate destruction of the abandoned mining town Niemeyer interprets as 'an admission of his failure to set the past aright'.[13]

The film's title, then, has implications beyond legal title to an ore deposit. Rather, it implies also

the emotional claim that his wife and daughter embarrassingly represent for Dillon. The social fabric of Casterbridge, with its economic dependency upon the weather for the harvest, is swept away and replaced by a very different community but one still dependent upon the land for gold-mining and the lucrative results of routing a railway through a particular area. The bones of the story are still there but their significance is transformed by the dynamics of the society in which they are found.[14]

The Claim, then, with its different setting is not so much an adaptation as a translation of the original novel. Screenwriter Cottrell Boyce's altering the venue renders the key aspect of Hardy's plot, the wife-sale two decades prior to the story's principal action, more plausible and enables the film to make explicit for the audience the symbolism inherent in the arrival from Sacramento of surveyor Dalglish (Wes Bentley) and the Central Pacific Railroad survey crew: here is the Age of Technology supplanting the ethics and entrepreneurs of the previous era, as surely as Donald Farfrae's knowledge of modern business practices and farm machinery counterposes Michael Henchard's less formal knowledge derived purely from experience in Hardy's novel. The exchange of the Polish wife[15] and infant for a rich claim in the California Gold Rush of 1849 transpires not merely in the Sierra Nevada while a blizzard rages outside Burn's chaotic cabin, but also in a bygone, lawless epoch, and a savage region in which Western society's imposition of its mores was tentative at best.

Although a much freer adaptation of the novel than the two television versions, the film nevertheless retains a vividly realised flashback of the wife-sale (more properly, an 'exchange'). The flashback sequence of the wife-sale is not triggered within the memory of the Susan figure, the tubercular Mrs Burn (Nastassja Kinski), but within the guilt-laden consciousness of Mayor Dillon. Having received Mrs Burn's token from her daughter's hands, Dillon rushes to his old shack where the negotiation was conducted years before in the snows above the town. Here he scrutinises a silver-framed daguerreotype of a young couple and their infant – presumably a picture of himself, the girl's mother, and the girl herself. That he locates it so quickly in the old wooden box, and that it has been so well preserved, suggest its significance to him.

In an extended flashback, Dillon reverts to the time when he sold Elena and her child for the claim. Two figures struggle through a white-out, the woman dragging a box (the very chest in which the photograph has been stored) on a sled, the man laden with an enormous pack. The young immigrant couple have (we infer) met on shipboard or at their North American port of disembarkation – he from Dublin, she from Poland. Perhaps a year later, they are now down on their luck and need a break. Nursing her infant, Elena excites the attention of the host, whose gold is no compensation for loneliness: 'I need a woman', he remarks. Having lost his kit and his mules, Dillon owns 'nothing but her'. Her retort, 'You don't own me', seems a perfunctory concession to the audience's sense of political correctness, for in no way does she interfere with the bargain on which the two men shake hands. The date initially superimposed on the screen, 1867, combined with Hope's remark to Dalglish that her parents were 'Forty-niners', leads us to conclude that she is the infant of Dillon's flashback.

Aside from the scenes of the daughter and mother arriving in the mayor's town and the flashback to the sale (the order reversed in the film), the two stories have little in common structurally. For example, the romance between the railroad man Bellanger and the prostitute with the tender heart, Anny, has no parallel in Hardy's novel. The conflagration that engulfs Dillon's abandoned town has no counterpart either, and does not, as does Henchard's self-imposed exile from Casterbridge after Elizabeth-Jane's marriage to Farfrae, imbue the former mayor with an Aristotelian grandeur. The past, in fact, appears not to weigh upon any of the characters of *The Claim* with the force it exerts in Hardy's text.

Conclusions

Since the film-maker lacks the full range of narrative devices available to the novelist – notably, a controlling narrative voice, replete with allusion, metaphor, and direct revelation – the screenwriter and director must ensure that the viewer will be able to follow the thread of narrative implicit in a coherent succession of images. In the case of a film adaptation of a novel, the screenwriter must not rely on the viewer's actually having read the book: the film must, as it were, speak for itself. Although the occasional superscript may supply such details as time and place (duplicating the literary conventions of prologue and epilogue), everything else in the film must be self-explanatory, communicated either by sound track or by images. Thus, when an adaptor of Hardy's *The Mayor of Casterbridge* chooses to dramatise the material of the first three chapters, specifically the wife-sale and Henchard's oath, its connection to the main action of two decades later must be made immediately manifest to the audience.

The use of flashbacks in the 1978 mini-series goes beyond dramatising the opening chapters; rather, in the Ring as at Weydon Fair previously, the past momentarily supervenes in a character's mind, so that the flashback gives the viewer access to the thoughts and feelings of first Susan and then Michael Henchard. Given also the intensity of Alan Bates's portrayal of Henchard, the audience can assess and appreciate Henchard's atavistic impulsiveness and peremptory nature on the one hand, and his genuine contrition and yearning for absolution through a suitable act of atonement on the other. Thus, in the 1978 series Henchard's motivations are transparent, enabling the audience to make emotional identification with him and, at the end, experience a species of catharsis.

Even though *The Claim* has transformed Henchard's rise and fall into a more straightforward story, and one certainly less dependent upon coincidence than the original novel, it fails to demonstrate fully what motivates Dillon's self-destruction because the screenwriter so rarely permits the mayor of Kingdom Come to articulate the magnitude of his sense of shame regarding, and obligation to, the woman he bartered away and the child he consigned to a stranger's care. While both Alan Bates and Ciarán Hinds elicit the audience's sympathy and thereby create a profound feeling of loss and regret in the final sequences, Peter Mullan's reticence and aloofness undermine the concluding tragic moments of *The Claim*. Hardy's multiple coincidences, while they may work against the reader's or viewer's suspension of disbelief, must have conveyed to his late-nineteenth-century readers the sense of destiny at work in human affairs, and of its testing in a Job-like manner in the crucible of domestic complication and financial ruin the mettle of Michael Henchard. By radically paring down the plot of the Hardyan original, screenwriter Cottrell Boyce has diminished the heroic proportions of the protagonist's character and rendered him less accessible to our sympathetic identification. The relationship between the flashback events and those of the main narrative should provide the audience with the grounds for Henchard's Lear-like need for affection and atonement; this relationship is clear in both Dennis Potter's screenplay for the 1978 mini-series and Ted Whitehead's for the

2003 made-for-television film, but fails to explicate the development of Mayor Dillon's character in Frank Cottrell Boyce's visually stunning but much reduced 'westernised' version of Hardy's 1886 novel.

NOTES

1. The Progress Company was governed by a contract of February 1921 stipulating, 'No alteration or adaptation being such as to burlesque or otherwise misrepresent the general character of the novel' (Richard Little Purdy and Michael Millgate (eds.), *The Collected Letters of Thomas Hardy*, 7 vols. (Oxford: Clarendon Press, 1978–88), vol. VI, p.72. All subsequent references to this work are given is brackets in the text). This must have been awkward, given Hardy's insistence on a measure of authorial control with film adaptations. This film actually predates the first dramatic adaptation, namely the professional production of John Drinkwater's stage adaptation starring Lyn Harding as Michael Henchard that opened at the Barnes Theatre, Greater London, on 8 September 1926.

   In the summer of 1921, Sidney Morgan of the Progress Film Company directed the first screen version of *The Mayor of Casterbridge*, Hardy having signed an agreement with that production company earlier that year that gave him a certain measure of control over the cinematic adaptation. However, in a letter to Morgan on 22 March 1921 Hardy apparently sanctioned some changes in the plot of the 65-minute film: the character of Farfrae was eliminated; Elizabeth-Jane became Henchard's daughter rather than Newson's; she was courted by an unnamed doctor; and the film ended with Henchard's departure rather than his death. Despite the fact that the Company's studios were located in Sussex, certain scenes involved location-shoots at Maiden Castle, Grey's Bridge at Dorchester, and the city's Hangman's Cottage. In a letter to Florence Henniker dated 2 July 1926, Hardy wrote that he had met the cast of the movie that morning on location in Dorchester; he reported having talked to The Mayor (Fred Groves), Mrs Henchard (Pauline Peters), Elizabeth-Jane (Mary Clare), and 'the rest, in the flesh' (*Letters*, VI, 93).

2. The production failed, according to Paul Niemeyer, *Seeing Hardy: Film and Television Adaptations of the Fiction of Thomas Hardy* (Jefferson, N. C.: McFarland, 2003), p. 24, because the Associated British Corporation felt that it would be too expensive and likely have little 'commercial value in America'.

3. The three-DVD boxed set announced for release on 27 May 2003 by the British Broadcasting Corporation (through Acorn Media of Silver Spring, Maryland) does not provide Alistair Cooke's original introductory commentaries, but does offer brief 'filmographies' of the five principal actors, Sir Alan Bates, Anne Stallybrass, Janet Maw, Anna Massey, and Jack Galloway. There is also a rather odd note on Hardy himself which alludes to his having prepared technical drawings for his father's restoration of 'Woodsford Castle'. The list of films in which each actor has played a role usually involves half-a-dozen titles from the 1970s to 2002, as if to imply the currency of the 1978 series.

4. Norman D. Prentiss, 'Compilation and Design in *The Mayor of Casterbridge'*, *Thomas Hardy Journal* 11 (1995) 70.
5. Thomas Hardy, *The Mayor of Casterbridge*, ed. Keith Wilson (Harmondsworth: Penguin, 1997; revised 2003), ch. two, p.18. All quotations from the novel, unless otherwise stipulated, are from this edition, the only one currently available that reproduces the Barnes illustrations.
6. *The Claim* does not make the same error, casting a couple in their early twenties for the younger counterparts of Dillon and Elena in the first flashback's transaction scene and the second flashback's awakening scene. The dates on Susan's tombstone in the 1978 film (1808–47) establish her age at the time of the sale in 1829 as twenty-one, making Susan her husband's senior by perhaps a year.
7. Although he was seen in *A Kind of Loving* (1962), *The Entertainer* (1964), *The Fixer* (1968), *Butley* (1972), *Impossible Object* (1973), *Plaintiffs and Defendants* and *Two Sundays* (BBC, 1975), Bates's most memorable pre-*Mayor* performances, aside from his leading role as Gabriel Oak in *Far From the Madding Crowd*, were in *Georgie Girl* (1966) and *The Three Sisters* (1969). By 1978, he had already worked with such cultural icons as Sir Laurence Olivier, Harold Pinter, John Schlesinger, John Frankenheimer, and, of course, his co-star in *Far From the Madding Crowd*, Julie Christie.
8. While Richard Newson is introduced in the uniform of a British tar, with black hat and pigtail, blue jacket and silver buttons, at the climax of the wife-sale in the 1978 mini-series, Ted Whitehead's Newson is more likely a merchant-sailor. In the text, Hardy's narrator eight times in the course of two pages in chapter one refers to him as a 'sailor', and Henchard himself in both films and the text finalises the bargain with his wife by remarking, 'I take the money: the sailor takes you' (MC, i, 12–13).
9. Although Ciarán Hinds had been seen in supporting roles as Finn McGovern in *Road to Perdition* (2002) and as President Nemerov in *The Sum of All Fears* (2002), his was hardly the household name in mid-2003 that Bates was in 1978. In fact, the five principal members of the cast have between them a respectable list totalling 146 film credits. Both Jodhi May (22 credits) and Polly Walker (29 credits) worked on the 1997 adaptation of Hardy's *The Woodlanders*, the former starring as the long-suffering Marty South, the latter as Felice Charmond. Hinds, with 41 film credits, had recently appeared as the villainous Jonathan Reiss in *Lara Croft Tomb Raider: The Cradle of Life* (2003), so that his face would undoubtedly have been much more familiar to viewers than that of any other cast member, except perhaps that of Jean Marsh (Mrs Goodenough) of *Upstairs Downstairs* fame. Since Hinds has tended to specialise in playing 'heavies' (he appeared as Sir Danvers Carew in *Mary Reilly* (1996), Edward Rochester in *Jane Eyre* (1997), Brian de Bois-Guilbert in *Ivanhoe* (1997), and John Traynor in *Veronica Guerin* (2003)), his characterisation of Michael Henchard brings with it a dour screen presence that may have inhibited viewers from identifying him completely with Hardy's misunderstood hero-victim.
10. The figure, based upon the Wessex Edition of 1912, which extended the oath from twenty to twenty-one years, suggests that Henchard's oath still has two

years to run and that the babbling infant of the opening scenes should now be about twenty years of age, if we are not privy to the novel's plot-secret about the death of the first and the birth of the second Elizabeth-Jane. Thus, Hardy's specifying 'a well-formed young woman of eighteen' (MC, iii, 19) is perfectly consistent with the lapse of almost two decades and with Newson's account to Henchard of the early phase of his common-law marriage: 'Your child died; she had another, and all went well' (MC, xli, 288). However, Henchard's assertion that his step-daughter has been dead about a year (as in the text) does not square with the date of the arrival of the women at Casterbridge.

11. As quoted by David Selwin in 'The Birthday Weekend', *Thomas Hardy Journal* 19 (2003) 22.
12. Niemeyer, *Seeing Hardy*, p.203.
13. *Ibid.*, p.204.
14. Patricia Ingham, *Thomas Hardy* (Oxford: Oxford University Press, 2003), p.226.
15. Thirty-eight-year-old Nastassja Kinski curiously brings to her role in *The Claim* little that one might associate with her previous Hardy characterisation, that of Tess Durbeyfield in Polanski's 1979 classic *Tess*.

10   *The Woodlanders*: the conflicting visions of Phil Agland and Thomas Hardy

Dale Kramer

The ending

'Grace, what do you feel for me?'
[pause]
'Nothing.'

This is the last piece of language in the film version of *The Woodlanders*. With her one-word Ibsenist reply to his question Grace rejects the returned and chastened, and eloquently pleading, unfaithful husband Fitzpiers; then she turns away and slowly walks towards the carriage on the hilltop, where Marty South is awaiting her. Concluding the film with this exchange between Fitzpiers and his wife the former Grace Melbury marks the clearest divergence in director Phil Agland's vision of the story from that of Hardy. Or so it seems. But a fuller examination suggests that Agland resuscitates something of the vision Hardy may have been working towards before social and editorial considerations of the late nineteenth century led to the printed novel as we know it. Nevertheless, if we expand the discussion to include the nature of the two media – film and fiction – we may find, finally, an opaque barrier between the two visions. Perhaps we may also find that, contrary to nearly a century of seeing Hardy's fiction as precursors to film versions, what makes Hardy 'Hardy' in *The Woodlanders* is not friendly to cinematography.

In the novel, the ending of the story continues past the second drama-tised surreptitious meeting of Grace and her estranged husband, in chapter forty-six, which in its own terms provides a rough analogy to the film's final dialogue (I will discuss this meeting in the novel in due course). The denouement of the story in the novel unfolds for dozens of pages, beginning with Grace's thinking of the stupendousness of her wed-ding vows, thoughts that delay her setting out for another of her meetings with Fitzpiers. Hurrying through the area behind the Tangses' garden, she is tripped up by a man-trap – which had been set on an impulse by Tim Tangs, the embittered husband of Suke, Fitzpiers's former sex partner, to avenge himself upon Fitzpiers just before the Tangses leave for Australia. The man-trap tears her dress and alarms Fitzpiers. Reunited by the emotion of the narrow escape, Grace and Fitzpiers go to a nearby hotel, the Earl of Wessex, and take a room, the likely consequence being unstated but obvious. Because Grace had not told her family of her meetings with her estranged husband, her father George Melbury collects a group of his employees and neighbours, who burdened with heavy ropes and clumsiness go in search of Grace. Finding the couple eventually at the Earl of Wessex and dumbfoundedly acquiescing to their reconciliation, Mr Melbury makes his famous prediction about Fitzpiers that his daughter 'may take him back to her bed if she will', but he will in due course find other women's necks to 'col' (embrace).[1] Passing the graveyard on their way home from their search, they see Marty South, who overhears their conversation and realises that Grace has returned to Fitzpiers, that now she (Marty) will have the memory of Giles Winterborne to herself, and that Grace is unworthy of the sacrifice of life that Giles had made for her. Marty whispers that *she* will never forget, or be false to, Giles, 'For you was a good man, and did good things!' In the novel, *these* are the concluding words.[2]

The novel does not end inappropriately, although the film-makers evidently found Marty's paean of love too sentimental for use in the twentieth century.[3] In the novel Marty South is nearly on a par with Grace, representing the true (i.e. honest and consistent) sufferer. In closing the novel and in effect becoming a sexless novice, she gives Giles his due. In the film, however, Marty scarcely exists other than as a background figure whose main purpose is to cut spar-gads, to help Giles plant trees, and to cut her hair to provide a wig for Mrs Charmond (although the wig is not again referred to in the film).

At least two aspects of the final dialogue in the film stand out in a study of Agland's adaptation of *The Woodlanders*. One is that the film's last dialogue is a stereotypic consequence of a certain mode of late-twentieth-century feminism. The second is that this dialogue turns a less pivotal exchange in the novel into Grace's dramatic declaration of self. Agland's vision required a contretemps and denouement that Hardy did not see as achievable – not surprisingly, since Grace's attitude in the film's last dialogue represents an accommodation to a century of thoughts about women, their sexuality, their expectations from society and relationships.

That the film ends with this dialogue rather than with the novel's complex concluding alternations between slapstick comedy, foreboding, and rhapsodic if humble bathos speaks volumes about the differences between film and fiction. The two versions of *The Woodlanders* show that fiction can better handle generically ambivalent material than film (or at least a film aimed at a mass audience). It will become evident that the differing conclusions are not the only differences between film and novel. Many striking events in the novel are modified or elided (in part, no doubt, because to include all of the novel's major incidents while keeping the film to ninety or so minutes would have made the film cluttered and stunningly hard to follow).[4] In addition to its entire concluding sequence, elisions from the novel include Grace's actual first visit to Mrs Charmond early in the novel (during which Felice notices that she looks old in contrast to Grace and thus decides not to invite her to be her companion to Italy), Old South and his (accurate) superstitions, the lifehold on Giles's cottage (which in the novel ties together several local families and Mrs Charmond), and Fitzpiers's opportunistic seduction of Suke on the same night that he first kisses Grace. Some of the omissions lead to almost certainly unintended implications. In the film 'Grandma Oliver' (who is 'Grammer Oliver' in the novel, unrelated to the Melburys) is at Giles's 'warming' party, and sits down next to her employer Mr Melbury. This may be a consequence of the film's combining the roles of Mrs Melbury and Grammer the servant; but it is still interesting that none of the English film reviewers seems to have commented on this neglect of class etiquette.

Another unusual filmic moment is Fitzpiers and Grace's first kiss, after Grace runs into his arms during the turmoil of the husband-conjuring ceremony involving the village maidens: Fitzpiers intercepts the fleeing Grace and they kiss; she walks away, glancing behind her, and the camera pans to the darkening evening above a dense grove. A viewer who hadn't read the novel but was familiar with the 'language' of films might deduce from the pan-to-the-sky that Fitzpiers has followed her and they're having sex. Thus, a standard film-maker's device can create a (presumably) false impression in the audience. One can guess that the film-crew shot a scene with Suke Damson, didn't use it, but left in the suggestive grove of trees anyway, perhaps to provide an omen of danger for Grace in her feelings for Fitzpiers, but in any case creating a piquant moment for the viewer who *has* read Hardy. Moreover, several characteristic 'Hardyan' moments are altered, not always for clear reasons. For instance, in the novel's initial embarrassed meeting between Giles and Grace, Giles is holding a seedling apple tree in a muddy market, expecting Grace in an hour; in the film he is being bemused by a galvanic trick performed by a street hawker seconds before Grace comes into sight. The film thus turns him from a taciturn rural businessman into a bemused yokel.

To state it directly, the film *The Woodlanders* is not a redaction of the novel. There is nothing surprising in this. Expectations are different for the two art-forms. Much about the film is excellent, especially the casting, and the directing of individual scenes. But too many features in the novel that are essential to Hardy's intentions are skirted or modified by the film. I say this knowing that Hardy, were he still around, would not necessarily criticise the film. He himself, as Keith Wilson has shown in chapter eight of this volume, tried to write stage versions of several of his stories, and was familiar with the difficulty of transposition from printed page to stage. He would probably have been sympathetic to Zadie Smith's response to the TV version of *White Teeth*: 'The truth is, it [the novel] could do with some touching up.'[5] But the film not only bypasses several characters, motifs, and events but settles on a twentieth-century morality that, while not false to nineteenth-century emphases, drastically simplifies its portrayal. It also makes no effort to reproduce in a different medium the novel's multi-focus narration or to render pictorially the novel's bitter (or bitter-sweet) presentation of the Unfulfilled Intention, the struggle for survival within nature's fauna and flora.

This takes us to the core of Agland's vision in relation to Hardy's. Although Agland neglected many defining moments of the novel's narrative he adhered closely to others (even falsely, as in his poor location selection to portray the argument between Mrs Charmond's carriage driver and the carters of Giles's timber-waggon). Indeed, at times the method appears to be to photograph vignettes or tableaux. There is, then, a puzzling push-pull between casualness and slavishness. What is most damaging is when this push-pull seems to exhaust Agland, and the result is perfunctoriness, even creative apathy. Sometimes Agland seems determined to have his film reflect the novel, as in Grace and Giles's stroll through the ecclesiastical building during their renewed courtship. Why are they there? Where is it? It is of course a striking moment in the novel, during which (in the late versions) the tombs of Fitzpiers's aristocratic forebears are mentioned. But without any justification of this kind it just seems to be a 'Hardyan moment' to appease people who have read the novel. I'm not sure that the peculiarities of this scene would even be noticed by the non-reader of the novel, but that is exactly the point: what are scenes like this doing in the film *except* assuring readers of the novel that they are watching Hardy? Also, think of the bare-bones, obligatory portrayal of Grace and Giles's interactions in the hut towards the end of the film, as if Agland didn't believe in the events and morals/feelings that are so powerfully evoked in the novel but felt he didn't dare leave out *this* portion of the novel.

One of the causes of the adaptation's uncertain focus is the twentieth-century film-makers' assumption that the strength of conventions that are both evident and taken-for-granted in the novel would transfer to twentieth-century audiences. Already in 1887 these conventions were crumbling – which is why Hardy could portray them successfully in a traditional rural setting, but needed to intensify unconventional moments by outspoken clarifiers in post-1887 additions to the text of the novel such as 'He's had you!' and *'Come to me, dearest! I don't mind what they say, or what they think of us any more'*[6] (Hardy's emphasis). In other words, Hardy realised that times were changing (a change led in part by himself), and that to keep his works current for his ever-renewing audience he needed to dramatise the conventions that were being broken.[7] Agland shifted Hardy's revolutionary stress on the power of female sexual desire to a standard twentieth-century feminist rejection of dependency on the male. This discrepancy – not a discrepancy from audience expectations but a discrepancy from what Hardy presented in a quite basic fashion – constitutes the film's most problematic re-vision. By omitting the novel's conclusion, Agland discarded Hardy's nineteenth-century unconventionality for the sake of a twentieth-century feminist cliché.

The film *Jude* of course did something comparable, in allowing Jude to survive; but Jude is still, as in the novel, separated for ever from Sue, and that is his true death. Dying corporeally allows a few further ironies at the expense of Arabella and permits a departing Job-like blast at God. With *The Woodlanders*, the film's altered meaning strips out a very large portion of what Hardy had been driving at, a point he made explicit in the novel's Preface, written in 1895 and reiterated in 1912, namely how a man and woman can 'find a basis for their sexual relation'.[8] Hardy's sympathy clearly is with the woman, but structurally he does not challenge his times. He allows the man to dominate, and in a comic-satiric fashion makes all well with the world at the end. Melbury's prediction of Grace's future unhappiness with Fitzpiers does not loosen the reins of patriarchy. Grace's freedom of choice is minimal: Melbury has told his daughter that she can continue to live apart from her husband, but he (like most fathers) gives no weight to his daughter's sexual feelings. Hardy risks offending his readers by drawing attention to this.

Numerous passages in the novel indicate that Grace has powerful sexual instincts, for example when she realises that Fitzpiers is visiting Mrs Charmond, sees Giles, and ponders Nature's bounty:

her senses revelled in the sudden lapse back to Nature unadorned. The consciousness of having to be genteel because of her husband's profession, the veneer of artificiality which she had acquired at the fashionable schools, were thrown off, and she became the crude country girl of her latent, early instincts.

Nature was bountiful, she thought. No sooner had she been cast aside by Edred Fitzpiers than another being, impersonating chivalrous and undiluted manliness, had arisen out of the earth, ready to her hand. (W, xxviii, 186)

In the course of the novel Hardy revises Grace into abjuring '*all* fastidiousness now', not just 'all *such* fastidiousness now' (W, xxxviii, 250;

Illustration 14. Grace Melbury (Emily Woof) and Giles Winterborne
(Rufus Sewell) in *The Woodlanders*, Pathé (UK), 1997.

my emphases), and into speaking to Giles 'invitingly' rather than just
'archly'.[9] Finally, climaxing the revisions in Grace's pleading with Giles
to come into the hut at the end of the novel are the additions in 1912 of
the intensifiers '*dearest*' and '*of us*' (W, xli, 279). Clearly, Hardy is making her plea a sexual invitation, and this underscores Rebekah Owen's
comment to Hardy about Grace that 'she was willin'' when Giles was
not.[10] The posters for the film advertise the romance between the two
(see Illustration 14), yet the film itself makes relatively little of the final
scenes between them.

It is interesting, for example, that the film employs a call by Grace to
Giles to return to the hut that is tamer than in any printed version of
the novel. Her words in the film, 'Giles, come back!', carry little sexual
energy because in context Grace is mainly distraught at Fitzpiers's having
just returned. Even the earliest version in the novel at least makes clear
that what sends Giles outside into the rain and his flimsy lean-to are the
sexual implications of an adult male and female being alone, even if one
of them is desperately ill. In other words, while the nineteenth-century
novel stresses Grace's acceptance of her own sexual drive, the twentieth-
century film underplays Grace's sexual nature, instead emphasising her
role in the social/class drama of rural yeomanry and local aristocracy. This
displacement of Grace's sexuality extends as far back in the time of the
film as Grace's presumed (not presented) meeting with Mrs Charmond.

It seems a loss that the novel's presentation of Grace's first visit to Mrs Charmond is absent from the film, in which Mrs Charmond does not make her first physical appearance until Giles's timber-waggon blocks her carriage's way. It is 'Grandma Oliver' therefore who has to make the observation to the woeful Grace when Mrs Charmond goes to Italy without her, 'For all your schooling, for the likes of her you're still a country lass.' The film, in other words, emphasises the social or class element while in the novel Hardy operates here on a more personal level: Mrs Charmond realises that she looks older and shopworn beside Grace and that the younger woman's freshness will outshine hers if they travel together.

In short, both versions of *The Woodlanders* carry a feminist theme, but they do so in different ways.[11] To the question, 'Who needs a man?' the film basically replies, 'What does that question mean? I am my own person, and will hold true to my principles', whereas the novel replies resoundingly, 'Any decent woman who wants sex.' I accept that the film offers the more appropriate answer for the late twentieth century. But it is not Hardy's answer. For him, Grace's life does not end at the conclusion of the narrative. Indeed it took him several post-1887 revisions, with continuing evolution of Melbury's comment after he and his workers have found Grace with Fitzpiers in the Earl of Wessex Hotel, to make explicit that Grace's denouement will involve a repetitively unfaithful husband.

Despite the truncation of the plot, however, the film is not unfaithful to Hardy's vision of the clash of generational and class attitudes in an era of shifting foundations. Both book and film make a feminist point through Grace. In the book, her sexuality defies her father and returns her to Fitzpiers's bed. Grace is allowed to be a sexual woman, and Hardy points up the painful dilemma of Victorian marriage. In the film, Grace rejects the philandering husband, with the 'sisterly' support of Marty South sitting in the carriage at the top of the hill of their meeting-place. Thus, in the novel, the pain of life is perpetual; in the movie, Grace's future is more open. That the visions of Hardy and Agland do not clash more than they do depends upon the irony that Agland's independent Grace almost certainly resembles the Grace that Hardy might have ended with had not the mores of the time made a male-less future of a heroine require an incredible leap of imagination.

To return to chapter forty-six of the novel, where the film ends. The exchange between Fitzpiers and Grace in the novel parallels that of the film, as I began by saying. Fitzpiers urges to Grace, 'Say "husband."' '"No, no – I cannot"', replies Grace as she slips away through the garden-hedge (W, xlvi, 312). In both of these meetings, in the novel and in the film's last dialogue, Fitzpiers attempts to elicit some expression of emotion from Grace, which in the novel she refuses to give mostly because it might falsely suggest she was softening towards him. The impulse Hardy stresses is her Artemis-quality, her devotion to the self-effacing Giles, and the residue of her guilt at possibly having caused Giles's death. But the novel, at this stage, is unfinished. It *needs* an ending. Hardy supplies one which sees Grace responding to the sexual needs of her nature in the only venue available to a daughter of the socially sensitive Melbury. Agland, less imaginatively, falls back on a non-complex feminist assertion of the self over social expectation. This reflects a world outlook in which premarital sex and faithless marriages are not unusual – it would be a stretch in our times to rely on a sexual insight arising from societal repression to drive a woman back to an unsatisfactory marriage. The ending of the film is unadventurously feminist. Fitzpiers has come back to Melbury's house (although Melbury refuses to see him), apologising profusely to Grace ('I have done you so much wrong' and 'I have never loved any woman as I love you now'), giving no word of what has happened to Mrs Charmond. No longer do woman's frailty and the dictates of society require Grace to try again with Fitzpiers. One could legitimately ask if the film-makers expected the audience to remember the novel's ending and project it onto the film. But I think the answer has to be no, that the film-makers in responding to their own times accidentally made a film that in this respect more closely resembled what Hardy might have approved.

The narrator

Although it can be argued that Agland managed to hew a striking and appropriate conclusion from the materials of Hardy's novel, important characteristics of the novelist were immune from modification, or even utilisation, in the film. The novel *The Woodlanders*, unusually in Hardy's *oeuvre*, has a proportionately large number of narrative passages analysing character and meditating upon life. Consider, for example, all the narratorial evaluations of Grace's state(s) of mind as her feelings for Winterborne wax and wane, both before and after Giles's financial losses, her courtship and early relationship with Fitzpiers, and her life post-marriage with Fitzpiers. The novel is far richer in its portrayal of a non-steady romantic situation than a film could possibly be. In the film she is changeable, but on a large-scale evolution which takes her from early finishing-school complacency to confused passion vis-à-vis Fitzpiers to disenchantment with Fitzpiers and renewed truthful affection for Giles.

This steady cinematic development is sharply different from the highly contingent inconsistency in the novel.

These considerations point up another major discrepancy in the management of the author's and director's visions. The end of *The Woodlanders* (the film) can be acceptable in terms of audience. The greater cause of my unease with *The Woodlanders* as film is its failure to find a cinematic equivalent to the narrator. The novel *The Woodlanders* offers a sober, understated but consistent disenchantment with life's possibilities, in a variety of carefully observed descriptive passages which are distinct in tone from the outrage of *Tess* and the bitter nihilism of *Jude*. The sense of an observing consciousness is far more pervasive in *The Woodlanders* than similar narratorial contributions in, say, *The Trumpet-Major*, *The Well-Beloved*, or *Under the Greenwood Tree*. If the narrative's sexuality needed to be updated for the film's audience, and if many plot elements and characters had to be elided or altered for purposes of time and structure, other, more strictly purely 'Hardyan' elements of the novel *The Woodlanders* are totally absent from the film. The reason for their absence may well be that they are aspects of his fiction that film can only sporadically represent. This absence may be less of a problem for other Hardy novels than for *The Woodlanders*, which takes meditation as one of its larger concerns, announcing in its opening pages that the woodland is 'one of those sequestered spots outside the gates of the world where may usually be found more meditation than action' (W, i, 7–8).

Among the many themes upon which the narrator of the novel meditates is the effect of mutually struggling nature exemplified by the 'overcrowded branches in the neighbouring wood which were rubbing each other into wounds' and by the 'vocalized sorrows of the trees' (W, iii, 15). A film can cast an image but it has a hard time projecting the connotations of the 'bleared white visage of a sunless winter day' emerging 'like a dead-born child' (W, iv, 21); nor can a film show what is *not* there, as in the ensuing reference to 'Owls that had been catching mice in the outhouses, . . . and stoats that had been sucking the blood of the rabbits' that are no longer to be seen when humans get up in the morning (W, iv, 22). Without a commenting narrator (and voice-over would be inappropriate for this), there is simply no cinematic equivalent for these philosophical passages in the novel.

The narrator of *The Woodlanders* also fulfils a number of other roles, pointing up the significance of events apart from the perception of a particular character or more generally shaping the situation. For example, Grace's observation of the animals outside the hut, 'these neighbours who knew neither law nor sin' (W, xli, 275), is an effective spur to her impassioned invitation to Giles that they share the hut. Descriptions of nature under stress can also be made to echo human situations: 'Sometimes a bough from an adjoining tree was swayed so low as to smite the roof in the manner of a gigantic hand smiting the mouth of an adversary, to be followed by a trickle of rain, as blood from the wound' (W, xli, 277). Again, there is no cinematic equivalent for passages such as this.

As I say, these absences of Hardyan attention from the movie *The Woodlanders* are attributable to the nature of film. Agland isn't to blame for this – other than perhaps for the decision not to try to incorporate a narrator in some way (which of course is a highly problematic tactic in a movie). What is troubling in considering the movie *The Woodlanders* in relation to the book is that in the novel *The Woodlanders* these qualities are essential, to a degree not true for any of his other novels. It is a novel without a single focused-upon character (i.e., it has no main protagonist) because the nature of existence affects all persons, from Marty with her hair desired by Mrs Charmond, to Mrs Charmond whose hair is derided by the no-longer enchanted Fitzpiers, to the Continental admirer who kills Mrs Charmond who is in pursuit of Fitzpiers, back to Fitzpiers's chastisement of Marty ('O Marty those locks of yours – and that letter! . . . . But it was a kindness to send it, nevertheless' (W, xliv, 300, ellipsis Hardy's)). The film reduces all of this to the first scene with Percomb and Marty sadly cutting her hair after seeing Giles invited into the Melbury house. There is no further reference in the movie to hair or wig, or to Marty's letter that had alerted Fitzpiers to Mrs Charmond's wig. Time and clarity may require such truncations, but the differences remain immense.

Consider also the analysis of Fitzpiers's mind and attitude on the morning that Grace comes to plead for Grammer Oliver (W, xviii, 111–15). It becomes clear in the novel that Fitzpiers has no friendships in the community, and would never have considered taking Grace seriously as a love object had there been anything interesting to do in the early winter time. What these and other early passages in the novel do is to create in Fitzpiers mixed dimensions of admirableness and weakness beyond those of a mere seducer or cad. In the film, the intellectual dimension of Fitzpiers is scarcely noted, and he *is* primarily simply an attractive shallow womaniser. At the time Grace comes for this visit, Fitzpiers has had no previous thought of her whereas in the novel he has by the time of her visit seen her several times, spied on her over the fence, and been detected doing so by Giles. The narrator points out that Fitzpiers as a stranger in Hintock doesn't have the support of friends and associations, thus is liable to overreact emotionally. His seeing Grace in his half-awake-half-dream state and his ensuing confusion lead him to give her theatrical compliments that in effect make him a suitor – in opposition to the intention he has just recently settled on, that any relation with her could only be casual, a matter of flirtation only. His reassertion of non-seriousness towards Grace after she leaves is therefore undermined by his increasing (though unconscious) propulsion towards marriage. The point is that Hardy, who *understands* Fitzpiers and his situation, sets him up to be ambushed by Grace. In contrast, in the film everything stems from Grace's physical presence in his living/consulting room. Both actors perform excellently: Emily Woof is skittish, curious, attractive; Cal MacAinch is clear-eyed and politely domineering, deferential and accommodating towards Grandma Oliver's request that he cancel his purchase of her head. But neither actor can reproduce the narrator's controlling voice.

Conclusion

Taken all in all, Phil Agland and Thomas Hardy have much in common – sympathy for women, love of nature, and the skill and means to present both. Agland's forte, and the film's best moments, in my view, occur during efforts at faithful reproduction of the novel. I think especially of the scene where the errant Fitzpiers going towards Middleton disappears from the lower left of the screen just as Giles and his apple-press appear at the upper right. The portrayal of Melbury eager to have the young doctor court his daughter is perfect in detail and implication. But the film is not entirely coherent, and I think one of the main reasons is, ironically, Agland's determined fidelity to much of Hardy's story. Whether Agland is thinking in terms of adaptation, imitation, reproduction of a cultural artifact classed as 'Hardyan', or creating a film that is strictly speaking a film and not a cinematic novelisation, the slavishness of certain imitations that one might expect in the dramatisation of something entitled *The Woodlanders* creates structural oddities such as the opening with Percomb (who does little in the rest of the story), and Marty making the gads with her own hands. Occasionally Agland's desire to make a 'Hardy film' leads him astray, as in the scene where Giles refuses to move his timber-waggon to let Mrs Charmond's carriage go by on its way to the Continent.

This is a core moment in the story, and a crisis in the novel because Giles forces Mrs Charmond's carriage to back up, delaying (insignificantly) her departure for the Continent and earning him her ill-will that eventually leads to her refusal to renew his leases. The novel prepares for this scene by emphasising the narrowness of the lane. But, to judge from the image of the encounter in the film, it would be a simple matter for draymen of any skill at all to get past one another in the level open spaces alongside the road, which has a fairly wide sward on the right side of the screen. Giles in the film does refer to the availability of a 'siding' (i.e., a turn-out) nearby, but the viewer can see that all that would be necessary is a little adjustment on the part of each vehicle. Clearly, Agland (or the screenwriter) thought this to be such an essential '*Woodlanders*' scene that he/they included it even though they could not find an authentic location. In the novel, Hardy ensures that the reader understands the constrictiveness of the road-bed and the extreme difficulty Giles's carters would have if they were to attempt to back up their heavily loaded vehicle. Mrs Charmond is shown to have no consideration either for ordinary common sense or for the rural economy, ruining Giles out of petulance. The film reproduces the whole scene 'faithfully', transferring the dialogue verbatim from the novel. But the effect on screen is seriously diminished since viewers can *see* the obvious solution to the problem.

So keen was Agland to produce a film of *The Woodlanders* faithful to Hardy's novel that he shot it over a two-year period, to get the seasons right. It is clearly an adaptation made with love and respect. Nonetheless, what results is not a Hardyan story as presented by Hardy. Both the credit and the blame for that can be ascribed to Agland and to the difference between words on a page and images on a screen.

NOTES

1. This prediction appears only in post-first editions of the novel. Hardy had been stung by heavy criticism from magazine and newspaper reviewers of the first book version of the novel for letting Fitzpiers off so easily despite his infidelities. Melbury's prediction of Grace's future unhappiness first appeared in the one-volume edition of 1887, and was given greater specificity in the 1896 Osgood, McIlvaine edition, to the extent that he even included Suke Damson among Fitzpiers's previous lovers, although he has not previously known of this particular liaison. Readers interested in full details may consult my critical edition of *The Woodlanders* (Oxford: Clarendon Press, 1981); variants in Melbury's comment are on p.335. Most readers will have easier access to my Oxford World's Classics Edition of this novel (1985; new edn Oxford: Oxford University Press, 2005), where this passage's variants are in a textual note to p.328. In subsequent notes and in parenthetical citations, I cite the Clarendon volume as 'Clarendon' and the World's Classics volume as 'W', with the 2005 pagination. The interpretive introduction to the 2005 Oxford World's Classics edition is by Penny Boumelha.

2. A valuable discussion of the ending of the film is Peter Widdowson, 'Thomas Hardy at the End of Two Centuries: From Page to Screen', in Tim Dolin and Peter Widdowson (eds.), *Thomas Hardy and Contemporary Literary Studies* (Basingstoke: Palgrave Macmillan, 2004), pp.194–8.

3. Emily Woof (who starred as Grace in the film), email interview, 5 October 2003. Other reasons to remove Marty's paean appear to have been a shift towards emphasising Grace and a concern that to end with Marty would have confused the audience. It is obvious that Marty's role in the film is

much reduced from that in the novel (where she is one of eight or nine 'main' characters).

4. An initial cut of the film was evidently shortened by some twenty minutes in editing, after production. According to Emily Woof, recalling what happened, 'It was mainly Marty's story which was cut. Grace's story was re-ordered. A few of my scenes which the director felt made Grace seem too assured were also cut or re-edited' (email interview, 5 October 2003). Woof also observed that the ending was changed after filming. She did not explain how, but said that it was at the request of American distributors who 'felt that the original ending did not have enough "closure"'. Woof also had an interesting response to my query about Grace's final scene as 'an expression of female independence': 'Yes that is the case. Grace was given a show-down at the end of the film in order to get away from Hardy's more suffocating sense of compromise. But this was not the ending we shot. This was changed for the second edit after the American distributors got involved.'

5. *The* [Sunday] *New York Times*, 11 May 2003, section 2, pp.1, 10.

6. For the textual history of 'He's had you!' see Clarendon, p.228, or the textual note to p.219 of W. For that of '*Come to me* . . .' see p.287 of Clarendon, or the textual notes to p.279 of W.

7. Note his advice to a would-be dramatist of the novel that in 1887 he couldn't say things that the dramatist could hope to say in 1889 (*The Life and Work of Thomas Hardy by Thomas Hardy*, ed. Michael Millgate (Athens: University of Georgia Press, 1985), pp.230–1).

8. Preface to W, p.[3].

9. These variants can be found in my Clarendon edition on p.259.

10. A comment written by Owen in her copy of the novel; given by Carl Weber, *Hardy and the Lady from Madison Square* (Waterville, Maine: Colby College Press, 1952), p.89.

11. I am by no means the first to notice the film's post-Victorian posture of feminism. Of particular pertinence are Paul J. Niemeyer, *Seeing Hardy: Film and Television Adaptations of the Fiction of Thomas Hardy* (Jefferson, N. C.: McFarland, 2003), p.193 and Patricia Ingham, *Thomas Hardy* (Oxford: Oxford University Press, 2003), pp. 229–32.

11 Dissonance, simulacra, and the grain of the voice in Roman Polanski's *Tess*

John Paul Riquelme

> . . . a novel is a mirror being carried down a highway.
>
> Stendhal, *The Red and the Black*[1]

Thomas Hardy's *Tess of the D'Urbervilles* (1891) contains vivid, detailed representations of scene, action, and speech, but it does not fit comfortably into the tradition of realism that Oscar Wilde decries in 'The Decay of Lying', which appeared in his *Intentions* in the same year as Hardy's novel. In *Tess*, and generally in his novels from *The Mayor of Casterbridge* (1886) onwards, Hardy deserves the exemption that Wilde grants to Hardy's friend and early mentor George Meredith, who, according to Wilde's Vivian, 'is not a realist', but rather 'a child of realism who is not on speaking terms with his father'.[2] In his third-person autobiography, Hardy himself claims that '"realism" is not Art'.[3] Hardy's *Tess* is a book of displacements and dislocations in style as well as narrative. Roman Polanski includes both kinds of dislocation in his film adaptation of the novel, *Tess* (1979), an adaptation that has sometimes been misunderstood as a realistic work, as has Hardy's novel.[4] Extending the assertion by Stendhal's narrator in *The Red and the Black*, we could describe a film with sound as an 'acoustic mirror' that travels.[5] But Polanski's acoustic mirror is obviously constituted by a variety of lenses whose recorded images have been edited. Sometimes the editing creates the illusion of realism, the impression of a mirror, a surface that passively reflects. That realistic impression is not the exclusive or even the dominant effect of camera work, editing, spaces, or sound in Polanski's film. Instead, because of various kinds of dissonance we recognise the world of the film's narrative as a simulacrum comprised of many component simulacra, large and small. The dissonant and simulacral effects make it difficult for the viewer to forget that what might be understood as a moving mirror is the edited result of work, of camera work and editing, that is, of acts of construction. The effects allow us to perceive what Roland Barthes called 'the grain of the voice',[6] the process, including the labour, by which the work of art comes into being. That evocation of the grain, which gives us access to the origin of the work of art, takes Polanski's film beyond realism in a way that expresses Hardy's modernity as well as Polanski's, a modernity that has a surprisingly Beckettian tinge.[7]

A critic would require a more vivid imagination than mine to think, independently of the facts, that a late twentieth-century film-maker from Eastern Europe, someone who had experienced the Holocaust, modernism and surrealism in the arts, and Beckett, would have the ambition to present faithfully and successfully on the screen the greatest novel of a Victorian novelist, born almost a century before the film-maker. Fortunately, we are not dependent on the limits of critical imagination concerning Polanski's *Tess*, which drew large audiences in Europe and North America and won three academy awards, for cinematography, art direction, and costume design.[8] Arguably, the film and its director deserved even more recognition than that. Both the initial acclaim and the subsequent critical attention, which has been scant, may well have been muted because of Polanski's difficulties with the authorities in California, which resulted in his leaving the United States to work abroad.[9] The effect of the scandal deserves comparison with the effect of scandal on Oscar Wilde's career, though the circumstances were quite different. In both cases, however, the artist under a cloud became for many a taboo subject or a subject of silent scorn. Moral issues unquestionably arise concerning the behaviour of both Wilde and Polanski, specifically regarding the responsibilities of older, influential artists towards the young, but silence about their art is implicit censorship by intentional avoidance. Hardy, too, faced restrictive public attitudes reflected in publishers' requirements when he attempted to publish *Tess* serially.[10] In the cases of both Wilde and Polanski, scandal has contributed to a distortion in the history of the media in which they worked. The history of literary modernism was affected by the critical neglect of Wilde for over half a century, followed in recent decades by a great deal of attention. The recent attention, however, has not resulted in the kind of rethinking of literary modernism's development that is needed. Nor has the increased attention paid to Polanski since he won an Oscar in 2003 as Best Director for *The Pianist* made up for the paucity of serious commentary on his work for a quarter of a century.[11] The increased interest has, however, given us easier access to his films and more information about them. This is particularly the case with *Tess*, which was released as a 'special edition' DVD in 2004. The DVD contains a documentary by Laurent Bouzereau about the making of *Tess*, presented in three parts, that includes recent interviews with Polanski and with a number of the other principals involved in the filming.[12]

Contributing to the comparative silence among critics concerning *Tess* is the difficulty of rendering discursively its richly paradoxical virtues,

virtues that translate Hardy's arresting changes of register in style and his memorable mixture of realistic and anti-realistic elements into vivid cinematic forms. Both Hardy's *Tess* and Polanski's contain strongly realistic scenes, but the texture of the scenes and their structural relations to other portions of the narrative frequently do not contribute to realistic illusion. In the novel, the anti-realistic elements are evident in Angel's allegorical name and in the fluctuations of the style from reported dialogue to reported thoughts and to commentary by the narrator that is by turns ironic and learned. The narration regularly breaks the illusion of realism that it also fosters. In considering Polanski's relationship to realism, it is worth remembering that he had made a strange, at times surrealistic, film, *The Tenant* (*Le locataire*, 1976), just prior to filming *Tess*. The comparatively more realistic texture of his *Tess* appears to be a turn away from the dominantly expressionistic character of much of his earlier work. But the apparent realism of his *Tess* is combined, as in Hardy's novel, with its own apparent opposite, an assault on the limits of realism from within a veneer that invites us to understand it at times in realistic terms as part of a process of overturning the effects and implications of realism.

Both Polanski and Hardy are at odds with realism in a way that amounts to an aesthetic protest against the expectations and limitations imposed on their central character. *Observation* and *protest* are no more distinct in their works than they are in Wilde's 'The Decay of Lying: An Observation', which is also a protest.[13] Each develops a stylised mask that enables us to recognise the apparently realistic style for what it is, not a natural perspective but one that has been constructed by cultural processes that are related to the cultural pressures faced by their protagonist. We see through the style and by means of it to a cultural situation in which rigid conventions constrict and deform people in arbitrary, unjustified ways. Society provides a script for the lives of the characters, and it provides a marketable, conventional style, realism, for rendering the narrative in prose and in film. But the script and the style are conventions symptomatic of hierarchies of power that need not be accepted. The writer's style and the film-maker's emerge from the refusal to accept such conventions. In the case of Hardy, we have a late-Victorian writer who contributed with *Tess* to the first crest of literary modernism, whose experiments in style involve questions of value that are political and moral as well as aesthetic. With Polanski, we have a post-Holocaust, post-surrealist artist attracted to Hardy's narrative who translates Hardy's subversions of realism by means of cinematic strategies.

The motivations and implications for Polanski's act of recovering Hardy are multiple. They include his evident concern with exploitative social situations in some of his earlier films, including the short works *The Fat and*

the Lean (1961) and *Mammals* (1962). A central motivation to undertake
Tess involves Polanski's dead wife, the actress Sharon Tate, who was cruelly murdered in 1969 while eight months pregnant. She had left Hardy's
book for him in their bedroom because she was attracted to the role. The
film's dedication, 'To Sharon', which appears just below the title, makes
clear his association of the work with her. Hardy's narrative provided
Polanski with the opportunity to make a film about a beautiful young
woman who dies, but more importantly the woman is not murdered by a
man in a senseless act of violence; quite the reverse: the man is murdered
in a motivated act by the woman he has damaged, though the act can
arguably be called mad. Additionally, the narrative involves flight from
the authorities in the wake of the murder, but the flight turns out to be
directed into the hands of the police. Escape may have been impossible,
but it appears that Tess wishes to be taken, that she has chosen to die by
her own hand through committing an act that results in her apprehension
and execution; in effect, she is already dead before being apprehended.[14]
I do not mean to reduce the film to the director's biographical projections
or to draw undue attention to resonances between the film and the life,
but it is reasonable to assume that many viewers know about the death
of Polanski's wife and about his own flight from prosecution. In Hardy's
narrative, he found a vehicle for treating again the social effects of power
while paying homage to his dead wife; the result aesthetically reverses
and rechannels elements of experience that he knew first hand. Polanski
makes out of the book, however, not autobiography but dissonant expressionist art that can be mistaken for an exercise in realism.

Polanski and Beckett: tramps, crossing the Channel, foreign accents

The opening of Polanski's film presents briefly the ensemble musical procession of the club-walking in which Tess participates as part of the May
Day celebration. She is not singled out for the viewer as she later is after
the procession has reached its destination, when Angel happens on the
dancing and impulsively joins in. As in Hardy's narrative, the first indi-
vidualised characters to whom we are introduced are John Durbeyfield
(Tess's father, played by John Collin) on foot and Parson Tringham on
horseback, who patronisingly tells Durbeyfield about his defunct ances-
tral line. Unlike the procession with its horizontal movement and engag-
ing music, the scene with the Parson and the one that follows involving Angel and his disparaging brothers project hierarchical relations and
class distinctions. These are reflected in the Parson's elevated position on
horseback and in the distance he and then Angel's brothers dismissively

put between themselves and the peasants by literally turning their backs on them and moving away. Hardy glosses the Parson's elevation and irony in a bitterly ironic way when his narrator returns to the D'Urberville aristocratic past in the book's closing paragraph. There the narrator evokes the hierarchical world of Greek tragedy by alluding to Aeschylus and the 'sport' (T, lix, 384) of the gods, who toy with humans. Not a god but a man of God, the Parson is toying with an uneducated member of the agricultural labouring class, someone whose life is almost beneath his notice.

The Parson and the ragged peasant inhabit different worlds socially. Durbeyfield in the film, however, occupies a different world from the Parson in a surprising aesthetic way. He does so because Polanski creates a double temporal perspective by bridging Hardy's late-nineteenth-century English text and post-WWII European perspectives. Rather than linking the English narrative with an ancient Greek dramatist, as Hardy does, Polanski links it implicitly with a post-war dramatist, Samuel Beckett. Polanski makes no attempt to render the novel's closing passage, with its mention of Aeschylus, choosing instead to conclude the film visually with Tess and Angel's departure from Stonehenge in police custody. This crucial strategic decision to focus on Stonehenge in the film's closing is as important as opening with Durbeyfield, as I suggest later. Durbeyfield's clothes, his scruffy looks, and his statements now and later in the film qualify him to occupy a conceptual space from which the Parson is excluded: he is a tramp who would fit in on the stage of *Waiting for Godot*. Durbeyfield is by far the most arresting presence in these early moments of the film. His encounter with the Parson is both true to Hardy's novel and dissonant, considering the viewer's post-Beckettian position well past the mid-point of the twentieth century. The dissonant superimposition might seem to be merely circumstantial and coincidental, except that there is substantial evidence of Beckett's influence on Polanski's art before and after *Tess*. That is not surprising considering that Polanski's career as an actor and director in Europe began just at the moment that Beckett rose to prominence with *Waiting for Godot* (1952) and *Three Novels* (1950–3 French; 1955–8 English). Both works were published between the time Polanski started acting in the theatre in the late 1940s and the time he finished his studies at the Lodz Film School a decade later.

The short films from the 1960s concerned with the social effects of power that I have already mentioned, *The Fat and the Lean* and *Mammals*, were unquestionably influenced by Lucky's part in *Waiting for Godot*. In them, the exploitative relations between master and servant are presented by means of a chain used to restrict movement and the pulling of a heavy load.[15] Polanski also cast Jack MacGowan, the Irish stage actor who was a primary interpreter of Beckett, in two of his most successful films, *Cul-de-Sac* (1966) and *Dance of the Vampires* (1967).[16] In a prominent French television version of *Waiting for Godot* directed by Walter Asmus in the year of Beckett's death (1989), Polanski played Lucky.[17] It is worth remembering that Lucky's dance in scene two of *Godot* is called 'The Net' and that the dance's name evokes Aeschylus. Like Agamemnon in the *Oresteia* and like Tess in Hardy, Lucky is entangled, but his entanglement is part of a staging of being in the net. Although disturbing, Lucky's performance-within-the-play is not tragic in the mode of Aeschylus, because it is laughable and obviously a matter of performance. Something similar is true of John Durbeyfield as played by John Collin. However well he fulfills within a realistic frame our expectations for the character in Hardy's narrative, he is also a player in a post-Beckettian staging that, when he is on camera, can be laughable (as in the scene in which he offers to sell the right to his name for ever smaller sums of money, which drop from £1,000 to £20 with hardly a pause for a breath). The laughter, of course, disappears by the time Durbeyfield refuses to allow Tess's baby to be baptised. We recognise Durbeyfield as contributing to a simulacrum, one that has been produced with painstaking labour to give the look of Hardy's world. But this world looks back at us and reveals our implication in it because of various dissonances and crossovers that invoke the ostensibly much different world we share with the director.

The crossovers include many aspects of the production and its result. The most evident of these for the viewer is the casting of a German actress as Tess. Nastassja Kinski, however, is only one element in an international artistic situation of Beckettian proportions, especially in the crossover between French and English. As with Beckett's work, which he often self-translated between English and French, it is impossible to characterise Polanski's *Tess* as anything but a hybrid, an anomalous result that emerges through the interaction of elements that are often kept separate. It is a French film by a Polish film-maker, first released in France, but made jointly through French and British collaboration, that represents English locales using locations and a studio in France and that stars a German actress portraying an English country girl. The agricultural action on the land set in England would seem to be far removed from the experience of a Polish film-maker, but in fact after leaving Cracow as a child to escape Nazi persecution, Polanski lived in the Polish countryside, where he learned about agricultural life, including how to milk cows.[18] The type of farming he encountered in Poland must have been much closer to the sort presented in Hardy's novel than the more modern agricultural techniques that had already become established by 1900 in England and in Western Europe. The production company was a joint venture, a Franco-British co-production between Renn Productions in France and Burrill in England. Although based on Hardy's English, the first version of the screenplay was written in French by Polanski and his long-time screenwriting partner, Gerard Brach. In order to put the screenplay in its ultimate form, however, John Brownjohn, an English writer from Dorset, joined the team and helped invent English dialogue for scenes in which Hardy had provided none. These scenes are of particular interest in the film because of their central placement and distinctive camera work, as I suggest below. The cinematography was initially the responsibility of Geoffrey Unsworth, the famous British cinematographer, but Unsworth died while the film was still being shot. He was replaced by Ghislain Cloquet, a French cinematographer, who simulated Unsworth's style for the remainder of the shooting. Costumes were designed by Anthony Powell, who is British, but he worked, necessarily, in collaboration with Pierre Guffroy, the French production designer, and Jack Strange, the British art director. The film's three academy awards, then, went jointly to a British and a French cinematographer, jointly to the British art director and the French production designer, and to the British costume designer.

It is easy to imagine someone dismissing the boundary-crossing that characterises the film's production as aesthetically insignificant for viewers, as simply one of those oddities of the modern world. But culturally and aesthetically the boundary crossing is no more irrelevant than Beckett's situation in-between with regard to France and Ireland, the French language and the English language. The implications concerning the mixed national character of the artist's working methods and context have an aesthetic dimension with regard to language for both Polanski and Beckett, well beyond the quandary that French bookshops and libraries face when they try to identify these artists as French or as foreign. Their language is pervasively inflected in ways that militate against our reducing their works to responses appropriate to realistic art emerging from a single national origin. The perceptible, unavoidable trace of the heterogeneous origins of Polanski's *Tess* is evident whenever Nastassja Kinski speaks as Tess.

When I first saw *Tess* in the cinema twenty-five years ago, I disliked it intensely because my realistic expectations for the film were disappointed by what I heard and saw. My reaction was so strong that I left at the intermission. My main disappointment concerned the casting of Kinski in the lead. I probably could have accepted the delicacy of her features and her ethereal looks (in comparison with the other country girls), but I could not accept her voice. Kinski's English was without doubt fluent, but every word she spoke made it evident that she was a European actress playing a young rural woman from the south of England. Rather than being a flaw in the movie, however, her spoken performance is a brilliantly dissonant feature, one that makes it impossible for the spectator to mistake *Tess* for realism. The bold, unconventional casting of Kinski is comparable to Oscar Wilde's decision to cast Sarah Bernhardt as the first Salomé in the production that the English censor refused to license. Bernhardt at the time was in her forties, while her character was a nubile teenager. Both casting decisions have the effect of keeping the audience off balance through a refusal to fulfil expectations concerning details that are essential for realistic portrayal: age and voice.

That refusal puts Wilde's projected staging of his own play and Polanski's cinematic response to Hardy in an aesthetic space that Samuel Beckett identifies in 'Three Dialogues' as beyond 'the plane of the feasible'.[19] He means that the work of art cannot be mistaken for something that we have encountered before and have learned to accept as if it were natural and inevitable. Our spoken language is never natural, though we tend to behave as though it were. In Hardy's narrative, Tess herself asserts the often suppressed difference between the socially constructed and the natural when she says to Angel, 'I am only a peasant by position, not by nature!' (T, xxxv, 236). When a language is spoken with foreign inflections, even slight ones, its learned quality becomes perceptible to the listener, as does the physical, material process by which our vocal cords produce the apparently natural sounds of the languages that we acquire. Polanski's film as acoustic mirror respeaks Hardy's English and his narrative with a European accent and reflects a landscape that is not English, whose features are and are not real.

Echoes, mirrors, and shifting focus

Respeaking someone else's language is the work of the mythological figure Echo, whose story is entangled with the story of Narcissus, in which water acting as a mirror plays a central part. Hardy's narrative of Tess's life is a version of the tale of Echo and Narcissus, but Narcissus is doubled for her, since both Angel and Alec are egotistical. In the classical myth, Narcissus dies by wasting away in a kind of slow suicide. Angel comes close to experiencing that kind of self-destruction because of his wrong-headed relocation alone to Brazil. Tess becomes a vengeful Echo when she murders Alec. Twice in Hardy's narrative, Tess respeaks Angel's words. In chapter forty-six, she contributes to the undoing of Alec's religious conversion by repeating an argument to him that she has learned from Angel (T, xlvi, 315). When she and Angel are parting just before he goes to Brazil, she literally repeats his words in their conversation, and the narrator emphasises the repetition by pointing out that 'She simply repeated after him his own words' (T, xxxvii, 254). As director and as col-laborator on the screenplay, Polanski also plays an echoic role by enabling the repetition of Hardy's language through a translation first into French. As part of the echoic translation, he reproduces Tess's echoing of Angel by retaining her repetition in the conversation before they part.

Polanski also makes changes in Hardy's narrative, mostly excisions, such as the dropping of Angel's sleepwalking.[20] But there are also addi-tions and shifts in emphasis, notably ones that give Tess more to say and that emphasise her acts of writing. Together with Tess's letter-writing, her confession to Angel, which Polanski renders in detail even though Hardy does not, adds to our sense of her strength of will. The elaborated confes-sion scene in the film and the scenes that immediately precede and follow it constitute a significant, centrally placed sequence not only in the screen-play but in the camera work. Tess's confession is literally in the centre of the film; as it is divided into scenes on the 2004 DVD, the scene is four-teenth of twenty-eight. In his use of both a shallow space and rack focus, Polanski brings the film's expressionistic tendencies sharply to the fore.[21] The prelude to the confession includes shots of action not in Hardy's narrative in which Angel and Tess stand directly in front of a mirror washing their hands together and expressing their sense that their hands have become indistinguishable. The space is shallow, because the mirror hangs against a wall. But the mirror transforms the shallow space into a deeper one reflecting the room behind them. The effect is a visual illusion accompanying the characters' illusion, or delusion, about love that they voice sentimentally in terms that viewers are likely to find unconvincing. We may see *through*, as well as by means of, this visual illusion involv-ing a mirror. In other shots Polanski's use of mirrors is more complex. For example, in the scenes involving the milking of cows in Dairyman Crick's barn, Polanski uses a wall-sized mirror at the end of the barn to enlarge its dimensions visually. The mirror in the barn, however, is only perceptible in a still, not while the frames are in motion. The mirror in the handwashing scene can have quite a different effect, primarily because the reflection is unaccountably not in crisp focus and because it does not reflect us. We are observing the characters, seeing them and their profiles reflected in the mirror, but we are also looking directly into the mirror. This is an anomalous situation in the experiencing of a cinematic image that is supposedly to be understood as real. A real mirror would reflect us, but this one, of course, does not. The film, represented by the mirror we look at but not exactly into, looks back at us blankly and expresses the film's generation of visual illusions by suppressing our reflection.

The mirror in the middle of the shot in which we see the reflections of others but not ourselves is reminiscent of *Las Meninas* (1656) by

Velázquez, in which the mirror against the back wall of the salon reflects the images of the King and Queen of Spain, who are the subjects of the painting that Velázquez depicts himself as producing. The couple are also the spectators of the scene, as are we, but we are not reflected in the mirror. The connection might seem far-fetched, but Velázquez's painting and Polanski's out-of-focus mirror scene have in common a play on the singular and the doubled, the visible and the obscured, the illusion and the act of construction, the angle of vision and the manipulation of visual elements. Angel asks Tess whose hands are whose in the basin, and she replies that they are all one, specifically that they are all his. While they are having this exchange about two being one, the viewer is having a visual experience that gives rise to a recognition that the scene includes a doubling of action in the represented space that is reflected in the mirror and a simultaneous recognition that what we see in the mirror and the words we hear from the acoustic mirror of the film are constituted by illusion. Failing to see ourselves doubled by the mirror, we recognise the mechanism that generates realistic illusion, rather than accepting the illusion as if it were natural.

Velázquez employs the geometry of the various planes in the represented space of his painting in ways that disturb the realistic illusion for the viewer, who is then likely to consider the dynamics of the handling of space within the painting. To that extent, we participate in the artist's act of construction and recognise its immanent position within the represented space. Something similar emerges during the scene in which Tess confesses, shortly after the scene with the mirror, when Polanski uses rack focus, that is, a change in focus during the scene, to disturb our relation to the ostensibly realistic space. The changes in focus can remind us that the mirror in the earlier scene was, strangely, not quite in focus. Tess may well think of herself and Angel as one, but she also insists on parity with him when she refuses to let him ignore her determination to confess after he has. As soon as she begins to speak, Angel, who starts out standing, while Tess sits down, goes mildly out of focus. As she continues, he goes further out of focus and sits down, which creates the opportunity for the camera to present him as if he were in a lower space. The focus changes several times between the two characters, until finally the scene ends with Angel walking out of focus deeper and deeper into the space of the rooms, through two doorways until he is out of sight. The camera work is memorably effective in displacing the realism of deep focus (which presents the whole of a scene's action in sharp focus) by the expressionism of shifting focus. Deep focus is usually taken to contribute to the impression of realism because the camera work does not draw attention to itself. Our eye is supposedly free to roam where it will. Rack focus, by contrast, makes the effects of lenses and angles insistently evident. It is as though Tess's insistence on attention is matched by the director's camera. Rack focus often shifts our attention from one character or object in a scene to another, but as Polanski uses it multiply during the confession, the redirecting of our vision is ambiguous, aleatory, and potentially quite active. We are as likely to be drawn to the character in sharp focus as we are to the character who is out of focus. Or we might be looking back and forth between them in an energetically shifting way that resembles the effect of the ambiguous geometry of *Las Meninas* on the eye. The shifting intensifies the oscillation of the spectator's wandering vision created by the multiple changes in focus. As with Kinski's out-of-tune English voice, the in-and-out-of-focus, ambiguously directive camera work makes us aware of the process by which the work has been created.

In the next scene, during the conversation between Tess and Angel about their situation, Polanski changes Hardy's dialogue by having Tess repeat in echoic fashion Angel's words about her being a different woman now. This repetition, which prepares for the echoic speech at their parting, is followed by Tess's impassioned statement that she was a child when Alec seduced her. By the time the second act of repetition occurs, at the parting, Tess has accepted Angel's decision to live separately from her. But her glancing away from Angel during the second echoing and the measured character of the repetition indicate that Tess's passion and determination, exhibited in the earlier scenes, have not been extinguished. They are merely being held temporarily in check.

The scene much earlier between Tess and Alec, in which he insists that she allow him to put a strawberry in her mouth (see Illustration 15), provides a figure for understanding Tess's relation to Echo. For a time, she reluctantly accepts having things put in her mouth, strawberries and words, but ultimately she, like the German actress who plays her, has a voice of her own, and a will that refuses to accept. The refusal comes out visually in Sandbourne near the movie's conclusion in the scene that precedes Tess's taking her revenge on Alec. That scene sends us back to Tess's determination to confess and to tell her own story because the camera work again involves prominent use of rack focus. Tess's agitated will to act and to speak parallels the camera work's energetic, paradoxical expressive movements. As with the earlier scene involving the mirror, the position of the observer contributes to breaking the illusion. We initially observe the scene between Tess and Alec from outside the room through the keyhole with the landlady, but in mid-scene the viewing direction is abruptly reversed. We now look from inside the room directly towards the door behind which the landlady peeps as Tess walks towards it, inadvertently scaring the observer away. In effect, the change of direction asks us to

Illustration 15. Tess (Nastassja Kinski) refuses a strawberry in *Tess*, Pathé Renn Production (France), 1979.

look at our own obscured point of vantage, at our participation in the act of looking and our engagement with the scene. As Angel did earlier, Alec first stands and then sits, but Tess goes blurrily out of focus with her head on the table. When she stands, however, and the direction of observation is reversed, she is silent but in focus while Alec, now gone fuzzy, continues to speak words that are not in Hardy's narrative. Hardy's *Tess* reports that Alec called Angel 'by a foul name' (T, lvii, 372), but we witness Polanski's *Tess* experiencing Alec's attempt to put words in her mouth by suggesting an answer for his question about why she is upset. No longer willing to be ventriloquised, this now silent Echo acts.

Boots, simulacra, and the work of art's contradictory origin

The dissonance in Polanski's film is a matter of contradictions, including especially ones that involve the spectator's eyes and ears. The dissonance emerges as well through the linking of apparently incommensurate aspects of human experience in Hardy's narrative. Polanski replicates that linking in a way that enables the viewer to recognise the constructed quality of the human world by experiencing the act of aesthetic construction in the grain of the voice and in simulacra. Polanski expresses the humanly created quality of our world by labour inscribed in the film's techniques and by representations of labour, but also by the prominence he gives to non-representational constructions. We see the contrasting elements, representations of labour and the centrality of non-representational creations, in quite different moments of Hardy's narrative that Polanski retained. These include the scene involving Mercy Chant's taking of Tess's boots (at the conclusion of Tess's thwarted attempt to visit Angel's parents in Emminster) and the closing scene at Stonehenge.

These contrasting scenes, one set in an agricultural village and the other set on Salisbury plain, contain elements that Martin Heidegger uses to evoke the character and the origin of the work of art in his seminal essay, 'The Origin of the Work of Art'.[22] Heidegger discusses first Vincent van Gogh's representation (in more than one painting) of an agricultural worker's well-worn boots and then a temple, specifically a Greek temple. Like Stonehenge, another temple, the Greek temple is an architectural work of art that is not utilitarian or instrumental in the ordinary sense because it is not a tool, not a means to achieving a practical end. Van Gogh's painting, by contrast, presents objects that are utilitarian in character, though his painting, while representational, is, like the temple, not utilitarian. As Heidegger explains, the temple 'cannot be ranked as a representational art': 'A building, a Greek temple, portrays nothing. It simply stands there in the middle of the rock-cleft valley'.[23] His essay throws light on the contradictory mix that Polanski recognises in Hardy and reproduces, because Heidegger attempts to bridge by juxtaposition the difference (without reducing or effacing it) between the utilitarian, representational vector and the non-representational vector in the dynamic of the work of art. Any attempt to understand art, he implies, and, in effect, to understand what it means to be human, will attend to these apparently incommensurate realities of art.

Polanski's *Tess* renders cinematically the distance, the dissonance, and the mutually defining relevance of these contrasting realities. His Tess is able to occupy the spaces appropriate to both the utilitarian world of representational art and the non-representational space of the temple. She is equally at home and equally out of place in both spaces. Following Hardy, Polanski creates for us the surprising, unlikely linkage. A shorthand way to make that point is to repeat what the novel tells us repeatedly, that Tess is both Durbeyfield and D'Urberville, an assertion that Polanski realises in a creative process that crosses over between English and French. He also evokes the duality when Tess inhabits film spaces that would seem to belong to quite different films. Tess walks into and out of both scenes, but she is presented as if a different person in each. In the earlier one, she is solitary and, though dressed in her best clothes, obviously a woman who lives on the land. In the later one, she is accompanied and dressed in the fashion of the city, a fashion that marks her as urban. In the earlier scene, her boots are taken into custody by Mercy Chant, while Tess walks out of the village in a different direction. In the later scene, it is Tess who is taken into custody. The shots in the earlier scene give us first a view of Tess from behind walking out of the village space, then a contrasting shot of Mercy's back as she walks away at the same moment with Tess's boots. Without transition, Polanski cuts to Alec on horseback riding directly towards the camera. We know that he is headed towards Tess. By contrast, in the closing scene, the police on horseback move towards Tess, but they do so in a slow, steady motion that puts Tess under arrest and takes her up into a final movement out of the scene. The pace and the aggressive shifts into and out of the village space, with the virtual ejection of Tess while an important part of her is confiscated, have been displaced by a contrasting continuity of movement that has the feel of a cortège.

The most remarkable contrast, however, concerns the setting of the two scenes. The village, like the boots, is representable as intelligible and utilitarian. It is a space for living and working on what Beckett refers to as the 'plane of the feasible', though Tess finds no comfort there. The space could easily have been the context for a more realistic presentation of the action, had Polanski not edited the shots in such an exaggerated way. Stonehenge as temple, however, is both non-representational and a simulacrum of a non-representational structure. As a full-scale model of Stonehenge in a form similar to the original as Hardy knew it, Polanski's simulated Stonehenge, like the mirror earlier, stands paradoxically for the film itself in its genuine-seeming but obviously anti-realistic appearance. The viewer is likely to realise that this is and is not Stonehenge, which has been in a significantly greater state of ruin for many decades. Even twenty-five years ago it had become a protected space that would not have been available as a movie set and would not have been suitable for the scene because of its state of decay. A shot from the filming in Bouzereau's documentary shows Polanski looking at and adjusting a small model of the simulated Stonehenge, as if it were a toy, which, in fact, it is. The diminutive, simulated quality of the small model is also an aspect of the full-scale simulation. The simulacral effect resembles that of one of Alexander Calder's steel stabiles that mimic the monumental buildings also made of steel that tower over them; it turns the space into the space of human creation, despite the monumental, threatening surroundings, through an act of doubling, a repetition with a difference.

At the end of Hardy's novel, his narrator famously evokes the situation of humans as the playthings of the gods. But his own narrative combines the antithetical aspects of the work of art that Heidegger implies enable us to recognise ourselves not as playthings but as human agents who play and create in a double contradictory situation. Having meditated on the utilitarian, referential aspect of art and on its equal, opposite, and connected non-representational aspect, Heidegger suggests that we encounter in art its 'createdness',[24] its having come into being. The created, generating quality that we encounter is the grain of the voice. We recognise and experience our engagement with the act of creation in Nastassja Kinski's voice, in Roman Polanski's expressionist camera work, in boots that Vincent van Gogh painted and that Tess Durbeyfield walks in and then away from, and in the simulacrum of a temple as the film's dissonant, contradictory, genuinely illusory space. Our directions through that space take us not only to Tess's death but to recognitions of ourselves in the shifting, dissonant echoes and reflections of an acoustic mirror.

NOTES

I wish to thank Peter Lurie of the University of Richmond (USA) and Keble College, Oxford, for his advice about film theory and criticism.

1. Stendhal, *The Red and the Black*, trans. Lloyd C. Parks (New York: New American Library, 1970). The statement occurs twice in the novel, first as the epigraph to book 1, chapter thirteen, p.85, where it is attributed to 'Saint-Réal', and later in elaborated form in book 2, chapter nineteen, p.359.

2. Oscar Wilde, 'The Decay of Lying', in Isobel Murray (ed.), *The Writings of Oscar Wilde*, (Oxford: Oxford University Press, 1989), p.221. I discuss Hardy's relation to realism in the biographical and historical introduction to my edition of *Tess of the D'Urbervilles* (Boston and New York: Bedford/St Martin's, 1998), pp.9–10 and in the essay 'Echoic Language, Uncertainty, and Freedom in *Tess of the D'Urbervilles*', *ibid.*, pp.506–20.

3. Thomas Hardy, *The Life and Work of Thomas Hardy*, ed. Michael Millgate (Athens: University of Georgia Press, 1985), p.239.

4. Virginia Wright Wexman in *Roman Polanski* (Boston: Twayne Publishers, 1985) pronounces *Tess* Polanski's 'most "realistic" film' (p.110), though her use of quotation marks around the term is a telling, but unexplained, qualification. Niemeyer, by contrast, emphasises the film's anti-realism generated by the sound track's sometimes discordant details (such as the loud ticking of a clock while Tess and Angel sit in silence at table) and by the viewer's puzzled engagement with enigmatic aspects of the narrative caused by Polanski's omission of elements in the novel and by Kinski's impenetrably blank, ambiguous portrayal of Tess (Paul Niemeyer, *Seeing Hardy: Film and Television Adaptations of the Fiction of Thomas Hardy* (Jefferson, N. C.: McFarland, 2003), pp.132–43). Niemeyer does not discuss the cinematography. Wexman reduces the implications of Polanski's use of rack focus to psychological realism (p.114).

5. Kaja Silverman, *The Acoustic Mirror* (Bloomington: Indiana University Press, 1988).

6. Roland Barthes, 'The Grain of the Voice', in his *Image-Music-Text*, trans. Stephen Heath (New York: Hill and Wang, 1977), pp.179–89.

7. I suggest the relevance of Beckett to understanding Hardy's poetry, especially his late poetry, in my essay on Hardy's poetic modernity (John Paul Riquelme, 'The Modernity of Thomas Hardy's Poetry', in Dale Kramer (ed.), *The Cambridge Companion to Thomas Hardy* (Cambridge: Cambridge University Press, 1999), pp.221–2.

8. It was nominated as well for Best Picture, Best Director, and Best Original Musical Score.

9. Polanski left the US in 1978 to live in France when he was faced with a judicial proceeding on criminal charges having to do with his alleged relationship with an underage girl. In his remarks on the 2004 DVD, Burrill, the British co-producer, describes the difficulties he had in arranging for distribution of the film both in North America and in Britain, despite its success in France. Although he does not attribute the difficulties, which must have arisen from several causes, to Polanski's personal situation, it is reasonable to assume that some in the movie industry were intentionally refusing to consider his work. Columbia, for example, had dropped Polanski as director for *The First Deadly Sins* in 1977 after he was arrested. Some critics vilified Polanski when the film was released (see, for example, Jane Marcus, 'A *Tess* for Child Molestors', in Peter Widdowson (ed.), *Tess of the D'Urbervilles: Contemporary Critical Essays* (Basingstoke: Macmillan, 1993), pp.90–4).

10. See my introduction to Thomas Hardy, *Tess of the D'Urbervilles*, ed. John Paul Riquelme (Boston and New York: Bedford/St Martin's, 1998), pp.11–12. All future references to this novel will be to this text, which reprints the second impression (1920) from the Wessex Edition (1912), the last printing of the novel in which Hardy was involved.

11. There has been comparatively little written about Polanski's *Tess*. John Tibbetts and James Welsh, for example, make no mention of *Tess* in their *Novels into Film* (New York: Checkmark Books, 1999), a would-be 'encyclopedia' of books made into films.

12. The seventy-minute documentary is presented as '*Tess*: From Novel to Screen', 'Filming *Tess*', and '*Tess*: The Experience'. The segments

include interviews with Polanski, Claude Berri (producer), Timothy Burrill (co-producer), Nastassja Kinski (Tess), Leigh Lawson (Alec), Anthony Powell (Costume Designer), Pierre Guffroy (Production Designer), John Brownjohn (the British screenwriter), and others. The documentary includes shots taken of the production in progress. During the interview Polanski shows a map of France from the time of the production that marks the route the crew, which he describes as a communal circus troupe, travelled for eight months to locations in Normandy, Brittany, and north of Paris during all the seasons. He and Berri also describe the lengthy editing process that was extended even further when Berri insisted that Polanski shorten the film, which was originally over 3 hours, by 30 minutes. After unsuccessful interventions, by Francis Ford Coppola among others, Polanski himself cut the film to 172 minutes. It is this trimmed version which has been released on VHS and DVD.

13. Subtitled 'An Observation', the dialogue contains a version of itself as a single-voiced text, Vivian's 'The Decay of Lying: A Protest', in Oscar Wilde, 'The Decay of Lying', in Murray (ed.), *The Writings of Oscar Wilde*, pp.213–39.

14. This interpretation of Tess in both Polanski's narrative and Hardy's aligns her implicitly with Wilde's Salomé, another female victim who takes revenge, apparently knowing that doing so means her own death.

15. Wexman provides more detailed descriptions of these films in relation to Beckett (Wexman, *Roman Polanski*, pp.26–7).

16. In his *The Beckett Actor: Jack MacGowran, Beginning to End* (Beverly Hills, Ca.: Moonstone Press, 1987), Jordan R. Young discusses the details of MacGowran's work with Beckett and with Polanski. *Dance of the Vampires* is also known as *The Fearless Vampire Killers or Pardon Me, But Your Teeth Are in My Neck*.

17. Details about the cast are available from the movie database at www.imdb. com. Asmus, a distinguished German theatre director, worked with Beckett frequently starting in 1974.

18. Polanski explains the basis for his knowledge of agricultural life of the kind Hardy depicts in the special features on the 2004 DVD.

19. Samuel Beckett, *Proust and Three Dialogues with Georges Duthuit* (London: John Calder, 1987), p.103.

20. Niemeyer lists and discusses the major omissions (Niemeyer, *Seeing Hardy*, pp.132–5).

21. The association of shallow space and rack focus with expressionism and of deep focus with realism is widely accepted in film studies. See James Monaco, *How to Read a Film* (Oxford: Oxford University Press, 2000), p.86. Christian Metz, *The Imaginary Signifier: Psychoanalysis and the Cinema* (Bloomington: Indiana University Press, 1982) informs my own discussion of cinematic mirroring and voyeurism.

22. First delivered as a lecture in 1935, then published in a revised form in 1950, Heidegger's essay was republished with final revisions and a 1956 Addendum in 1960.

23. Martin Heidegger, 'The Origin of the Work of Art', in his *Basic Writings*, ed. David Farrell Krell (New York: Harper and Row, 1977), pp.149–87 (p.168).

24. *Ibid.*, p.181.

12 Romancing the text: genre, indeterminacy, and televising *Tess of the D'Urbervilles*

Richard Nemesvari

By the time Thomas Hardy reached the end of his career as a novelist it had become a critical commonplace to emphasise the controversial subject matter of his texts. Whether a reader was an attacker or a defender, and it is important to remember that Hardy had many defenders, it was his contentious decision to explore sexuality in its relation to social and cultural mores that seemed most to polarise his audience. What is sometimes still forgotten, however, is that Hardy's novelistic method, what at the time was called his 'style', also received a great amount of attention. In particular, Hardy's radical mixture of conflicting genres and his manipulation of narrative voice disconcerted a readership accustomed to the unified effects of Victorian realist fiction as constructed by George Eliot. This is especially obvious in *Tess of the D'Urbervilles*, where Hardy's conflation of realism with sensationalism, tragedy, melodrama, didacticism, the Gothic, and the pastoral is exacerbated by a third-person narrator who is sometimes omniscient, sometimes contradictory, sometimes part of the story, and sometimes apparently unable to describe the story at all. Such a method severely challenged his original audience, and it can cause serious difficulties for anyone trying to transfer the text from page to screen.

Thus the 1998 television version of the novel, originally broadcast in two parts in March by London Weekend Television in Britain, and by the Arts and Entertainment Network in September in North America, demonstrates that a change in medium radically alters function and ideology. Presented in the promotional material as 'Thomas Hardy's *Tess of the D'Urbervilles*', the programme makes what had become by the late 1990s a standard cinematic claim to legitimacy through its attachment of author's name to title. Yet its efforts to establish a unified generic representation, which entail the repression of Hardy's disjunctive ambiguity and 'unreal' characters/plot devices, significantly modify Hardy's method and effect. In particular, the television production removes the text's most extreme sensational and melodramatic elements and attempts to replace them with relationships acceptable as 'real' to a late-twentieth-century audience. This, connected with the decision to employ narrative voice-overs while at the same time filling in the narrational gaps that are the most distinctive element of *Tess of the D'Urbervilles*, creates what might be characterised (somewhat paradoxically) as romantic realism. I am using 'romance' in this sense not as the generically formal antithesis to realism, but rather in the more colloquial sense of a plot centred on sexual and emotional entanglements as developed in contemporary popular culture. What the LWT/A&E version of *Tess* does is re-establish mimetic elements intentionally unavailable in the novel while at the same time present-ing its tragedy in purely personal and relational terms, which requires that *all* elements of the central love triangle of Tess, Angel, and Alec be 'believable' and 'sympathetic' in modern mass-media terms. This creates a homogenisation of effect that is not in the original. If, as Linda Shires has argued, 'Hardy relies on multiplicity and incongruity. He . . . ques-tions the very foundations of traditional representation and belief. He wants his reader to become conditioned into thinking simultaneously in terms that are multiple and even contradictory',[1] such a viewing experi-ence is not achieved by the programme. Instead the text is 'romanced' in a way that erases its uncertainties and gives its television audience a less complex, and considerably less uncomfortable, experience of Tess's life and eventual destruction.

Ironically, it is the programme's attempt to imitate the text's intru-sive third-person narrator through equally intrusive voice-overs that first reveals their discrepancies in effect. The importance of this device is sig-nalled by its early appearance. Before the main titles roll Jack Durbeyfield is shown walking towards his meeting with Parson Tringham as a voice informs us, 'It was on the day of the May dance that Tess's father encoun-tered the parson who revealed to him what would have been better left forgotten. A chance encounter, a chance remark, yet such things deter-mine our fate.' There are seventeen such interventions spread throughout the film, and already their purpose is clear. The audience is given needed background information (it is a May Day dance we are about to witness), its reactions are pointed in the proper direction (what is about to be dis-covered 'would have been better left forgotten'), and themes are quickly established ('chance' is repeated twice, and the determinations of 'fate' are invoked). This last element is especially significant, since the idea that Tess is 'fated' is repeated in two other voice-overs. Paul Niemeyer, in his recent book *Seeing Hardy: Film and Television Adaptations of the Fiction of Thomas Hardy*, observes that '[t]hough it may seem that the narrator is a mere gadfly, he actually serves a clear ideological purpose of imposing a text on the serial. The narrator *makes* the viewer see the story as a tragedy of fate.'[2] The voice-over narrator is therefore constructed as a guide whose perspective is meant to be accepted by the viewer as authoritative.

This is very different from the shifting relationship with the narrator of the novel, which needs to be negotiated by the reader from encounter to encounter. One of the most notorious examples of this occurs at the end of chapter thirteen in 'Phase the Second: Maiden No More', when the narrator in one paragraph declares that 'the world is only a psychological phenomenon', yet insists in the very next paragraph that Tess's conventional feelings of guilt are 'moral hobgoblins . . . out of harmony with the actual world'.[3] These unreconciled antithetical statements (is the world a 'psychological' projection or is it 'actual'?) are simply left for the reader to work out, creating the kinds of uncertainty crucial to Hardy's purpose. The television production's treatment of this situation is revealing. Instead of providing complicated indeterminacies the text's two long paragraphs are boiled down to a single voice-over statement: 'She had broken the laws of society, but in her feelings of guilt and distress she believed, mistakenly, that she had broken the laws of nature itself.' This is clearly a version of the chapter's last sentence: 'She had been made to break an accepted social law, but no law known to the environment in which she fancied herself such an anomaly' (T, xiii, 121), but because it has been removed from the full narrative context the voice-over cannot recreate the complexity of Tess's response to her situation. She is simply 'mistaken' in her feelings, and the voice-over tells the audience exactly how to position itself in relation to the developing plot.

Perhaps the most startling voice-over intrusion in the television production, however, occurs after Tess makes her confession to Angel, and the two of them wander outside, he leading and she following. As they walk down a narrow street in the film, they pass a man going the opposite way who stops, bows slightly, and lifts his hat to Tess. As he begins his bow the voice-over declares 'I could never forget those lovers, their faces blind to time and place, each isolated in their mutual despair', and a sudden close-up reveals the character to be an aged version of Thomas Hardy himself. This apparently Fowlesian moment, however, has a completely different effect from the metafictional subjectivity insisted upon by the author's (multiple) intrusions into *The French Lieutenant's Woman*.[4] The narrative voice-overs are now unproblematically linked with the author himself, who becomes a chronicler of events which he has apparently researched, recorded, and on some level even witnessed. The television production does have partial warrant for such a reading, but again the difference between novel and programme is instructive. In the novel we get the following passage.

They wandered on again in silence. It was said afterwards that a cottager of Wellbridge, who went out late that night for a doctor, met two lovers in the pastures, walking very slowly, without converse, one behind the other, as in funeral procession, and the glimpse that he obtained of their faces seemed to denote that they were anxious and sad. Returning later, he passed them again in the same field, progressing just as slowly, and as regardless of the hour and of the cheerless night as before. It was only on account of his preoccupation with his own affairs, and the illness in his house, that he did not bear in mind the curious incident, which, however, he recalled a long while after. (T, xxv, 330)

Here ambiguities dominate. From the passive construction, 'it was said', through the filter of an unnamed and preoccupied cottager and the equally unspecific identity of the nameless 'two lovers', to the fact that their faces 'seemed' to indicate sadness and the 'long while after' passage of time, this entire paragraph calls into question narrative certainty. The text may hint at reporting, at several removes, something that actually happened, but there is no omniscient voice uttering definitive pronouncements. The television production's removal of this uncertainty, and its replacement by an explicitly authorial authority, is part of a concerted effort to achieve realism through a direct claim of presenting events reliably. Further, the TV version's refusal to include elements which are defined as too unrealistic to be acceptable, and its insistence on filming scenes which the novel explicitly elides, contributes to the focus on 'believable' relationships which will romanticise this realism and de-socialise its wider implications.

To start with a somewhat minor example of one such element, Hardy's inability to resist giving Angel a harp to play has been causing comment for quite some time. Margaret Oliphant, writing in the March 1892 *Blackwood's Magazine*, observes that 'it is perhaps not less unlikely that a parson's son in Wessex should carry a harp about with him, than that he should be called Angel Clare'.[5] This is her opening attack on the 'unlikely' nature of his entire character. Hardy's choice of musical instrument is ironic, intended to emphasise Angel's later, 'un-angelic' behaviour, but as with the Victorian reviewer this is considered too much for a contemporary television audience. At the risk of replacing the ironic with the ridiculous, the television adaptation provides Angel with, of all things, a *concertina* to play, and it is by producing mournful tunes on this that he attracts Tess. To be fair to the programme's writer, Ted Whitehead, in his original screenplay he has Angel playing a flute,[6] but obviously in either case Hardy's teasing prod at the reader is perceived as too disruptive to include. Someone named Angel cannot possess a harp and remain credible as a love interest in romance or realist terms, since this is too close to burlesque and the antithetical generic responses it creates.

Altering Angel's instrument is one thing, removing a central scene involving him is something else. A more telling example of the television production's desire for genre consistency is its erasure of the sleep-walking episode. Once again there is a Victorian precedent for finding this incident questionable, since the anonymous critic for the *Saturday Review* of 16 January 1892, whose distaste for the novel is palpable, mocked it by observing that Angel performs 'a feat that must have been almost unique in the history of strength, considering that he was not a Hercules, and that Tess was a tall and well-developed young woman'.[7] Obviously Angel's ability to lift Tess out of bed, and carry her down the staircase, out of the house, across the river over a narrow plank bridge, through the Abbey plantation, and into the Abbey church, all the while remaining sound asleep, is physically impossible. Equally obviously, however, Hardy is not concerned with physical realism here; he is concerned with externalising Angel's psychological conflict, and he does so by employing a Gothic trope which is fully successful in developing his purpose. Angel's constant refrains, 'Dead; dead; dead!' and 'My wife – dead, dead!' (T, xxxvii, 347–8), along with his unconscious, ritualistic 'interment' of Tess, communicate both his inability to cope with the destruction of the patriarchal fantasy he has created of her, and the deep love which he is suppressing. Tess's recognition that 'continued mental distress had wrought [Angel] into that somnambulistic state' (T, xxxvii, 347) is meant to be explanation enough for what follows, but it is insufficient if a projected audience is deemed unwilling to recognise the legitimate uses of 'unrealistic' events in fiction or on the screen.

The overall result of such alterations and omissions, among which also could be included the removal of the description of Alec's blood soaking through the ceiling of The Herons and forming that infamously 'gigantic ace of hearts' (T, lvi, 519) which so startles the landlady, is a flattening of affect that foregrounds the relationships in the LWT/A&E production. It is certainly possible to see that Angel is upset by Tess's revelation, but the depth of the blow he has suffered, let alone the gender ideology upon which it rests, so crucial to understanding the extremity of his reaction, is lost. In 1897 Hardy wrote that '[a]ll tragedy is grotesque – if you allow yourself to see it as such',[8] so that erasing the grotesque and the sensational – in essence preventing the audience from seeing the novel 'as such' – radically alters the text. A film may provide accurate period costumes and settings, as this production does, and even attempt accurate regional accents, as is also done, but the verisimilitude produced mitigates the tensions between realism and tragedy in a way that redraws the tragic significance of Tess's situation. And this is reinforced even further when the production actually fills in gaps which the text intentionally leaves blank.

There can be little doubt that the two most provocative and famous *aporiai* in the novel are Tess's rape/seduction and her murder of Alec, yet both are fully dramatised for the TV production. The clear belief is that each is too important to remain unviewed, and their filmatic representation wipes away Hardy's carefully constructed ambiguity. Although the interpretations inescapably generated are crucial individually, their reading in tandem is even more important, and confirms the film's use of contemporary realist/romance conventions in its generic structure.

What precisely happens in the Chase continues to be a source of disagreement, and although the novel's reader can never know for sure because it is simply not presented, a critical consensus appears to have been reached. The narrator's inability or unwillingness to describe this event, along with the conflicting comments concerning it which appear later in the text, has increasingly led commentators like Ellen Rooney to declare the 'complete inadequacy of [Hardy's] method'[9] in its attempt to problematise the rape/seduction dichotomy. This, in turn, has paved the way for later critics such as Jules Law to unify the issue, as he categorically declares that the 'second phase of the novel is initiated by a cataclysmic event – Alec d'Urberville's rape of Tess'.[10] Current theorisations of the novel are all but uniform in their descriptions of what happens to Tess as rape,[11] and this has clearly had a significant impact on the LWT/A&E production of the scene. It makes some effort to acknowledge the possibility of ambiguity, but its structure cannot successfully do so, and ultimately it provides the kind of certainty consistent with its overall presentation. Connected to this, it also takes care to provide specific foreshadowing. After Tess dismounts from the wagon that first brings her to the Slopes, and as she uncertainly tries to decide which direction to take, both she and the viewer are startled by a harsh off-camera sound. Looking around she sees an old workman sharpening his scythe with a whetstone, but the camera work films the blade of the scythe in near close-up, with Tess in the middle distance. Positioned like this she is framed directly under the blade, and although a jump-cut close-up of her face shows her smiling in relief at the mundane explanation of the noise, the camera quickly pulls back to its initial shot as the old man continues his loud sharpening, so that she remains under the blade as she turns and walks off towards her first meeting with Alec. The premonition of violence is obvious, and more than prepares the audience for what occurs later.

Thus although the film reproduces the fog which is so important in creating the 'obscurity' (T, xi, 102) on which the novel's description (or rather lack of description) depends, there is nothing obscure about Alec's actions. After he returns to where he has left Tess he first stands over her sleeping body and then, as ominous music begins to rise, he kneels down and starts to kiss her. Tess turns to him and begins to respond with kisses of her own, then shakes her head and attempts to partially push him away. This gesture, however, turns into a clasping of Alec's head as she is clearly shown kissing him back and responding sexually. When, however, Alec reaches down and tries to push up her dress, Tess cringes away and begins to protest. Gasping and crying she says, 'don't, don't, no, stop, no, no', and with a look of shock turns her head away as Alec penetrates her and is shown thrusting and finally grimacing in orgasm. The scene takes place in darkness, but its lighting makes the characters' reactions obvious, and there is only one interpretation available to a late-twentieth-century audience. Whatever attraction or sexual arousal Tess may have demonstrated at the beginning of the encounter, modern formulations of 'no means no' and the requirement for consent throughout intercourse mean that the second she says 'no' and 'stop', and Alec continues, the film presents him as raping her. I am not suggesting in any way that such contemporary constructions of rape are incorrect, only that the television production cannot adequately reproduce the ambiguity of the text through the device it has chosen, and this overt construction of Alec as rapist has major implications for the other plot gap it fills in: Alec's murder.

Once again the text provides the possibility of an after-the-fact reconstruction of the scene, but Mrs Brooks's spying and keyhole eavesdropping, along with Tess's later recounting to Angel of what she has just done, are both so disjointed that no absolute understanding of what transpired is available. The television viewer is not subjected to any such uncertainty. Alec's question after Tess re-enters their room, 'What's the matter?' (T, lvi, 517), literally his last words in the novel, opens up a fully dramatised exchange. Tellingly in an adaptation which seems at pains to remove unrealistic melodrama, this is the most melodramatic scene in the entire film. After Tess informs Alec that Angel has returned, the following dialogue is provided.

ALEC (surprised and concerned): 'He came back? When? Where? Now?'
TESS (gasping and sobbing): 'Now he's gone! Gone a second time! Oh God, I have lost him now forever! He won't love me the littlest bit anymore, only hate me. Oh yes I have lost him now. (angrily) You said he'd never come back!'
ALEC (pleading): 'I didn't believe he would, I swear.'
TESS: 'And I have lost him again because of you!'

ALEC: 'Tess, you lost him years ago, when you first told him the truth. He abandoned you then. I wouldn't have done that, no matter what you told me. And he wouldn't if he had ever truly loved you.'

TESS (staring into space): 'He loved me. He loves me still. That's why he came back.'

ALEC (shouting): 'Then why is he gone again!'

TESS: 'My sin! My sin! (Alec turns away in frustration) He looks as if he's . . . dying.'

ALEC (shouting): 'Tess, you rejected me a hundred times, and it never altered what I felt for you, because I loved you, that's all that mattered. I offered you everything that I had to offer, my soul, my life, everything.'

This is quite astonishing. Alec's declaration that he loves Tess has no basis in the text at all – certainly he never says it directly. The result of this dialogue is that Alec, instead of being the rake and cad of the novel, is turned into a sympathetic lover whose emotions are not adequately appreciated. Further, when later in the scene he reveals that he is a Stokes and not a D'Urberville, something which in the film Tess has not realised until this moment, he repeats his feelings: 'I helped your family for *your* sake, because I loved you! I would have done anything for you.' At this point it becomes difficult for the viewer not to think of Tess as unreasonable in her loyalty to Angel, a truly startling reversal of identification. The scene culminates in Alec's bitter declaration, 'Your own, true, husband is a spineless bastard!', at which point Tess, leaning against the breakfast table with her mouth open in shock, picks up the carving knife and plunges it into Alec's chest. Alec is killed for love.

This transformation of Alec is quite intentional. In an online interview Jason Fleming, the actor who plays him, states 'I think you have to find some endearing quality in a character . . . [h]is redemption is quite endearing to a point, and I tried to make him likeable, despite himself . . . any character that you can't sympathize with is a monster.'[12] The possibility that Alec is meant to be fully and completely unendearing, unlikeable, and unsympathetic is simply not an option available to this production, since he would then be unacceptable as 'real' to its modern audience. This is also made explicit by Whitehead who, in his own online interview, declares,

We were . . . interested in making the three characters a tragic trio . . . Alec, you know, is . . . a Victorian villain – twinkling eyes, mustaches, all that. But we wanted to make him a much more complex character . . . So we told the story of Alec as sympathetically as we could. And I think that . . . Jason Fleming has given it a very modern feeling.[13]

I have argued elsewhere that Hardy's portrayal of Alec as a melodramatic villain is crucial to his critique of masculinity in the novel,[14] and this 'modernising' of him helps nullify the novel's social criticism. Further, the idea that Alec is *also* a tragic character is consistent with the production's overall softening of Hardy's plot, since this shift can only be achieved by replacing issues of class, power, and gender with romance. Alec becomes as legitimate a potential love interest as Angel, and the relationships portrayed are divested of any political charge, or at least of the political charge that the original text produced. For in dramatising the two scenes left as gaps in the text, the LWT/A&E *Tess* potentially becomes involved with a different controversy: that of the redeemed rapist in soap-operas.

It is difficult to see how Alec's later protestations of love in the film can be reconciled with the unambiguous rape scene which has been provided, but it is completely appropriate that the 'resolution' to the apparent conflict in this televised version of the novel finds expression in a foundational television genre. Of course 'soaps' are explicitly a form of mass-media romance, and their staging in a recognisably current social setting is the thin veneer of verisimilitude needed to compensate for their absolute focus on shifting and exaggerated personal relationships. To this extent they qualify as the romantic realism that occurs in the televised *Tess*, so it is unsurprising the production falls back on a similar pattern of representation. Mary Buhl Dutta, in her article 'Taming the Victim: Rape in Soap Opera', observes that '[o]ne cultural myth endorsed by soap opera is that of the reformed rake, whose appearance and appeal can be traced back to eighteenth-century fiction. Soap opera presents him as the rapist redeemed by the woman who loves him, not uncommonly the same woman he raped.'[15] Dutta makes the connection that the film attempts to avoid, for the literary lineage from characters such as Richardson's Lovelace in *Clarissa*[16] passes directly through Victorian melodramatic bounders to end up at Alec D'Urberville. Hardy's resolute refusal to redeem Alec is, ironically, too radical for LWT/A&E's definition of 'complex', so that although Tess does not love Alec, the TV production nonetheless presents *his* declared love for *her* as mitigation of his rape. Deborah Rogers is very aware of the danger in this type of construction, and her warning about soaps holds true for this version of *Tess of the D'Urbervilles*: 'Most viewers are oblivious of the fact that reinterpreting soap rapes and brutality as romance denies – if not legitimates and glorifies – male violence by reading it as love.'[17] The film is not a soap-opera, but its use of this trope reinforces the ways in which the production counteracts Hardy's text. The ideology of the novel, which attempts to aggressively subvert patriarchal assumptions about sexuality and masculinity, is turned on its head as the audience is asked to sympathise with a rapist, and to view the consequences of his unrequited 'love' as a tragedy equal to that of the woman he has victimised. This, in turn, helps explain the film's closing scenes and rather confused final shot.

In his screenplay Whitehead holds relatively closely to the novel's conclusion. Tess and Angel arrive at Stonehenge, and the dialogue directly reproduces parts of the text, including Angel's observation, when Tess lies down on one of the stones, 'I think you are lying on an altar' (T, lviii, 536). Hardy's unsubtle suggestion that Tess is a tragic sacrificial victim, however, is too blatant (and potentially restrictive) for the film, which instead leaves out the line and creates the romantic tableau of Angel sitting on the stone while Tess lies with her head in his lap (see Illustration 16); it is in this position that they are discovered by the police. Whitehead's script omits any mention of Tess's sister 'Liz-Lu, but after a scene shift it still finishes with Angel climbing the hill outside Winchester, turning and watching the raising of the black flag which is the metonymy for Tess's execution, and then falling to his knees before rising and proceeding on his way. None of this appears in the LWT/A&E production. Instead, after Tess is apprehended, she is shown walking towards the rising sun surrounded by policemen while an onscreen text states 'Tess was convicted of murder and hanged at Wintoncester Prison.' This is followed by the final voice-over which, as Tess continues to stride into the distance, announces that 'Justice was done; mankind in time-honoured way had finished its sport with Tess.' This is an attempt to echo the novel's famously provocative statement '"Justice" was done, and the President of the Immortals (in Æschylean phrase) had ended his sport with Tess' (T, lix, 542), but again it cannot serve the same function. Understandably, the film hesitates to reproduce what for most viewers would be a totally unintelligible reference to Æschylus' *Prometheus Bound*, but removing this very specific allusion to tragedy, along with the image of her being sacrificed on the altar of social convention and hypocrisy, weakens the focus on Tess's tragic experience, a focus which has already been diluted through its expansion to include Alec, and even Angel. This being the case, however, how can 'mankind' be the source of what has happened, since the two men who apparently represent mankind are equally enmeshed in, and victimised by, the events dramatised, and how can those events be 'time-honoured', since they are portrayed as the results of primarily individual and personal failures? The film's final statement attempts to invoke a vaguely materialist explanation for what has occurred, but this idea is subverted by almost everything that has come before, and the only result is to create a brief incoherence that hints at issues the production has chosen *not* to pursue.

The furore that arose with the publication of *Tess of the D'Urbervilles* in 1891 centred on its didactic intent to question basic Victorian

Illustration 16. Tess (Justine Waddell) lies in the lap of Angel (Oliver Milburn) at Stonehenge in *Tess of the D'Urbervilles*, London Weekend Television, 1998.

assumptions. Perhaps predictably, the 1998 television version, in its attempt to ensure that a late-twentieth-century audience can relate to the story, makes a series of production decisions that downplay Hardy's disruptive style, and therefore the exploration of class conflict, the sexual double standard, and the oppressive gender roles which it highlights, and which so troubled its first readers. But weakening these 'period-specific' issues may in fact have rendered the action less, not more, relevant. The movement away from ambiguity, achieved by genre uniformity and the removal of indeterminacies in both narrative voice and plot, encourages a detachment which distances viewer response to what now becomes a story of drastically failed relationships, and not much more. Paradoxically, a more experimental attempt to transfer Hardy's idiosyncratic textual methods to the screen would have forced a more intense engagement with the film. The romantic realism provided paves an easy road for the viewer to follow; however, the specifics of the tragedy are diffused and lost, and the emotional impact of Tess's situation proportionately reduced. In the end, romancing Hardy's text for television makes it more accessible, but that accessibility removes the unique qualities of a novel whose impact depends on its refusal to cater to either nineteenth- or twentieth-century audience expectations.

NOTES

1. Linda Shires, 'The Critical Aesthetic of *Tess of the D'Urbervilles*', in Dale Kramer (ed.), *The Cambridge Companion to Thomas Hardy* (Cambridge: Cambridge University Press, 1999), p.147.
2. Paul Niemeyer, *Seeing Hardy: Film and Television Adaptations of the Fiction of Thomas Hardy* (Jefferson, N. C.: McFarland, 2003), p.237.
3. Thomas Hardy, *Tess of the D'Urbervilles*, ed. Juliet Grindle and Simon Gatrell (Oxford: Clarendon Press, 1983), ch. thirteen, p.121. All subsequent references, in brackets in the text, are to this edition.
4. John Fowles, *The French Lieutenant's Woman* (St Alban's: Triad/Panther, 1977). First published 1969. In his novel Fowles explicitly invokes Hardy, describing him as 'the great novelist who towers over this part of England of which I write' (p.235).
5. Margaret Oliphant, 'The Old Saloon', *Blackwood's Edinburgh Magazine* 151 (1892) 470.
6. I would like to thank Ted Whitehead, and Ms Gina Galoppi of Casarotto Ramsay & Associates Limited, for providing me with the screenplay for the production.
7. Unsigned review, *Saturday Review*, 16 January 1892, in R. G. Cox (ed.), *Thomas Hardy: The Critical Heritage* (London: Routledge and Kegan Paul, 1970), p.190.
8. Michael Millgate (ed.), *The Life and Work of Thomas Hardy by Thomas Hardy* (Athens: University of Georgia Press, 1985), p.315.

9. Ellen Rooney, '"A Little More than Persuading": Tess and the Subject of Sexual Violence', in Lynn A. Higgins and Brenda R. Silver (eds.), *Rape and Representation* (New York: Columbia University Press, 1991), p.104.

10. Jules Law, 'A "Passing Corporeal Blight": Political Bodies in *Tess of the D'Urbervilles*', *Victorian Studies* 40.2 (Winter 1997) 255.

11. See as well Melanie Williams, '"Is Alec a Rapist?" – Cultural Connotations of "Rape" and "Seduction" – A Reply to Professor John Sutherland', *Feminist Legal Studies* 7 (1999) 299–316.

12. Jason Fleming, AandE.com Interview, http://www.aande.com/tv/films/tess/alec.html.

13. Ted Whitehead, AandE.com Interview, http://www.aande.com/tv/films/tess/ted.html.

14. See Richard Nemesvari, '"The Thing Must be Male, We Suppose": Erotic Triangles and Masculine Identity in *Tess of the d'Urbervilles* and Melville's *Billy Budd*', in Phillip Mallett (ed.), *Thomas Hardy: Texts and Contexts* (Basingstoke: Palgrave Macmillan, 2002), pp.87–109.

15. Mary Buhl Dutta, 'Taming the Victim: Rape in Soap Opera', *Journal of Popular Film and Television* (Spring 1999), http://www.findarticles.com/cf_dls/m0412/1_27/55437790/print.jhtml.

16. Samuel Richardson, *Clarissa* (1747–8). In Richardson's novel the character Robert Lovelace falls in love with Clarissa Harlowe, rapes her, and then is later killed for his transgression.

17. Deborah Rogers, 'Daze of Our Lives: The Soap Opera as Feminine Text', *Journal of American Culture* 14 (1991) 38.

13   Adapting Hardy's *Jude the Obscure* for the screen: a study in contrasts

Robert Schweik

Two contemporary critical commonplaces – that 'fidelity' in screen adaptation is a multifaceted and treacherously complex concept, and that screen adaptations are works of art with claims to be judged with respect to their own goals[1] – have obvious relevance for this comparative study of Hugh David's 1971 BBC television adaptation of Thomas Hardy's *Jude the Obscure* and Michael Winterbottom's wide-screen version of 1996.[2] Not surprisingly, the two screen versions I consider are strikingly different both in the kinds of 'fidelity' they have to the novel and in their own very different artistic objectives. The 1971 BBC video version, shown in six episodes with a running time of 262 minutes, was calculated to have about it the aura of a literary 'classic'[3] – to create, that is, the appearance of earnest respect for Hardy's art deemed appropriate for a BBC production. Characteristically for such television adaptations in the early 1970s, it was shot mostly on sets, without much in the way of gradation in lighting or changes in camera focus, but with a goal to follow the outline of Hardy's narrative relatively closely and to incorporate much of Hardy's language in the script. On the other hand, the 1996 wide-screen version, with its far shorter running time of 122 minutes, was almost the reverse. Greater lighting variation – including black-and-white for its opening sequence – and other cinematic effects were more freely substituted for Hardy's prose. Box-office sales and time limitations of theatre screening were compelling considerations. Much was made of Kate Winslet's nudity; less attention was paid to period fidelity; and advertising quotations from both Winslet and Winterbottom stressed how very 'modern' the characters were. Moreover, Hardy's plot was eviscerated in the interests of a greatly compressed story line that ended with Sue leaving Jude – and so omitted the grimly powerful conclusion on which Hardy claimed to have had his mind 'fixed' when writing the novel.[4] In short, the 1971 and the 1996 versions exhibit the typical differences between the 'literary' tendencies and technical limitations of BBC productions of the early 1970s and some of the highly compressed and freer adaptations exemplified most recently in Michael Winterbottom's very loose screen transmutation of *The Mayor of Casterbridge* into an American gold-rush setting.[5]

But precisely because of such wide variations, a comparative consideration of some strikingly different choices made in the versions directed by Hugh David and Michael Winterbottom can illuminate some of the complex ways in which screen adaptations undertaken with such varied aims in such different production conditions may differ. It can also allow for a consideration of some of the multifarious ways they may – or may not – be 'faithful' screen adaptations of Hardy's *Jude* and how this 'fidelity' may relate to their achievement as independent works of art. For this purpose I have chosen five elements which have parallels in both screen versions and in the novel: (1) the opening, (2) Jude's meeting with Arabella, (3) the pig-killing episode, (4) the characterisation of little Father Time, and (5) the Remembrance Day procession scene.

The opening

The opening sequences of both screen versions are exemplars of their very different approaches to finding ways to convey what were taken to be the major themes rendered in the first five chapters of Hardy's *Jude*.

The 1971 production begins with a long shot of a blue sky flecked with clouds. The camera moves forward to reveal the spires and domes of Christminster, cuts to a close-up of one of the spires, slowly pans down that conventional icon of human aspiration, then abruptly cuts to a tightly framed and brightly illuminated image of a stone being chipped away by a hand-held chisel. It is possible to read that visual juxtaposition of spire and stone as a metaphor for the contrast in *Jude* between his aspirations and the hard economic and social realities that will confront them. But because the movement of the camera down the spire increasingly darkens the screen, the cut from spire to chisel also involves a shift from dark to light, so that the overall effect of the contrast is ambiguous. In the scenes immediately following, Jude's beating by farmer Troutham – certainly one of the more strikingly rendered episodes at the opening of the novel – is not dramatised at all but rather briefly reported by Jude, who appears crying, 'You said to be kind to the birds and beasts of the field' – an adaptation of a line of dialogue by Phillotson (I, i, 4–5), to which Phillotson replies with language drawn from Part First, chapter two, about the 'flaw in the terrestrial scheme, by which what was good for God's birds was bad for God's gardener'. This awkward set speech (Phillotson even lifts his eyes melodramatically heavenward at the mention of God's birds) is not Hardy's dialogue but adapted from the narrator's comment explaining that, after his beating, Jude was weeping *not* from the pain, though that was keen enough; *not* from the perception of the flaw in the terrestrial scheme, by which what was good for God's birds was bad for God's gardener; *but* with the awful sense that he had wholly disgraced himself. (I, ii, 11; italics added)

David's privileging of those words on the 'terrestrial scheme' by turning them into a speech by Phillotson is an attempt, certainly, to embed in his screen version what he takes to be one of the novel's major underlying ideas. But here as elsewhere the 1971 version stretches for 'fidelity' by clumsy conversion of narrative language into dialogue.

Michael Winterbottom in his 1996 *Jude* also attempts at the opening to epitomise one of the novel's major themes – but in a strikingly different way. The film opens with a black-and-white extreme long shot of a vast dark furrowed field rising to a brow, with the tiny figure of Jude outlined against a sliver of grey sky, the noise of his wooden clacker used to scare the rooks increasing as he approaches. In the left foreground stands a crude wooden gibbet with dead rooks ominously hanging from it. As the boy passes the dead rooks, he looks sympathetically at them, then stops his clacker and proceeds to cast bits of bread at other rooks feeding in the field. The perspective shifts to focus on Jude seen tightly framed from the front, bending over to throw crumbs to the rooks before being abruptly grabbed from behind by Farmer Troutham, who intrudes into the closely framed scene shouting angrily at the boy. In a series of shots Jude is seen being beaten repeatedly on his buttocks with the clacker, accompanied by shouts from the farmer and cries from the boy, cuts being made first to a more distant view and, finally, to a long overhead shot of the boy beaten and running from the farmer across the dark furrowed field. Subsequent scenes depict Jude, rubbing his buttocks, running home only to be greeted with scolding by Aunt Drusilla.

The contrast between those two openings could scarcely be greater. David's symbolism – if, indeed, that is what he attempts with those opening shots of spire and chisel – is ambiguous; his later use of a paraphrase of Hardy's narrator's words is in a limited way 'faithful' to the novel, but, as dialogue, stilted. By contrast, Winterbottom's use of black-and-white, his focus on the dark furrowed field with its makeshift gibbet of dead rooks that adumbrates the later hangings of Jude's children, the tightly framed image of Jude sympathetically feeding the birds into which the angry Farmer Troutham abruptly intrudes, followed by Aunt Drusilla's scoldings drawn from bits of dialogue in Part First, chapter two – all combine to render plangently one of the novel's main themes: the grimness of a world in which sympathy and tenderness may be harshly rewarded.

Jude's meeting with and marriage to Arabella

In one of the most memorable episodes in the novel, Jude is walking, dreaming of a future in which Christminster will be his alma mater and he 'a beloved son in whom she shall be well pleased', when suddenly 'something smacked him sharply in the ear . . . A glance told him what it was – a piece of flesh, the characteristic part of a barrow pig' (I, i, 35). Hardy's successive bowdlerisations of this episode are well known, and the final phrasing he adopted, 'the characteristic part of a barrow pig', is, as John Sutherland has noted, 'a devious and effective omission of frankness in a novel whose proclaimed boast is to eschew equivocation'.[6] But in other respects Hardy was remarkably frank, and the chapters that follow have, by comparison with many other parts of Hardy's *Jude*, limited and well-defined goals. Arabella's character is rendered in such passages as this: 'She had a round and prominent bosom, full lips, perfect teeth, and the rich complexion of a cochin hen's egg. She was a complete and substantial female animal – no more, no less' (I, vi, 36). What is not given over to amplifying that description of Arabella, and dramatising her efforts to manipulate Jude, is spent depicting the overwhelming sexual attraction Jude feels for her – one in which he singles her out 'in commonplace obedience to conjunctive orders from headquarters, unconsciously received by unfortunate men when the last intention in their lives is to be occupied with the feminine' (I, vi, 36). It is an attraction epitomised in chapter seven when Jude's resolve to re-read the Greek Testament dissolves: 'Η ΚΑΙΝΗ ΔΙΑθΗΚΗ was no more heeded', and in three minutes a 'predestinate Jude' rushes out of the house to meet Arabella (I, vii, 41). Chapter eight culminates in the sexually charged 'egg seduction' scene, and by the beginning of chapter nine Arabella has tricked Jude into agreeing to marry her. Again, the corresponding 1971 and 1996 adaptations of those episodes are strikingly dissimilar.

In the 1971 version of the 'pig's pizzle' episode in the novel, the pizzle is, indeed, a pig's, though for viewers not familiar with pig slaughtering David's close-up of it could be as puzzling as Hardy's words, 'the characteristic part of a barrow pig', might be to a reader without some editorial gloss at hand. David's version provides no such gloss in the form, say, of some verbal reaction from Jude but, instead, immediately injects into Hardy's sexually charged scene an irrelevant bit of dialogue in which Jude mutters, 'Pity about pigs . . . They have to die', to which Arabella replies, 'Well of course they do!' That exchange was appropriate for the pig-killing episode from which it was taken, but injected at this point it diffuses what was in Hardy's scene a tensely sexual relationship. And in other respects, too, the 1971 version of Jude's initial meeting with Arabella and the events leading up to their marriage lacks the concentrated focus of Hardy's narrative. Instead of the egg-seduction, there is an invented scene shot outside in a brightly sunlit field, with Jude giving an almost childishly earnest account of his studies. Again, that awkward speech is not taken from any dialogue in the novel but is an adaptation of the narrator's lengthy account of Jude's 'mental estimate of his progress' from Part First, chapter six. Still, something like the sexual power of Hardy's seduction scene is captured by dramatising Arabella's amusedly sensuous responses to Jude's account and by having her draw Jude's hand to her breast, after which the camera focuses on their feet – Jude's pushing frantically into the sod as a visual rendering of his sexual excitement.

That scene, however, is not followed immediately by a dramatisation of Arabella's manipulation of Jude into marriage, or of the marriage itself, but, rather, by an invented scene in which Aunt Drusilla tells Jude that his affair with Arabella is the talk of Marygreen – and that intrusion is followed by an abrupt cut to Christminster and yet a second invented scene in which Phillotson briefly meets Sue Bridehead who is working in Miss Fontover's religious art shop. The injection of two such irrelevant inventions into the middle of what could have been a concentrated depiction of Jude's sexual attraction for Arabella creates instead, a sequence that, by comparison with both Hardy's and Winterbottom's, seems diffuse and aimless. A subsequent attempt at 'fidelity' to Hardy's language also fails. In the episode that follows these intrusions, David's Jude is made to repeat the narrator's ironic words on marriage: that 'they would assuredly believe, feel, and desire precisely as they had believed, felt, and desired during the few preceding weeks' (I, ix, 56). But again, such use, almost verbatim, of the narrator's neatly parallel syntax sounds unpersuasive as dialogue. In short, this sequence in David's version – both through the irrelevance of its invented scenes and through its awkward use of language imported directly from Hardy's text – manages to combine the worst of both artistic worlds.

Yet, if the 1971 video seems perverse in its handling of Jude's encounter with Arabella, the 1996 version may seem in at least one respect even stranger. In the Winterbottom episode, Jude sits under a tree reading Greek when something plops on to his book – and so foreshadows the way Arabella will come between him and his studies. He picks it up, and, in a close-up, what appears in his hand is not a pizzle but a pig's heart. The animality of a pig's heart, however, works well enough to suggest the animality of Arabella's character, as does her subsequent reply to her comrade's inquiry, 'Did you catch anythin'?' with, 'Naw. I should have thrown somethin' else at him'. That reply elicits a giggle from her companion at the implication – exactly the reverse of the meaning of that line in Hardy's novel – that a pizzle would have been a clearer invitation.[7] Like David, Winterbottom also chose to adapt some of Jude's 'mental estimate of his progress' from chapter six of Part First, but in a truncated way that, as dialogue, flows more naturally. What follows is a seduction episode in which an archly sensuous Arabella mouths the egg before placing it between her breasts. The copulation takes place not in the upstairs of Arabella's house but adjacent to pig pens where the sheer animality of the scene – the erotic noises of Jude and Arabella mixing with those of the pigs – underscores the raw animal power of the sexual drives both respond to. Winterbottom heightens that intensity by eliminating any reference to Arabella's efforts to trap Jude into marriage and, instead, shifts immediately to a dramatisation of their marriage party where he continues the emphasis on animality by prominently featuring a pig as Arabella's wedding present.

In short, in the 1971 version, Jude's meeting with and seduction by Arabella is pointlessly interrupted both by David's awkward effort at 'fidelity' through his insertion of an irrelevant bit of dialogue derived from later in the novel, and also by his ill-considered invention of equally irrelevant scenes which intrude into what could have been a series of events charged with sexual tension. By contrast, Winterbottom, unencumbered by David's preoccupation with 'fidelity' but under pressures to compress Hardy's narrative, provides a highly simplified but closely focused concentration on the animality of the sexual attraction that will thwart Jude's aspirations.

The pig-killing episode

Contrasts of another kind appear in the way the two adaptations treat the pig-killing episode of Part First, chapter ten. One major significance it had in Hardy's novel was not only to contrast Jude's impractical sympathy and sensitive repulsion with Arabella's unfeeling practical acceptance of cruelty but also to dramatise vividly the horrifying brutality of the killing itself. In Hardy's version, a snowy pig sty is the setting for a graphically detailed account of the two noosing the frightened pig, looping the cord over its legs, hoisting the struggling and screaming animal on a stool, legs upward, Arabella insisting the pig must die slowly, and Jude impulsively plunging the knife into the animal's neck with deliberate force to end its suffering. Hardy's narrative is punctuated with repeated references to the squealing of the pig, whose notes change from a 'squeak' of surprise to 'cries of rage', then to a 'cry of despair', and finally to a 'shriek of agony' lasting until Arabella slits the animal's windpipe.[8] Arabella's anger over

Jude's accidental upsetting of the pail in which she is catching the pig's blood is the point at which Challow, the pig-butcher, belatedly appears.

The solution adopted in the David version was to centre attention not on the visual aspects of Hardy's scene but on the squeals of the pig and on Hardy's dialogue, with such additions as Jude's plaintively desperate cries: 'O God! O God!', 'I can't kill the pig!', 'She knows me. I've fed her!', 'She looks to us for life!', and 'Bella have pity!' Accordingly, for the pig-killing itself, David cuts away to focus on the pig-butcher listening with a knowing smile to the dialogue between Jude and Arabella and to the squeals of the animal. Only after the pig is killed does David again cut back to the scene of the slaughter.

The Winterbottom version, on the other hand, focuses on the horrors of the pig-killing – the struggle of Jude and Arabella to tie up the squealing animal, then to carry it wriggling and shrieking to a slaughtering bench, where Jude finally stabs it viciously in the throat accompanied by a final shriek from the dying pig, while Arabella rushes to get the bucket to catch the blood. Jude's 'Thank God he's dead!' and Arabella's response, 'What's God got to do with it?' echo snatches of the dialogue in Part First, chapter ten. The scenes immediately following provide images of Arabella hoisting the dead pig, scraping its skin, and butchering the animal, alternating with shots of Jude back in the house attempting to study, then finally giving up and walking out into a grim wintry landscape and trudging over a bleak snowy field.

In this episode, David chooses to rely upon the pig's squeals and over-heard dialogue – much invented – to create the impact of the scene; but he clumsily weakens that by adopting a smiling Challow as its visual focus. The Winterbottom version, by contrast, renders the horror of the pig's death in visual terms as well as in sound. Yet it is not only by deference to Hardy's text but by invented departures from it – particularly by alternating Arabella's pig butchering with scenes of Jude's futile attempt to study, and by evoking that unrelentingly bleak landscape into which he afterwards wanders – that Winterbottom tellingly juxtaposes the harsh realities of Jude's lower-class existence both with his sensitive repulsion from cruelty and with his scholarly aspirations.

Little Father Time

Hardy's characterisation of little 'Father Time' was strikingly inconsistent. Instead of the variety of realistic techniques he adopted for the bulk of the novel, some of the strategies he used to portray Time were, as I have pointed out elsewhere,[9] closer to the kind of literary expressionism that was emerging in Strindberg's dramas at this time. His 'Father Time' nickname is consistent with Strindberg's device of using general rather than specifically personal names. Time's face, too, is described with expressionist hyperbole – 'like the tragic mask of Melpomene' (V, iv, 294). Even some of Time's most memorable comments – 'I should like the flowers very very much, if I didn't keep on thinking they'd be all withered in a few days!' (V, v, 312) – might pass unnoticed in the dialogue of Strindberg's *To Damascus*. But, on the other hand, Sue's observation that 'these preternaturally old boys almost always come from new countries' (V, iv, 294) and Jude's report that the doctor has told him of other boys springing up who, like Time, seem to see all life's terrors before they are old enough to resist them, and are part of a coming universal wish not to live (VI, ii, 355), inject a more naturalistic account of Time's behaviour. This in turn seems inconsistent with the narrator's characterisation of Time as having a face that 'took a back view over some great Atlantic of Time, and appeared not to care about what it saw' (V, iii, 290). To add to these inconsistencies, elsewhere Hardy dramatises Time's discovery of the grimness of life in a more naively childlike way. It is that element of naive childlike discovery which dominates the final scene in which Time learns that Sue is to have another baby. To Sue's halting protest that her pregnancy is 'not quite on purpose', he responds,'Yes it is – it must be! For nobody would interfere with us, like that, unless you agreed! I'll never believe you care for me, or father, or any of us any more!' (VI, ii, 353). In short, Hardy's depictions of little Time – variously as preternaturally aware of life's tragic elements, or involved in a childlike process of coming to a naive understanding of them, or uncaring about what he saw, or overwhelmed by life's terrors and part of a coming universal wish not to live – posed in a highly concentrated way some of the larger problems any film adaptation of *Jude* would have in dealing with its manifold complexities and ambiguities.

The solutions to that narrower problem adopted by David and by Winterbottom are representative of their approaches to the novel as a whole. In neither screen version is Jude's child called 'Father Time', but, in other respects, David adapts extensively the language of Hardy's text, such as Time's comment, 'I should like the flowers very very much, if I didn't keep on thinking they'd be all withered in a few days!' (V, v, 312). He also invents scenes – e.g., the boy at play creating a little grave to which he is affixing a crude wooden cross – to suggest his prematurely aged and weirdly pessimistic vision of life. On the other hand, like Hardy, he also depicts the boy learning in a childlike way of life's terrors. For example, in one particularly intense scene David alters Hardy's story so as to have Mrs Edlin's account of Jude's and Sue's ancestors – the death by hanging of the husband, the subsequent madness of the wife – not, as in the novel, overheard (V, iv, 296–7), but, instead, told directly to the little boy, who listens wide-eyed. Important, too, is David's choice of a child actor whose face, marked with prominent wart-like growths on his eyebrow and the side of his nose, gives him an appearance at once child-like, but with a grotesqueness that sets him apart. By such varied means David renders some of the conflicting complexities of Time's character: his in part preternatural awareness of, in part indifference to, and in part childlike discovery of life's horrors.

By comparison, Winterbottom not only chooses a more normal-looking child, but, unlike David, elects to compress much of his character-isation into one vivid impression of the little boy's premature vision of life's terrors. For that purpose, he creates two successive connected episodes – neither in Hardy's *Jude* – in which the camera alternates between lit-tle Time's wide-eyed staring face and the terrifying scenes he watches. In the first, Jude and Sue take the boy to a magic lantern show titled 'Ghouls, Ghosts, and Apparitions' where, it is threateningly promised, 'Out of thin air the terrors come!' Images of spirits, skeletons, and other apparitions pass before Time's eyes with increasing rapidity, accompa-nied by flash-powder explosions, drum noises, shrill laughs, shouts, and a horde of hooded ghost-like figures that run screaming through the audi-ence. Then, from a hideous scream that dominates the final frames of this hallucinatory scene, Winterbottom abruptly jump-cuts to the spectacle of Sue Bridehead's scream in the agony of giving birth, her gory vulva and the bed sheets drenched with blood – on which scene little Time looks wide-eyed. By these two connected scenes Winterbottom attempts to convey something of the vision of life's terrifying horrors the wistfully sad-looking child has – though, as Winterbottom presents them, they tend to call attention more to themselves than to little Time.

The inconsistent mix of exaggerated metaphors, abstract generalisa-tions, bits of death-oriented dialogue, and childishly naive responses Hardy used to depict Time would be a challenge for any director engaged in adapting an otherwise relatively realistic novel. The more complex approach to the problem taken by David depends on the cumulative effect of many elements of dialogue, on such innovations as a scene in which Time plays at making a grave or listens to a terrifying account of hanging and suicide, and on the choice of an actor whose appearance has a curiously suitable grotesqueness. The result in many respects approx-imates cinematically to Hardy's complex and inconsistent treatment of Father Time. Winterbottom, on the other hand, adopts a solution at once more simplified yet more theatrically powerful – but at the risk that the scenes he creates call more attention to themselves than to the little boy whose vision of life's horrors they are intended to embody.

The Remembrance Day procession

One function of Hardy's first chapter of Part Sixth, 'At Christminster Again', was to situate Jude at the Remembrance Day procession and to contrast the festivity of the crowd with Jude's bitter acknowledgement of the death of his dream of admission to one of the Christminster colleges. His caustic remark, 'A lesson on presumption is awaiting me today! – Humiliation Day for me!' (VI, i, 342) epitomises his feeling. In response to a question from Uncle Joe, Jude's extended attempt to analyse the causes of his 'abandoned hopes' – in which he touches on chance, poverty, contemporary social restlessness, and misplaced confidence as possible reasons – leads, finally, to his conclusion, 'Well – I'm an outsider to the end of my days' (VI, i, 347). In this context, Hardy's references to a 'peal of six bells', 'the peals of the organ', and the cheers of the crowd (VI, i, 346–7) serve ironically to contrast the celebratory tone of the day with Jude's sense of humiliation. Both Hugh David's and Michael Winterbottom's recreations of this episode involve the use of background sound, but the choices they make are markedly different.

The David 1971 adaptation provides a highly abbreviated version of this scene – uncharacteristically including less of Hardy's language than Winterbottom's – but even then (David seems to have a penchant for such irrelevancies) he quickly shifts the visual focus away from Jude to Phillotson, who watches him. As part of the background for the procession, the David version includes a brief snatch of Handel's familiar music for 'See, the Conquering Hero Comes' from the oratorio *Judas Maccabaeus*:

> See, the Conquering Hero Comes,
> Sound the trumpets, beat the drums;
> Sports prepare, the laurel bring,
> Songs of triumph to him sing.[10]

David's choice of background music provides an ironic comment on what is anything but Jude's 'triumph', but Winterbottom, on the other hand, is far more innovative. He adapts some of Jude's responses to Uncle Joe's question about why he had failed – though he does not include the most emphatic of Jude's acknowledgements of his failure quoted above. Instead, Winterbottom prominently employs for musical background the final chorus of J. S. Bach's *St Matthew Passion*, Part 78. Bach's music here calls attention to itself by being altogether inappropriate for the Remembrance Day procession – but exactly right for the death of Jude's Christminster dreams, which it pointedly underscores. And for those who recall Bach's text on the burial of Jesus –

Wir setzen uns mit Tränen nieder
und rufen dir in Grabe zu:
Ruhe sanfte, sanfte ruh'.[11]
[With tears of grief we bury you
and call to you in the grave.
Sleep softly, softly sleep.]

– there is the additional poignant irony that those words anticipate a resurrection that Jude realises will never come for his hopes of a university education. David Lodge has pointed out the many allusions which relate Jude and Christ, particularly in Part Sixth of the novel. Like them, Winterbottom's musical allusion is, in Lodge's words, 'reductive and ironic, underlying the futility of Jude's sufferings, and the irrelevance of the Christian myth and its consolations to his plight'.[12] In short, David's choice of musical background seems pedestrian in comparison with the profoundly striking originality of Winterbottom's.

Conclusion

As I suggested at the beginning of this study, a comparison of two such very different screen adaptations of Hardy's *Jude the Obscure* can be a revealing way of considering some aspects of the slippery concept of their 'fidelity' as well as of their individual achievements as independent works of art. Of course the David version is more 'faithful' to the novel in the sense that it captures much more of the narrative line in Hardy's plot – including that final successive frustration of Jude's ever-diminishing aspirations and some of the painfully ironic contrasts of its ending that Hardy spoke of as being fixed in his mind while he was writing the novel. But clearly the 'fidelity' achieved by having a running time that allows for more representations of the sequential events in Hardy's *Jude* does not necessarily translate into 'fidelity' to the effects Hardy achieved in narrating those events nor to cinematic achievement on its own terms. In fact, this comparative consideration of how each production renders five significant portions of Hardy's *Jude* tells a different story: that a more limited running time may prompt greater ingenuity in creating cinematic effects that can sometimes yield results superior both as independent cinema and as effective screen adaptation. In at least three of the examples considered – the opening scenes, Jude's meeting with and marriage to Arabella, and the pig-killing episode – the Winterbottom version not only more effectively exploits cinematic means to create an equivalent for some major element of Hardy's text but also succeeds more fully in accomplishing its own more limited artistic objectives. In at least two – Jude's meeting with Arabella and the pig-killing episode – David's more leisurely developed version interposes scenes and dialogue not in the novel that actually weaken the concentrated effect of the novel without gaining any clear artistic advantage. On the other hand, Winterbottom's elimination of Jude's death and the events leading up to it deprives his film of the power of Hardy's stark and bitterly ironic conclusion. Moreover, although Winterbottom relies more often on strongly heightened cinematic effects, they do not always succeed. His attempt to use such means to convey little Father Time's vision of life's horrors, for example, seems more overpowering than functional when compared to David's more subtle and complex approach.

Yet Winterbottom's creativeness can be remarkably original – as in his use of Bach's *St Matthew Passion* as background for the Remembrance Day procession – and even his failures can be interesting in their innovativeness. Given such complexities, it would be futile to attempt to generalise about whether the 1971 Hugh David *Jude the Obscure* is, either as a 'faithful' adaptation or as a work of art in its own right, more successful than the 1996 Michael Winterbottom *Jude*. Certainly someone who simply wants to see a screen version that more closely approximates to the sequence of events in Hardy's plot should view the David version. For the most part it is a workmanlike adaptation of major portions of *Jude*, though with a regrettable tendency to convert Hardy's narrator's words to awkward dialogue in naive attempts at 'fidelity', as well as to create scenes whose effect is to inject an aimlessness into some of Hardy's most striking episodes without any notable artistic gain. On the other hand, for someone willing to accept an adaptation that is far more uneven, incomplete, and, as a whole, a less moving tragedy, the Winterbottom version – in part prompted by commercial considerations to seek greater compression and heightened cinematic effects – offers the compensation that it can at moments rise to screen innovations that rival in their own originality some of Hardy's most impressive achievements in prose.

NOTES

1. For a recent particularly trenchant analysis of the concept of 'fidelity' in screen adaptation, see Robert Stam, 'Beyond Fidelity: The Dialogics of Adaptation', in James Naremore (ed.), *Film Adaptation* (London: Athlone Press, 2000), pp.54–76.
2. References to the text of *Jude the Obscure* are to the World's Classics edition, ed. Patricia Ingham (Oxford: Oxford University Press, 1998). Page references to this edition are inserted parenthetically in the text along with book and chapter number.

3. See Paul J. Niemeyer's discussion of BBC policy in his *Seeing Hardy: Film and Television Adaptations of the Fiction of Thomas Hardy* (Jefferson, N. C.: McFarland, 2003), pp.206–7. For differences between the 'classic novel TV serial' and the 'classic novel film adaptation', see Ian MacKillop and Alison Platt, '"Beholding in a Magic Panorama": Television and the Illustration of *Middlemarch*', in Robert Giddings and Erica Sheen (eds.), *The Classic Novel: From Page to Screen* (Manchester: Manchester University Press, 2000), pp.71–92.

4. Richard Little Purdy and Michael Millgate (eds.), *The Collected Letters of Thomas Hardy*, 7 vols. (Oxford: Clarendon Press, 1978–88), vol. II, p.105.

5. For comment on a similar development in recent television adaptations of literary classics, see Sarah Cardwell, *Adaptation Revisited: Television and the Classic Novel* (Manchester: Manchester University Press, 2002), p.82.

6. John Sutherland, 'A Note on the Teasing Narrator in *Jude the Obscure*', *English Literature in Transition* 17 (1974) 160.

7. In *Seeing Hardy*, pp.180–1, Paul J. Niemeyer argues that the use of the pig's heart and a more sympathetic treatment of Arabella in later parts of the novel make it 'impossible to conclude that [in the Winterbottom version] Arabella's feelings are anything other than loving'. But there is no getting around the aura of animality that Winterbottom associates with Arabella in the first part of his film: his later creation of a loving Arabella is simply inconsistent with the 'female animal' he effectively renders in those earlier scenes.

8. In his 'Postscript: The Film of *Jude*' in *On Thomas Hardy: Late Essays and Earlier* (Basingstoke: Macmillan, 1998), pp.188–95, Peter Widdowson has argued that Arabella has a 'satiric' role in the novel. But although Hardy's narrator occasionally comments on Jude's idealised ambitions, Hardy portrays Arabella's unfeeling acceptance of cruelty as having no more than a kind of raw animal survival value. 'Satire' it is not. Hardy's stance, rather, is a more nuanced one, poising different ways of coping with the human condition against one another, none of which he portrays as satisfactory, though some – particularly those which include sympathy and loving kindness – he tends to depict with greater respect.

9. Robert Schweik, 'The "Modernity" of Hardy's *Jude the Obscure*', in Phillip Mallett and Ronald Draper (eds.), *A Spacious Vision: Essays on Hardy* (Newmill: Patten Press, 1994), pp.54–7.

10. G. F. Handel, *Judas Maccabeus* (London: Novello and Company, 1906), p.32.

11. J. S. Bach, *Matthäus Passion*, ed. Hans Grischkat (London, Zürich, Mainz, and New York: Ernst Eulenburg, 1968), pp.317–36.

12. David Lodge, *Working with Structuralism: Essays and Reviews on Nineteenth- and Twentieth-Century Literature* (London: Routledge and Kegan Paul, 1981), pp.112–13.

Filmography: film and television adaptations of Thomas Hardy

1913 (Famous Players Film Co.; USA): *Tess of the D'Urbervilles*
Presenter: Daniel Frohman
Director: J. Searle Dawley
Cast: Millie Maddern Fiske (Tess Durbeyfield), David Torrence (Alec D'Urberville), Raymond Bond (Angel Clare), John Steppling (John Durbeyfield), Mary E. Barker (Mrs Durbeyfield), Kate Griffith (Mrs D'Urberville), Franklin Hall (Parson Clare), Camille Dalberg (Mrs Clare), J. Liston (Parson Tringham), James Gordon (Crick).
Category: Feature Film

1915 (Turner Films, Ltd; UK): *Far From the Madding Crowd*
Screenwriter/Producer/Director: Larry Trimble
Cast: Florence Turner (Bathsheba Everdene), Henry Edwards (Gabriel Oak), Malcolm Cherry (Farmer Boldwood), Campbell Gullan (Sergeant Troy), Marion Grey (Fanny Robin), Dorothy Rowan (Lyddie), John McAndrews (Farmhand), Johnny Butt (Farmhand).
Category: Feature Film

1921 (Progress Film Company; UK): *The Mayor of Casterbridge*
Screenwriter/Director: Sidney Morgan
Producer: Frank Spring
Cast: Fred Groves (Michael Henchard), Pauline Peters (Susan Henchard), Mavis Clare (Elizabeth-Jane), Warwick Ward (Newson), Nell Emerald (The Furmity Woman).
Category: Feature Film

1924 (MGM; USA): *Tess of the D'Urbervilles*
Screenwriter: Dorothy Farnum
Director: Marshall Neilan
Presenter: Louis B. Mayer
Cast: Blanche Sweet (Tess Durbeyfield), Conrad Nagel (Angel Clare), Stuart Holmes (Alec D'Urberville), George Fawcett (John Durbeyfield), Victory Bateman (Joan Durbeyfield), Courtenay Foote (Dick), Joseph J. Dowling (The Priest).
Category: Feature Film

1929 (British International Pictures; UK): *Under the Greenwood Tree**
Screenwriters: Sidney Gilliat, Monckton Hoffe, Harry Lachman, Frank
   Launder, Rex Taylor
Director: Harry Lachman
Cast: Marguerite Allan (Fancy Day), John Batten (Dick Dewey), Nigel Barrie
   (Shinar), Maud Gill (Old Maid), Wilfred Shine (Parson Maybold),
   Roberta Abel (Penny), Antonia Brough (Maid), Tom Coventry (Tranter
   Dewey), Robison Page (Grandfather Dewey), Tubby Phillips (Tubby).
Category: Feature Film
* Also known as *The Greenwood Tree* (USA)

1940 (Ente Nazionale Industrie Cinematografiche (ENIC); Italy):
   *Una Romantica Avventura**
Screenwriter/Director: Mario Camerini (based on 'The Loves of Margery')
Producer: Giuseppe Amato
Cast: Assia Noris (Annetta), Gino Cervi (Luigi), Leonardo Cortese (Il Conte),
   Armando Migliari (Il Padre di Annetta), Olga Solbelli (La Vedova Cavara),
   Ernesto Almirante (Berni), Calisto Bertramo (Silvestro), Adele Mosco (La
   Nonna de Annetta), Adelmo Cocco (Don Antonio), Edoardo Borelli
   (Il Farmacista).
Category: Feature Film
* also known as *A Romantic Adventure* (UK)

1953 (Merton Park Studios; UK): *The Secret Cave*
Screenwriter: Joe Mendoza (based on 'Our Exploits at West Poley')
Director: John Durst
Producer: Frank Hoare
Cast: David Coote (Steve Draycott), Susan Ford (Margaret Merriman),
   Nicholas Edmett (Lennie Hawkins), Lewis Gedge (Miller Griffin), Johnny
   Morris (Charlie Bassett), Trevor Hill (Job Tray).
Category: Children's Drama

1967 (Vic Films/Appia/MGM; UK/US): *Far From the Madding Crowd*
Screenwriter: Frederic Raphael
Director: John Schlesinger
Producer: Joseph Janni
Cast: Julie Christie (Bathsheba Everdene), Terence Stamp (Sergeant Troy),
   Peter Finch (William Boldwood), Alan Bates (Gabriel Oak), Fiona Walker
   (Liddy), Prunella Ransome (Fanny Robin), Alison Leggatt (Mrs Hurst),
   Paul Dawkins (Henery Fray), Julian Somers (Jan Coggan), John Barrett
   (Joseph Poorgrass).
Category: Feature Film

1969 (BBC; UK): *The Distracted Preacher*
Screenwriter: John Hale
Director/Producer: Brandon Acton-Bond
Cast: Stephanie Beacham, Christopher Gable.
Category: TV Drama

1971 (BBC; UK): *Jude the Obscure*
Screenwriter: Harry Green
Director: Hugh David
Producer: Martin Lisemore
Cast: Robert Powell (Jude Fawley), Fiona Walker (Sue Bridehead), John Franklyn-Robbins (Phillotson), Daphne Heard (Drusilla), Alex Marshall (Arabella).
Category: TV Mini-series

1973 (BBC; UK): *Wessex Tales*
Producer: Irene Shubik
The Withered Arm
Screenwriter: Rhys Adrian
Director: Desmond Davies
Cast: Billie Whitelaw (Rhoda), Yvonne Antrobus (Gertrude), Edward Hardwicke, William Relton, John Welsh, Esmond Knight.
Fellow Townsmen
Screenwriter: Douglas Livingstone
Director: Barry Davis
Cast: Kenneth Haigh, Jane Asher, Terence Frisby, Susan Fleetwood, John McKelvey, Ann Curthoys, Robert Hartley, William Simons, Colin Edwyn, Anthony Edwards.
A Tragedy of Two Ambitions
Screenwriter: Dennis Potter
Director: Michael Tuchner
Cast: John Hurt (Joshua Harlborough), David Troughton (Cornelius Harlborough), Paul Rogers (Joshua Harlborough, Sr), Lynne Frederick (Rosa Harlborough), Heather Canning (Selimar), Edward Petherbridge (Squire Fellmer), Betty Cooper (Mrs Fellmer), Dan Meaden (Countryman), Andrew McCulloch (Farm Labourer), John Rainer (Clergyman).
An Imaginative Woman
Screenwriter: William Trevor
Director: Gavin Millar
Cast: Claire Bloom, Norman Rodway, Maureen Pryor, Paul Dawkins, Barbara Kellerman, Anne-Louise Wakefield.
The Melancholy Hussar
Screenwriter: Ken Taylor
Director: Mike Newell
Cast: Mary Larkin, Ben Cross, Emrys James, Richard Kay.
Barbara of the House of Grebe
Screenwriter: David Mercer
Director: David Hugh Jones
Cast: Ben Kingsley (Lord Uplandtowers), Joanna McCallum (Barbara), Nick Bramble (Willowes), Leslie Sands (Sir John Grebe), Richard Cornish (Drenkard), Jean Gilpin (Mrs Drenkard), John Boswall (Tutor), Robert Rietty (Sculptor), Janet Hanfrey (Mary), Charles Rae (Bailiff).
Category: TV Mini-series

1978 (BBC; UK): *The Mayor of Casterbridge*
Screenwriter: Dennis Potter
Director: David Giles
Producer: Martin Lisemore
Cast: Alan Bates (Michael Henchard), Janet Maw (Elizabeth-Jane), Jack
Galloway (Donald Farfrae), Anne Stallybrass (Susan Henchard), Anna
Massey (Lucetta Templeman), Avis Bunnage (Mrs Goodenough), Richard
Owens (Newson), Peter Bourke (Abel Whittle), Joe Ritchie (Buzzford),
Douglas Milvain (Concy).
Category: TV Mini-series

1979 (Renn/Burrill; France/UK): *Tess*
Screenwriters: Gérard Brach, Roman Polanski, John Brownjohn (based on
Tess of the D'Urbervilles)
Director: Roman Polanski
Producer: Claude Berri
Cast: Nastassja Kinski (Tess Durbeyfield), Peter Firth (Angel Clare), Leigh
Lawson (Alec D'Urberville), John Collin (John Durbeyfield), Rosemary
Martin (Joan Durbeyfield), Sylvia Coleridge (Mrs D'Urberville), Richard
Pearson (Vicar of Marlott), Fred Brynat (Dairyman Crick), Carolyn
Pickles (Marian), Suzanna Hamilton (Izz).
Category: Feature Film

1985 (Children's Film and Television Foundation; UK): *Exploits at West
Poley* (based on 'Our Exploits at West Poley')
Screenwriter: James Andrew Hall
Director: Diarmid Lawrence
Producer: Pamela Lonsdale
Cast: Anthony Blake (The Man Who Has Failed), Brenda Fricker (Aunt
Draycott), Charlie Condou (Leonard), Jonathan Jackson (Stephen),
Jonathan Adams (Miller Griffin), Noel O'Connell (Job Tray), Frank Mills
(Ned Jones), Thomas Heathcote (Farmer Will Gant).
Category: Children's Drama

1987 (BBC; UK): *The Day After the Fair*
Screenwriter: Gillian Freeman (adapted from the play by Frank Harvey,
based on 'On the Western Circuit')
Director: Anthony Simmons
Producer: Louis Marks
Cast: Jonathan Adams (Parnell), Sammi Davis (Anna May Dunsford), Jane
Garnett (Grace), Hannah Gordon (Edith Harnham), Kenneth Haigh
(Arthur), Roy Holder (Jim), Anna Massey (Letty), Martyn Stanbridge
(Charles), Sophie Thursfield (Sarah), Veronica Clifford.
Category: TV Film

1994 (BBC; UK): *The Return of the Native*
Screenwriter: Robert W. Lenski
Director: Jack Gold

Producer: Craig Anderson, Nick Gillott, Richard Welsh
Cast: Catherine Zeta Jones (Eustacia Vye), Clive Owen (Damon Wildeve), Ray
Stevenson (Clym Yeobright), Steven Mackintosh (Diggory Venn), Claire
Skinner (Thomasin), Paul Rogers (Captain Vye), Joan Plowright (Mrs
Yeobright), Celia Imrie (Susan Nunsuch), Richard Avery (Humphrey),
Peter Wright (Timothy).
Category: TV Film

1996 (BBC/Revolution/Polygram; UK/US): *Jude*
Screenwriter: Hossein Amini (based on *Jude the Obscure*)
Director: Michael Winterbottom
Producer: Andrew Eaton
Cast: Christopher Eccleston (Jude Fawley), Kate Winslet (Sue Bridehead),
Liam Cunningham (Phillotson), Rachel Griffiths (Arabella), June Whitfield
(Aunt Drusilla), Ross Colvin Turnbull (Little Jude), James Daley (Jude as a
boy), Berwick Kaler (Farmer Troutham), Sean McKenzie (1st
Stonemason), Richard Albrecht (2nd Stonemason).
Category: Feature Film

1997 (Pathé; UK): *The Woodlanders*
Screenwriter: David Rudkin
Director: Phil Agland
Producer: Phil Agland, Barney Reisz
Cast: Emily Woof (Grace Melbury), Rufus Sewell (Giles Winterborne), Cal
Macaninch (Dr Fitzpiers), Tony Haygarth (Mr Melbury), Jodhi May
(Marty South), Polly Walker (Mrs Charmond), Walter Sparrow (Old
Creedle), Sheila Burrell (Grandma Oliver), Amanda Ryan (Sukey [*sic*]
Damson).
Category: Feature Film

1998 (LWT; UK): *Tess of the D'Urbervilles*
Screenwriter: Ted Whitehead
Director: Ian Sharp
Producer: Sarah Wilson
Cast: Justine Waddell (Tess Durbeyfield), Jason Flemyng (Alec D'Urberville),
Oliver Milburn (Angel Clare), John McEnery (Jack Durbeyfield), Lesley
Dunlop (Joan Durbeyfield), Rosalind Knight (Mrs D'Urberville), Anthony
O'Donnell (Crick), Christine Moore (Mrs Crick), Bryan Pringle (Kail),
Debbie Chazen (Marian).
Category: TV Film

1998 (Granada; UK): *Far From the Madding Crowd*
Screenwriter: Philomena McDonagh
Director: Nicholas Renton
Producer: Hilary Bevan Jones
Cast: Paloma Baeza (Bathsheba Everdene), Nigel Terry (Mr Boldwood),
Nathaniel Parker (Gabriel Oak), Jonathan Firth (Sergeant Frank Troy),

Natasha Little (Fanny Robin), Tracy Keating (Liddy), Robin Soans (Henery Fray), Victoria Alcock (Temperance Miller), James Allen (Will Coggan), James Ballantine (Joe Coggan).
Category: TV Mini-series

1998 (Scarlet Films; UK): *The Scarlet Tunic.*
Screenwriter: Colin Clements (based on 'The Melancholy Huzzar')
Director: Stuart St Paul
Producers: Daniel Figuero, Zygi Kamasa
Cast: Jean-Marc Barr (Matthaus Singer), Emma Fielding (Frances Groves), Simon Callow (Captain Fairfax), Jack Shepherd (Dr Edward Grove), John Sessions (Humphrey Gould), Lynda Bellingham (Emily Marlowe), Thomas Lockyer (Christoph Singer), Andrew Tiernan (Muller), Gareth Hale (William Parsons), Lisa Faulkner (William Parsons).
Category: Feature Film

2000 (Revolution Films/Canal+/Alliance Atlantis; UK/FR/CA):
*The Claim**
Screenwriter: Frank Cottrell Boyce (based on *The Mayor of Casterbridge*)
Director: Michael Winterbottom
Producer: Andrew Eaton
Cast: Peter Mullan (Daniel Dillon), Milla Jovovich (Lucia), Wes Bentley (Dalglish), Nastassja Kinski (Elena Burn/Elena Dillon), Sarah Polley (Hope Burn), Shirley Henderson (Annie), Julian Richings (Bellanger), Sean McGinley (Sweetly), Randy Birch (Priest), Tom McCamus (Burn).
Category: Feature Film
* also known as *Rédemption* (Fr), *Le Maître de Kingdom Come* (Ca, French title).

2003 (A&E/Pearson/Sally Head; USA): *The Mayor of Casterbridge*
Screenwriter: Ted Whitehead
Director: David Thacker
Producer: Georgina Lowe
Cast: Ciarán Hinds (Michael Henchard), Juliet Aubrey (Susan Henchard), Jodhi May (Elizabeth-Jane), James Purefoy (Donald Farfrae), Polly Walker (Lucetta Templeman), Darren Hawkes (Auctioneer), Jean Marsh (Furmity Woman), Michael Beint (Coachman), Clive Russell (Newson), John Surman (Tent Auctioneer).
Category: TV Mini-series

Bibliography

Ahmad, Suleiman M. 'Far from the Madding Crowd in the British Provincial Theatre.' Thomas Hardy Journal 16 (2000) 70–83.

AngliaCampus. 'The Mayor of Casterbridge (1972).' http://www.angliacampus. com/athome/feat/screen/2001_09/page02.htm

Allingham, Philip V. 'Robert Barnes' Illustrations for Thomas Hardy's The Mayor of Casterbridge as Serialised in The Graphic.' Victorian Periodicals Review 28 (Spring 1995) 27–39.

'Sensation Novel Elements in The London Graphic's Twenty-Part Serialisation of Hardy's The Mayor of Casterbridge.' Thomas Hardy Yearbook 31 (2001) 34–64.

'Six Original Illustrations for Hardy's Tess of the d'Urbervilles Drawn by Sir Hubert Herkomer, R. A., for The Graphic (1891).' Thomas Hardy Journal 10 (1994) 52–70.

'The Original Illustrations for Hardy's Tess of the d'Urbervilles Drawn by Daniel A. Wehrschmidt, Ernest Borough-Johnson and Joseph Syddall for The Graphic.' Thomas Hardy Yearbook 24 (1998) 3–50.

'The Wife Sale in The Mayor of Casterbridge.' http://www.victorianweb.org/ authors/hardy/pva283.html

Andrew, Dudley. 'Adaptation.' In Film Adaptation. Ed. James Naremore. London: Athlone Press, 2000, pp.28–37.

Barthes, Roland. 'The Grain of the Voice.' Image-Music-Text. Trans. Stephen Heath. New York: Hill and Wang, 1977, pp.179–89.

Beach, Joseph Warren. The Technique of Thomas Hardy. Chicago: University of Chicago Press, 1922.

Beckett, Samuel. Proust and Three Dialogues with Georges Duthuit. London: John Calder, 1987. First published 1965.

Benjamin, Walter. Illuminations. London: Fontana, 1973.

Berger, Sheila. Thomas Hardy and Visual Structures: Framing, Disruption, Process. New York: New York University Press, 1990.

Bignell, Jonathan, Lacey, Stephen, and Macmurraugh-Kavanagh, Madeleine, eds. British Television Drama. Past, Present and Future. Basingstoke: Palgrave, 2000.

Bird, Daniel. The Pocket Essential Roman Polanski. Harpenden, Herts: Pocket Essentials, 2002.

Bird, Dennis L. 'The First Hardy Film.' Thomas Hardy Journal 11 (October 1995) 43–4.

Bloom, Harold, ed. *Thomas Hardy's 'The Mayor of Casterbridge'*. New York: Chelsea House, 1988.

Bordwell, David. *Narration in the Fiction Film*. Madison: University of Wisconsin Press, 1985.

Boumelha, Penny. *Thomas Hardy and Women: Sexual Ideology and Narrative Form*. Brighton: Harvester Press, 1982.

Boumelha, Penny, ed. *'Jude the Obscure': Contemporary Critical Essays*. New Casebooks. Basingstoke: Macmillan, 2000.

Bourdieu, Pierre. *Distinction: A Social Critique of the Judgement of Taste*. Trans. Richard Nice. Cambridge, Mass.: Harvard University Press, 1984.

Bracewell, Michael. *The Nineties: When Surface Was Depth*. Hammersmith: Flamingo, 2002.

Brooke-Rose, Christine. 'Ill Wit and Sick Tragedy: *Jude the Obscure*.' In *'Jude the Obscure': Contemporary Critical Essays*. Ed. Penny Boumelha. New Casebooks. Basingstoke: Macmillan, 2000, pp.122–44.

Bullen, J. B. *The Expressive Eye: Fiction and Perception in the Work of Thomas Hardy*. Oxford: Clarendon Press, 1986.

Butler, Lance St John, ed. *Alternative Hardy*. London: Macmillan, 1989.

Butler, Lance St John, ed. *Thomas Hardy After Fifty Years*. London: Macmillan, 1977.

Cardwell, Sarah. *Adaptation Revisited: Television and the Classic Novel*. Manchester: Manchester University Press, 2002.

Cartmell, Deborah, and Whelehan, Imelda, eds. *Adaptations: From Text to Screen, Screen to Text*. London: Routledge, 1999.

Chalfont, Fran E. 'From Strength to Strength: John Schlesinger's Film of *Far From the Madding Crowd*.' In *Thomas Hardy Annual No. 5*. Ed. Norman Page. London: Macmillan, 1987, pp.63–74.

Clarke, Graham, ed. *Thomas Hardy: Critical Assessments*. 4 vols. Mountfield: Helm Information, 1993.

Cohen, Keith. *Film and Fiction: The Dynamics of Exchange*. New Haven: Yale University Press, 1979.

Collins, Jim, Radner, Hilary, and Collins, Ava Preacher, eds. *Film Theory Goes to the Movies*. New York: Routledge, 1993.

Constabile, Rita. 'Hardy in Soft Focus.' In *The English Novel and the Movies*. Ed. Michael Klein and Gillian Parker. New York: Frederick Ungar, 1981, pp.155–64.

Cooke, Alistair. *'The Mayor of Casterbridge'*. *A Decade of Masterpiece Theatre Masterpieces*. Television Archive. http://www.ffolio.com/abarchive/television/mayor.html

Cooke, Lez. *British Television Drama: A History*. London: BFI, 2003.

Costanzo, William. 'Polanski in Wessex: Filming *Tess of the D'Urbervilles*.' *Literature/Film Quarterly* 9 (1981) 71–8.

Cox, R. G., ed. *Thomas Hardy: The Critical Heritage*. London: Routledge and Kegan Paul, 1970.

Dalziel, Pamela. 'Whose *Mistress*? Thomas Hardy's Theatrical Collaboration.' *Studies in Bibliography* 48 (1995) 248–59.

Davis, Gwenn, and Joyce, Beverley A., compilers. *Drama by Women to 1900: A Bibliography of American and British Writers*. London: Mansell, 1992.

Dolin, Tim. 'Jude Fawley and the New Man.' In *Jude the Obscure: Contemporary Critical Essays*. Ed. Penny Boumelha. Basingstoke: Macmillan, 2000, pp.209–27.

Dolin, Tim, and Widdowson, Peter, eds. *Thomas Hardy and Contemporary Literary Studies*. Basingstoke: Palgrave Macmillan, 2004.

Dutta, Mary Buhl. 'Taming the Victim: Rape in Soap Opera.' *Journal of Popular Film and Television* (Spring 1999) http://www.findarticles.com/cf_dls/m0412/1_27/55437790/print.jhtml

Eagleton, Terry. 'Flesh and Spirit in Thomas Hardy.' In *Thomas Hardy and Contemporary Literary Studies*. Ed. Tim Dolin and Peter Widdowson. Basingstoke: Palgrave Macmillan, 2004, pp.14–22.

Ebbatson, Roger. *Hardy: The Margin of the Unexpressed*. Sheffield: Sheffield Academic Press, 1993.

Empson, William. *Some Versions of Pastoral*. London: Chatto and Windus, 1986. First published 1935.

Fish, Stanley. *Is There a Text in This Class?* Cambridge, Mass.: Harvard University Press, 1980.

Fleming, Jason. AandE.com Interview. http://www.aande.com/tv/films/tess/alec.html

Freeman, Mark. 'Michael Winterbottom's *The Claim*.' 2001. http://home.vicnet.net.au/~freeman/reviewsah/claim.html

Friedberg, Anne. *Window Shopping: Cinema and the Postmodern*. Berkeley: University of California Press, 1993.

Gardiner, Judith Kegan, ed. *Masculinity Studies and Feminist Theory: New Directions*. New York: Columbia University Press, 2002.

Gatrell, Simon. *Hardy the Creator: A Textual Biography*. Oxford: Clarendon Press, 1988.

   Thomas Hardy and the Proper Study of Mankind. Basingstoke: Macmillan, 1993.

   Thomas Hardy's Vision of Wessex. Basingstoke: Palgrave, 2003.

Giannetti, Louis D. *Understanding Movies*. 5th edition. Englewood Cliffs, N.J.: Prentice Hall, 1990.

Giddings, Robert, and Sheen, Erica, eds. *The Classic Novel: From Page to Screen*. Manchester: Manchester University Press, 2000.

Gilbert, W. Stephen. *The Life and Work of Dennis Potter*. London: Hodder and Stoughton, 1995.

Girard, René. *Deceit, Desire and the Novel*. Baltimore: Johns Hopkins, 1966.

Gregor, Ian. *The Great Web: The Form of Hardy's Major Fiction*. London: Faber and Faber, 1974.

Grundy, Joan. *Hardy and the Sister Arts*. London: Macmillan, 1979.

Guerard, Albert J. *Thomas Hardy*. New York: New Directions, 1964. First published 1949.

Hardy, Florence Emily. *The Life of Thomas Hardy 1840–1928*. London: Macmillan, 1962. First published 1928.

Hardy, Thomas. *The Life and Work of Thomas Hardy*. Ed. Michael Millgate. Athens: University of Georgia Press, 1985.

Halliwell, Martin. *Images of Idiocy: The Idiot Figure in Modern Fiction and Film*. Aldershot: Ashgate, 2004.

Heidegger, Martin. 'The Origin of the Work of Art.' *Basic Writings*. Ed. David Farrell Krell. New York: Harper and Row, 1977, pp.149–87.

Higonnet, Margaret R., ed. *The Sense of Sex: Feminist Perspectives on Hardy*. Urbana: University of Illinois Press, 1993.

Ingham, Patricia. *Thomas Hardy*. Oxford World's Classics Authors in Context. Oxford: Oxford University Press, 2003.

Jackson, Arlene M. *Illustration and the Novels of Thomas Hardy*. Totowa, N.J.: Rowman and Littlefield, 1981.

Klein, Michael, and Parker, Gillian, eds. *The English Novel and the Movies*. New York: Frederick Ungar, 1981.

Kozloff, Sarah. *Invisible Storytellers: Voice-Over in American Fiction Film*. Berkeley: University of California Press, 1988.

'Where Wessex Meets New England: Griffith's *Way Down East* & Hardy's *Tess of the d'Urbervilles*.' *Literature/Film Quarterly* 13 (1985) 35–41.

Kramer, Dale, ed. *The Cambridge Companion to Thomas Hardy*. Cambridge: Cambridge University Press, 1999.

Critical Approaches to the Fiction of Thomas Hardy. London: Macmillan, 1979.

Critical Essays on Thomas Hardy: The Novels. Boston: G. K. Hall, 1980.

The Woodlanders. By Thomas Hardy. Oxford: Clarendon Press, 1981.

Laird, J. T. *The Shaping of 'Tess of the D'Urbervilles'*. Oxford: Clarendon Press, 1975.

Law, Jules. 'A "Passing Corporeal Blight": Political Bodies in *Tess of the D'Urbervilles*.' *Victorian Studies* 40 (1997) 245–70.

Lerner, Laurence, and Holmstrom, John, eds. *Thomas Hardy and His Readers: A Selection of Contemporary Reviews*. London: Bodley Head, 1968.

Lodge, David. *Working with Structuralism: Essays and Reviews on Nineteenth- and Twentieth-Century Literature*. London: Routledge and Kegan Paul, 1981.

MacKillop, Ian, and Platt, Alison. '"Beholding in a Magic Panorama": Television and the Illustration of *Middlemarch*.' In *The Classic Novel: From Page to Screen*. Ed. Robert Giddings and Erica Sheen. Manchester: Manchester University Press, 2000, pp.71–92.

MacKinnon, Kenneth. *Uneasy Pleasures: The Male as Erotic Object*. London: Cygnus Arts, 1997.

Mallett, Phillip, ed. *The Achievement of Thomas Hardy*. Basingstoke: Macmillan, 2000.

Thomas Hardy: Texts and Contexts. Basingstoke: Palgrave Macmillan, 2002.

Mallett, Phillip, and Draper, Ronald, eds. *A Spacious Vision: Essays on Hardy*. Newmill: Patten Press, 1994.

Marcus, Jane. 'A *Tess* for Child Molesters.' In *'Tess of the D'Urbervilles': Contemporary Critical Essays*. Ed. Peter Widdowson. New Casebooks. Basingstoke: Macmillan, 1993, pp.90–3.

Monaco, James. *How to Read a Film*. Oxford: Oxford University Press, 2000.

Mascia-Lees, Frances E., and Sharpe, Patricia. *Taking a Stand in a Postfeminist World: Toward an Engaged Cultural Criticism*. Albany: State University of New York Press, 2000.

Mast, Gerald, Cohen, Marshall, and Braudy, Leo, eds. *Film Theory and Criticism*. 4th edition. Oxford: Oxford University Press, 1992.

McFarlane, Brian. *Novel to Film: An Introduction to the Theory of Adaptation.* Oxford: Clarendon Press, 1996.

Miller, J. Hillis. *Thomas Hardy: Distance and Desire.* Cambridge, Mass.: Harvard University Press, 1970.

Millgate, Michael, *Thomas Hardy: A Biography.* Oxford: Clarendon Press, 1982.

Millgate, Michael, ed. *Thomas Hardy's Public Voice: The Essays, Speeches, and Miscellaneous Prose.* Oxford: Clarendon Press, 2001.

Mitchell, Judith. 'Hardy's Female Reader.' In *The Sense of Sex: Feminist Perspectives on Hardy.* Ed. Margaret R. Higonnet. Urbana: University of Illinois Press, 1993, pp.172–87.

The Stone and the Scorpion: The Female Subject of Desire in the Novels of Charlotte Brontë, George Eliot and Thomas Hardy. Westport, Conn.: Greenwood Press, 1994.

Mitchell, Lee Clark. *Westerns: Making the Man in Fiction and Film.* Chicago: University of Chicago Press, 1996.

Moore, George. *Conversations in Ebury Street.* London: Heinemann, 1936.

Morgan, Rosemarie. *Cancelled Words: Rediscovering Thomas Hardy.* London: Routledge, 1992.

Women and Sexuality in the Novels of Thomas Hardy. London: Routledge, 1988.

Naremore, James, ed. *Film Adaptation.* London: Athlone Press, 2000.

Nemesvari, Richard. '"The Thing Must be Male, We Suppose": Erotic Triangles and Masculine Identity in *Tess of the d'Urbervilles* and Melville's *Billy Budd*.' In *Thomas Hardy: Texts and Contexts.* Ed. Phillip Mallett. Basingstoke: Palgrave Macmillan, 2002, pp.87–109.

Niemeyer, Paul J. *Seeing Hardy: Film and Television Adaptations of the Fiction of Thomas Hardy.* Jefferson, N. C.: McFarland, 2003.

Page, Norman. 'Hardy's Pictorial Art in *The Mayor of Casterbridge*.' *Etudes Anglaises* 12 (1972) 486–92.

Page, Norman, ed. *Oxford Reader's Companion to Hardy.* Oxford: Oxford University Press, 2000.

Paterson, John. *The Making of 'The Return of the Native'.* Berkeley: University of California Press, 1960.

Pettit, Charles P. C., ed. *Celebrating Thomas Hardy: Insights and Appreciations.* Basingstoke: Macmillan, 1998.

Peck, John. 'Hardy and Joyce: A Basis for Comparison.' *Ariel* 12 (1971) 71–86.

Phelan, James. *Reading People, Reading Plots: Character, Progression, and the Interpretation of Narrative.* Chicago: University of Chicago Press, 1989.

Phillips, Gene D. *John Schlesinger.* Boston: Twayne, 1981.

Potter, Dennis. *The Changing Forest: Life in the Forest of Dean Today.* London: Secker and Warburg, 1962.

Prentiss, Norman D. 'Compilation and Design in *The Mayor of Casterbridge*.' *Thomas Hardy Journal* 11 (February 1995) 60–74.

Purdy, Richard Little, and Millgate Michael, eds. *The Collected Letters of Thomas Hardy.* 7 vols. Oxford: Clarendon Press, 1978–88.

Ray, Robert B. 'The Field of "Literature and Film".' In *Film Adaptation.* Ed. James Naremore. London: Athlone Press, 2000, pp.38–53.

Riquelme, John Paul. 'Echoic Language, Uncertainty, and Freedom in *Tess of the D'Urbervilles.*' In *Tess of the D'Urbervilles.* By Thomas Hardy. Ed. John Paul Riquelme. Boston and New York: Bedford/St Martin's, 1998, pp.506–20.

'The Modernity of Thomas Hardy's Poetry.' In *The Cambridge Companion to Thomas Hardy.* Ed. Dale Kramer. Cambridge: Cambridge University Press, 1999, pp.204–23.

Rogers, Deborah. 'Daze of Our Lives: The Soap Opera as Feminine Text.' *Journal of American Culture* 14 (1991) 29–41.

Rooney, Ellen. '"A Little More than Persuading": Tess and the Subject of Sexual Violence.' In *Rape and Representation.* Ed. Lynn A. Higgins and Brenda R. Silver. New York: Columbia University Press, 1991, pp.86–114.

Ross, Harris, ed. *Film as Literature, Literature as Film.* New York: Greenwood Press, 1987.

Ruskin, John. *Modern Painters.* 6 vols. London: George Allen, 1898. First published 1843–60.

Sadoff, Dianne, and Kucich, John, ed. *Victorian Afterlife: Postmodern Culture Rewrites the Nineteenth Century.* Minneapolis: University of Minnesota Press, 2000.

Scholes, Robert, and Kellog, Robert. *The Nature of Narrative.* Oxford: Oxford University Press, 1966.

Schweik Robert. 'The "Modernity" of Hardy's *Jude the Obscure.*' In *A Spacious Vision: Essays on Hardy.* Ed. Phillip Mallett and Ronald Draper. Newmill: Patten Press, 1994, pp.49–63.

Selwyn, David. 'The Birthday Weekend.' *Thomas Hardy Journal* 19:3 (2003) 20–2.

Seymour-Smith, Martin. *Hardy.* London: Bloomsbury, 1994.

Shires, Linda. 'The Radical Aesthetic of *Tess of the D'Urbervilles.*' In *The Cambridge Companion to Thomas Hardy.* Ed. Dale Kramer. Cambridge: Cambridge University Press, 1999, pp.145–63.

Showalter, Elaine. 'The Unmanning of the Mayor of Casterbridge.' In *Critical Approaches to the Fiction of Thomas Hardy.* Ed. Dale Kramer. London: Macmillan, 1979, pp.99–115.

Shubik, Irene. *Play for Today: The Evolution of Television Drama.* Manchester: Manchester University Press, 2001.

Silverman, Kaja. *The Acoustic Mirror: The Female Voice in Psychoanalysis and Cinema.* Bloomington and Indianapolis: Indiana University Press, 1988.

Sinyard, Neil. *Filming Literature: The Art of Screen Adaptation.* Beckenham: Croom Helm, 1986.

Small, Helen. 'Chances Are: Henry Buckle, Thomas Hardy, and the Individual at Risk'. In *Literature, Science, Psychoanalysis, 1830–1970.* Ed. Helen Small and Trudi Tate. Oxford: Oxford University Press, 2003, pp.64–85.

Sonnet, Esther. 'From *Emma* to *Clueless*: Taste, Pleasure and the Scene of History.' In *Adaptations: From Text to Screen, Screen to Text.* Ed. Deborah Cartmell and Imelda Whelehan. London: Routledge, 1999, pp.51–62.

Stam, Robert. 'Beyond Fidelity: The Dialogics of Adaptation.' In *Film Adaptation.* Ed. James Naremore. London: Athlone Press, 2000, pp.54–76.

Literature through Film: Realism, Magic, and the Art of Adaptation. Oxford: Blackwell, 2005.

Stam, Robert, and Raengo, Alessandra, eds. *Literature and Film: A Guide to the Theory and Practice of Film Adaptation.* Oxford: Blackwell, 2005.

Starr, Sandy. 'A *Claim* on Hardy's Legacy.' 9 February 2001. *Spiked Culture.* http://www.spiked-online.com/articles/00000000548C.html

Stendhal. *The Red and the Black.* Trans. Lloyd C. Parks. New York: New American Library, 1970.

Stottlar, James F. 'Hardy vs. Pinero: Two Stage Versions of *Far From the Madding Crowd.*' *Theatre Survey* 18 (1977) 23–43.

Sutherland, John. 'A Note on the Teasing Narrator in *Jude the Obscure.*' *English Literature in Transition* 17 (1974) 159–62.

Taylor, Richard H., ed. *The Personal Notebooks of Thomas Hardy.* London: Macmillan, 1978.

Tibbetts, John C., and Welsh, James M., *Novels into Film: The Encyclopedia of Movies Adapted from Books.* New York: Checkmark Books, 1999.

Tompkins, Jane. *West of Everything.* New York: Oxford University Press, 1992.

Vuuren, Nancy van. *The Subversion of Women.* Philadelphia: Westminster Press, 1974.

Wagner, Geoffrey. *The Novel and the Cinema.* Rutherford, N.J.: Fairleigh Dickinson University Press, 1975.

Weber, Carl. *Hardy and the Lady From Madison Square.* Waterville, Maine: Colby College Press, 1952.

Webster, Roger. 'Visual Imagination in the Novels of Thomas Hardy.' Unpublished PhD thesis, University of London, 1979.

Wexman, Virginia Wright. *Roman Polanski.* Boston: Twayne, 1985.

Whitehead, Ted. AandE.com Interview. http://www.aande.com/tv/films/tess/ted.html

Widdowson, Peter. 'A Tragedy of Modern Life.' In *'Tess of the D'Urbervilles': Contemporary Critical Essays.* Ed. Peter Widdowson. Basingstoke: Macmillan, 1993, pp.95–108.

Hardy in History: A Study in Literary Sociology. London: Routledge, 1989.

On Thomas Hardy: Late Essays and Earlier. Basingstoke: Macmillan, 1998.

'Thomas Hardy at the End of Two Centuries: From Page to Screen.' In *Thomas Hardy and Contemporary Literary Studies.* Ed. Tim Dolin and Peter Widdowson. Basingstoke: Palgrave Macmillan, 2004, pp.178–98.

Widdowson, Peter, ed. *'Tess of the D'Urbervilles': Contemporary Critical Essays.* New Casebooks. Basingstoke: Macmillan, 1993.

Thomas Hardy: Selected Poetry and Non-Fictional Prose. London: Macmillan, 1997.

Wilde, Oscar. 'The Decay of Lying.' In *The Writings of Oscar Wilde.* Ed. Isobel Murray. Oxford: Oxford University Press, 1989, pp.213–39.

Williams, Melanie. '"Is Alec a Rapist?" – Cultural Connotations of "Rape" and "Seduction" – A Reply to Professor John Sutherland.' *Feminist Legal Studies* 7 (1999) 299–316.

Wilson, Keith. *Thomas Hardy on Stage.* London: Macmillan, 1995.

'Checklist of Professional Productions Staged in Hardy's Lifetime.' *Thomas Hardy Drama Page*, Thomas Hardy Association. http://aix1.uottawa.ca/~kgwilson/

Woolf, Virginia. 'Modern Fiction.' In *20th-Century Literary Criticism: A Reader*. Ed. David Lodge. London: Longman, 1972, pp.86–91.

Wright, Sarah Bird. *Thomas Hardy A to Z: The Essential Reference to His Life and Work*. New York: Facts on File, 2002.

Wright, T. R. *Hardy and His Readers*. Basingstoke: Palgrave Macmillan, 2003.

Young, Jordan R. *The Beckett Actor: Jack MacGowran, Beginning to End*. Beverly Hills, Ca.: Moonstone Press, 1987.

Index